CONVERSION AND SOCIAL EQUALITY IN INDIA

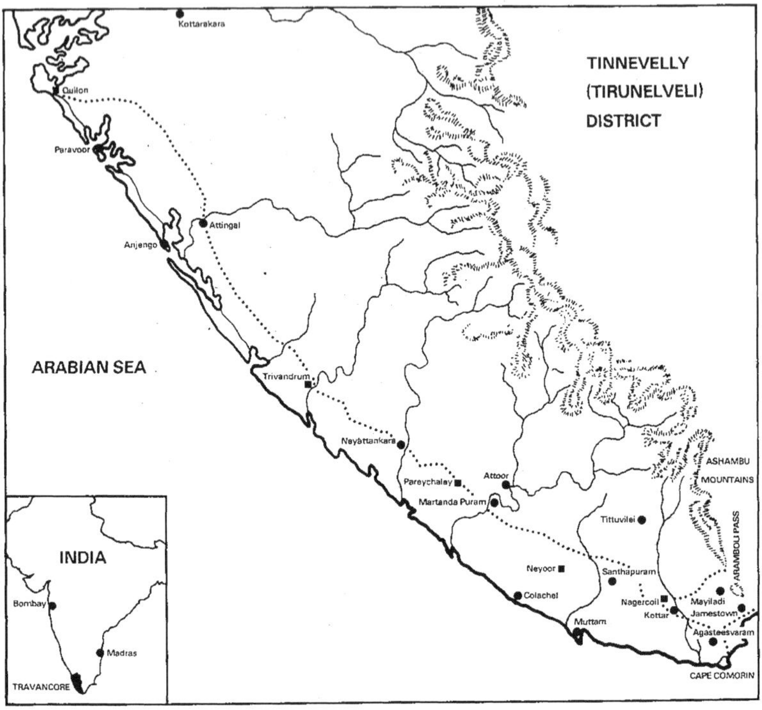

MAP OF TRAVANCORE (19TH CENTURY)
SHOWING LMS STATIONS

Conversion and Social Equality in India

The London Missionary Society in South Travancore in the 19th Century

DICK KOOIMAN

MANOHAR
2020

First published 1989
POD reprint 2020

ISBN 978-81-85054-78-0

Published by
Ajay Kumar Jain *for*
Manohar Publishers & Distributors
4753/23 Ansari Road, Daryaganj
New Delhi 110 002

Printed at
Replika Press Pvt. Ltd.

Contents

VI. Emergence of Coffee Plantations

VII. The Fight against Civil Disabilities

VIII. Conversion and Cultural Change

List of Tables, Maps and Pictures

TABLES

MAPS

PICTURES (placed between pages 108–109)

(Pictures 1–4, 8–12 and 14 are from LMS Archives, Council for World Mission, London; pictures 5–7 and 13 are from Ecclesiastical Archives, UTC Bangalore. Apart from portraits 3 and 4, all pictures are photographs made somewhere between 1885 and 1900.)

Preface

Monographs are seldom the work of one single person. This book is no exception. Several institutions, academic and non-academic, and their personnel have rendered valuable assistance to make the writing of this book possible.

First of all I would like to mention the Department of Cultural Anthropology and Sociology of Non-Western Peoples at the Amsterdam Free University, where I am working as a Reader in South Asian history. Participation in this Department's joint research program 'Religion, Power and Development' stimulated my interest in the socio-economic effects of conversion movements among untouchables in India and enabled me to benefit from discussions among my fellow-researchers. Colleagues like Pim Schoorl, Hans Tennekes, Matthieu Schoffeleers and Philip Quarles van Ufford saw parts of this book in draft and offered suggestions for improvement. The annual meetings of the Dutch Contact-Group for Tropical Asia (KOTA) proved a useful platform to submit draft texts as conference papers to the critical comment of researchers from other universities, and parts of chapters III, IV, V and VIII saw already the light of day in a modified form as contributions to the *Indian Church History Review* (Bangalore), the *Economic and Political Weekly* (Bombay), and the *Journal of Kerala Studies* (Trivandrum).

The Faculty of Socio-Cultural Sciences of the Amsterdam Free University granted me the necessary funds to consult historical source material in London and Bangalore. In London I spent many hours in the libraries of the India Office and the British Museum. Mrs. Rosemary Seton and Rev. J.T. Hardyman proved patient guides and advised me in finding my way in the archives of the London Missionary Society, now on deposit in the London School of Oriental and African Studies. Barrie D. Scopes, general-secretary to the Council for World Mission, the successor organization to the London Missionary Society, kindly permitted me to use the Council's remaining files and reports, and to reproduce old photos from its archives for publication. Mrs. Rosemary Keen drew my attention to the Hobbs Papers on the 'Ceylon Tamil

Cooly Mission' in the collection of the Church Missionary Society, now in Birmingham.

In Bangalore, Mrs. E. Adiappa and Rev. M.K. Kuriakose, librarians of the Ecclesiastical Archives of the United Theological College, did everything possible to make my period of research in Bangalore a fruitful one. They also permitted me to reproduce old photographs preserved in their library, some of which are published in this book. Mr. C.S. Mohanavelu was so kind as to search after a detailed map of the south Travancore region in several libraries and institutes in Madras, but his efforts proved in vain. Therefore, a rough map of this region was skilfully drawn by Kees Bos of the Free University's Photography Department.

Large parts of the London Missionary Society's archives are also available on microfiche in the Interuniversity Institute for Missiological and Ecumenical Research in Leiden, the Netherlands. There, Mrs. Leny Lagerwerf proved kind enough to adjust her lending-policies to my research needs. The same ought to be said of Mrs. Trudy van Koot and her colleagues of the Free University's library for Social Geography and Cultural Anthropology, who always showed a pleasant touch of leniency in interpreting library rules for researchers.

A lecture tour, granted under the Indo-Dutch Cultural Agreement, enabled me to visit universities and research institutes in Kerala and Tamilnadu, and to discuss some of the arguments presented here with colleagues and fellow-researchers who shared my interest in the history of the untouchables in the former Travancore state. Prof. Dr. K.K.N. Kurup of the University of Calicut, Dr. K.K. Kusuman of the University of Kerala, Dr. J.W. Gladstone of the Kerala United Theological Seminary, and Dr. P.K. Michael Tharakan and K. Ravi Raman M.A. of the Centre for Development Studies in Trivandrum offered valuable comments on my oral presentations or critically reviewed (parts of) draft chapters. I also travelled about Kanyakumari district to see with my own eyes the places where the numerous missionary letters and reports were produced which I have been studying in archives and libraries for so many years. In this venture I was happy to receive expert guidance from K. Rajappan, professor of history at Scott Christian College in Nagercoil, who in Aramboli described to me the course of 1809 battle with a vivacity as if it was fought only the day before.

My wife, Tineke Kooiman-Dokter, typed various draft chapters before she was dethroned by the entrance into our home of a personal computer. Our cousin, Wietske Wielenga-Hockey, fulfilled the arduous job to make my English more intelligible to an English-reading public. Any shortcomings that remain are all mine.

DICK KOOIMAN

I. Introduction

I.1 The Problem

Meenakshipuram is a small, dusty village in Tamilnadu's Tinnevelly (Tirunelveli) district, very close to the south Kerala border. In 1981, this inconspicuous place, and several other villages in its immediate neighbourhood, made big headlines in the Indian daily papers, when thousands of *harijans* or ex-untouchables decided to leave Hinduism and to embrace Islam. This spectacular case of mass conversion created a terrible shock among caste Hindus and threatened to upset the always precarious communal balance. Rumors circulated about Arabian *sheikhs* who had come to give tangible expression to the immense richness of Islamic belief by handsome distributions of oil-dollars. More serious investigation,[1] however, showed that the *harijans* in this region have been suffering from oppression by aggressive landlords, harassment by police authorities and acute prejudices by caste Hindus for a very long time. A growing awareness of this social degradation has led many of these ex-untouchables to convert to Islam.

The chronic recurrence of these conversion movements—Meenakshipuram does not stand as an isolated incident—indicates that the groups involved consider religious identity to be an important factor in their attempts to acquire a better and more dignified place in society. The reference to oil-dollars may remind us that conversion movements are never completely devoid of considerations of material improvement. But it is also important to remember that by converting to Islam the new Muslims of Meenakshipuram lost all the benefits and concessions which they were lawfully entitled to receive from the government as Hindu *harijans*. Apparently, other considerations have weighed more heavily than a right to government support.

A small number of Christian *harijans* also went over to Islam. They had nothing to lose in terms of government benefits which are denied equally to Muslim and Christian *harijans*, but much to

[1] See for instance Mathew, 1982.

win in Tamilnadu's caste ridden society and church. "By becoming Christians, we cannot raise our social status", one of their village leaders declared, "by becoming Muslims, we can."[2]

The Meenakshipuram case also reminds us that the ex-untouchables still form a heavily oppressed section of Indian society. Economically exploited and socially despised, the degradation of this minority—which actually contains well over 85 million people—is further reinforced by their ritual impurity. One may conceive of a social system, in which different groups serve each other in turn by the performance of polluting but necessary tasks, i.e. those related to death, decay and dirt. In Hinduism, however, occupations involving impurity are permanently assigned to specialists like sweepers, tanners, midwives and toddy-tappers. Relegated to the lower fringes of Hindu society, these "specialists in pollution" are considered unfit for social contact: untouchable. A government policy of "positive discrimination" does not seem to have effected substantial changes, whereas it lends itself to various kinds of abuses. And as far as *harijans* are able to avail themselves of government aid, they risk to incur the wrath of jealous caste Hindus, as can be gleaned from the regular newspaper reports on "*harijan* atrocities". It is true that the Constitution of independent India states that untouchability is abolished and its practice in any form forbidden. But a simple stroke of the pen cannot change an age-old social practice, so deeply entrenched in Indian society and Hindu religion. This book deals with the problem of untouchability from a historical perspective by focusing on developments among some untouchable communities in southern India.

It is generally accepted that Hinduism is a way of life more than a set of transcendental beliefs and values. The social and religious aspects of life not only overlap but largely coincide. Nevertheless, many scholars have tried to analyse the caste system primarily, if not exclusively, in terms of religion or social economy.

Dumont takes hierarchy to be the central principle and describes it as a holistic and religious ranking system. The purity of the Brahmin is harmoniously linked to the impurity of the untouchable, as both depend upon the mutual performance of very specific and indispensable services.[3] Other scholars, especially those of a Marxist school of thought, contend that the caste system has been

[2] *Indian Express*, 3.7.1981, quoted in Mathew, p. 1033.

[3] Dumont, Chapter III.

studied too exclusively from the point of view of groups at the top. If looked at from the bottom up, caste is not a system of interdependence and reciprocity, but of economic exploitation. Intermediate viewpoints argue that the stigma of pollution and the material deprivation of the untouchable poor, reinforce one another.[4] In this book I will largely conform to the latter view.

Untouchable communities never had much scope to escape from their miserable position on the lower fringes of Hindu society. They joined sects or movements that stressed social equality and since Independence some of them have started to fight for their rights through militant organizations (e.g. the *Dalit Panthers*). But the way out resorted to most frequently and by the greatest number has always been to leave the Hindu body *en masse* and to adopt a new religion. It is this phenomenon that has come to be known as "mass conversion" or "mass movement".

When from A.D. 1200 Muslim tribes succeeded in establishing their rule in north India, many low caste Hindus and untouchables began to adopt the creed of their new political masters. This steady drift of socially underprivileged people resulted in a situation, whereby at the end of Muslim rule about a quarter of the whole population professed adherence to Islam. Seen from this perspective the violent breakaway of (Muslim) Pakistan from India in the 1947 Partition assumes a still more dramatic character.

After Independence, Buddhism proved to be the main objective of the mass movements. Buddhism, although practically extinct in India at that time, was a religion of the soil and enjoyed the additional advantage of an image not besmirched by connections with political power. In the 1950s the *Mahars*, the main untouchable community of Maharashtra, decided to change their faith in favour of Buddhism, and today India numbers about 4 million (neo) Buddhists, less than 1 per cent of the Indian population.

The English East India Company never showed any interest in missionary work. But under the Charter Act of 1813 the Company had to concede the Christian missions some freedom of operation in its Indian territories. From then onwards, the mass movements were almost exclusively directed towards Christianity, starting in 1818 when 3000 *Shanars* (*Nadars*) were baptized in south Kerala.[5]

[4] Béteille, pp. 411 ff.

[5] Nevertheless, conversion to Islam did not stop under colonial rule. Thurston, II, p. 60 observed that no less than 40,000 *Cherumars* of Malabar (north Kerala) accepted Islam between 1871 and 1881.

Yet, in spite of the many great mass movements under colonial rule, the number of Christians in India has remained small and the Christian community dwindles into insignificance if set against the huge mass of the Indian population. At Independence, Christians, the Syrians included, numbered less than 3 per cent of the population. Geographically their spread is very uneven: 70 per cent of the Christians are to be found in the four southern states, and in Kerala about 25 per cent of the people belong to one of the many Christian denominations. Kanyakumari district, on the extreme southern tip of the peninsula, numbers several *taluks* with a majority of Christian inhabitants. This book deals chiefly with that region, which was formerly part of the princely state of Travancore.

I.2 The Source Material

When I started my research on the history of Indian untouchables, I was not motivated by any special interest in religious conversion movements. Rather, I was drawn towards untouchability as a developmental problem of historical dimension. What I wanted to investigate were the ways that had been tried to improve the lot of the *harijans*, by others as well as by themselves, and to find answers to the question, why up till now all these efforts had yielded so little result. My decision to narrow down this research to Kerala was mainly based on the intriguing fact, that this state had always been notorious for the extreme rigidity of its caste system, whereas nowadays its successive left front governments have given it a progressive image. A side-reflection was also the availability of Dutch East India Company records on Kerala in the "Algemeen Rijksarchief" in The Hague.

After some preliminary investigations, however, I had to draw the highly unpleasant conclusion that source material on the history of Kerala's untouchables is extremely scarce. Indigenous authorities had never shown much interest in the existence of these communities. As untouchables generally had no property and paid no revenue, they were simply left out of the government record. And although European trading companies extensively dealt with coastal merchants and inland rulers, the poor untouchables were not likely to enter their narrow sphere of commercial interest. Hence, as Protestant missionaries started working amongst these communities from the beginning of the nineteenth century, their reports and correspondence (in European languages) at first sight represent an invaluable source of historical documentation. The Catholics had started missionary efforts among the fishing population on the coast at a much earlier date. In the first decade of the nineteenth century they were followed by the Protestants, the Basler Mission in the north, the Church Missionary Society in the centre, and the London Missionary Society in the south of Kerala. At Independence, the combined efforts of these societies had resulted in many thousands of native converts. These new Christians were almost exclusively recruited from the poorest and most degraded sections of society.

In view of the scarcity of source material on untouchability, these missionary archives are absolutely unique and seem to offer much-promising avenues for research. Nevertheless, a cursory exploration of the files of correspondence (LMS and CMS) turns out to be quite disappointing.[6] That disappointment is not caused by any complexity or intransparency in the structure of the collections. All the incoming letters and reports—and those are the most important for our purpose—are neatly arranged and kept in a sequence numbered for each year according to the missionary district concerned. But most of these papers deal with the health of the missionaries' families, the problems of church building, and the numbers in attendance at divine services. A study of these papers may produce interesting information on the history of the Christian mission, but far from satisfies our need for historical information on indigenous society. Of course, there always are the proverbial exceptions, as some missionaries made pioneering studies in the field of linguistics or produced fascinating descriptions of particular castes or communities. But generally, missionaries who did report on the local population lacked the subtlety and understanding necessary to give a reliable picture of their social surroundings. Much of their correspondence is heavily biased by open aversion to "dark heathenism" with its "evil habits and barbarous customs",[7] and clearly reflects the feeling of Western superiority inherent in the imperial situation.

[6] A discussion of the usefulness of the missionary archives has also been given in Kooiman, 1983.

[7] Nagam Aiya, I, p. 501–2, is of the opinion that the missionaries were very much out of touch with the persons and institutions they wished to describe and that their channels of information were generally tainted. But he adds that the same applied to virtually all Englishmen, even when they spent a lifetime in India.

Yet, we have to bear in mind that every historical source has its own particular bias and limitations. Archives of the East India Company are strongly focused on commerce and related interests. They extensively document a short-weight in a consignment of pepper, whereas the researcher is desperately looking for data on the formation of the Travancore State on the mainland. And to give another example, my previous research on the emergence of Communism in Bombay has convinced me that Intelligence reports and Communist Party documents have to be treated with much caution. Policemen as well as party leaders had their own professional and political reasons to exaggerate the importance of the Communist menace, laying a dangerous trap for later historians. The conclusion must be that all primary sources have to be dealt with very carefully, first and foremost by taking account of the specific viewpoints and concerns of the producers of those sources.

As far as the missionary archives are concerned, we have to realize that the missionaries were hard pressed by demands for success, i.e. a growing number of baptisms and church members. Many of their letters were half-conscious defences, primarily meant to assure the missionary authorities at home that their money was well spent. In the interest of our research, therefore, we have to guard ourselves against appraising the effects of evangelism and social service from the missionaries' point of view. The emphasis should not be on the spread of the Christian faith or the expansion of western imperialism. That kind of approach tends too much to consider the local people as helpless victims of attempts to convert and subjugate them. Instead, we have to shift the focus of our analysis to the receiving end of the missionary effort. To poor and underprivileged groups in indigenous society, the activities of the Christian mission could offer new and hitherto unprecedented opportunities to improve their social and economic position. As a new ally entering the social arena, the mission could also heighten existing tensions between competing communities with violent conflicts as a possible result. In short, receiving groups could perceive the implications of the Gospel in accordance with their own needs and aspirations, and actively use the mission to serve their own particular purposes. Entirely in agreement with Boel[8], I want to start from the assumption that a new religion is not

[8] Boel, Chapter I, especially p. 9.

only *imposed* by an outside agency, but also *adopted* by certain groups of people, who have their own reasons for accepting a new religious tradition. That adoption must be seen in the context of the wider socio-cultural changes that take place as a result of increasing contact with western imperialism.

I.3 The Research Questions

This study will focus on the southern tip of India. In the next chapter a short introduction will be given to the history of that area. During the nineteenth century it formed part of Travancore, a so-called native state that managed to maintain its semi-independence up to 1947. Whereas the Church Missionary Society established its headquarters in the north of Travancore, the activities of the London Missionary Society (LMS) were concentrated in the south. Since our study is largely based on the archives of the LMS, the area that will be dealt with here is in fact south Travancore. Our narrative begins in 1806 with the arrival of the first LMS missionary in Travancore and ends, somewhat arbitrarily, around 1900.

Because of the large number of Christians in south Travancore, missionary activity and the rise of a native Christian community in this region have attracted at least some degree of scholarly attention.[9] Studies of the missionaries themselves, however, are conspicuous by their absence. Pointing at this remarkable lack in our knowledge, a prominent scholar recently observed that it would be both useful and interesting to have "a much more thorough breakdown of the class backgrounds of missionaries from various societies than has so far been attempted."[10] Therefore, apart from analysing the position and aspirations of the untouchable communities, we will also make some investigations into the personal background of the fifty LMS missionaries who started working in south Travancore during the nineteenth century. In the third chapter an analysis will be made of their personal motivation and socio-economic position in British society.

Like elsewhere in India, the LMS in Travancore recruited its main following from the untouchable communities among whom

[9] Mention may be made of the studies by Yesudas and Gladstone.

[10] Frykenberg, 1985, p. 332.

locally the most important were *Shanars, Pariahs* and *Pulayas*. Because of their association with the London Mission, we have at least some information about these groups and, therefore, they will figure very prominently in this book. Nowadays, *Shanars* are better known by their more prestigious name of *Nadars,* whereas *Pariahs* and *Pulayas* prefer to be called Scheduled Castes or ex-untouchables, if any reference to caste is made at all. In this book I have chosen to use the old names, not for lack of respect or sympathy, but for the only reason that I want to remain close to the written sources. Moreover, we are writing about the nineteenth century and at that time these communities were still only known under their old names. Wherever possible, the expressed views of these people themselves will be recorded, but unfortunately, even from the missionary reports they seldom speak to us in a direct way.

As these *Shanars, Pariahs* and *Pulayas* belonged to the poorest strata of Travancore society, we may assume that material concerns played an important part in their decision to adopt another religion. But that does not mean that the perspective of converts from these communities was necessarily restricted to expectations of material improvement. A change of religion is a far more complicated process and, as we have seen from the Meenakshipuram case outlined in the first paragraphs of this chapter, it may even involve material loss. Duncan Forrester has rightly pointed out, that the nineteenth century mass conversions were a kind of group identity crisis, in which social, economic, psychological and spiritual motives were blended together in one complex whole.[11] For Travancore's untouchable communities religion used to cover all aspects of life. Thus, when we raise the question why people entered into an association with the Christian mission, we should not consider economic considerations to be the opposite of turning to religion, but rather as an essential part of it.[12]

Starting from the assumption that Christianity is adopted by people as part of a process of adaptation to a new situation created by western imperialism, our next question must be under what conditions imperialism came to Travancore and more especially under what circumstances Christianity was presented to its people.

[11] Forrester, 1977, p. 45.

[12] See also Luke & Carman, p. 42.

We shall turn to that part of Travancore's history in its due place. What should be emphasized here is that imperialism as a system of political domination implies an unequal relationship of power. So, we should ask ourselves, to what extent this unequal power relationship was also transferred to the mission field and may have influenced people in adopting the Christian religion. In this connection power should be understood in its widest sense, including not only the scarce resources the always needy LMS itself was able to command, but also the missionaries' easy access to the highest government offices, their ability to mobilize outside political support for programs of social reform, and the benevolent assistance they received from wealthy capitalist planters on the spot.

Power, however, was vested not only in imperialist authority or missionary organization. Indigenous society had its own power structure with a landholding community and native bureaucracy holding dominant positions. Since the untouchable groups were held in subjection both by economic force and the stigma of pollution, a decision to shed their old religion implied at the same time an attempt to shake off all economic exploitation. For that reason, we may expect a change of religion to arouse strong reactions from Travancore's dominant castes and classes, and we will try to trace the effects of the conversion movements on the internal social structure.

To place Christian conversion in the wider context of the colonial dispensation, we have to look for other changes that took place under the imperialist aegis at the same time. Therefore, an enquiry will be made into the introduction of English education in Travancore and the opening of plantations in the hills. In the second half of the century, Travancore became increasingly integrated into a growing world economy. Since the untouchable communities, however marginal, were also affected by this social and economic transformation of the country, it becomes relevant to ask about the relation between Christian conversion, expanding education and the commercialization of agriculture. We will turn to that question in the central chapters of this book.

Some of the most persistent misunderstandings concerning the nature of Indian society—sometimes strongly reinforced by missionary perceptions of that society—were that religious values represented the sole status determinant and that social mobility was altogether impossible. Empirical research, especially after

World War II, has drastically changed this traditional picture. First, it was established that castes were ranked not only according to ritual purity, but also according to economic position and political power. Next, research demonstrated that there was no general agreement about the existing ranking order and that many groups objected to the places assigned to them. And finally, most important of all, it was unmistakably proved that Indian society did allow social mobility, in the past as well as in the present, its most conspicuous form being Sanskritization.[13]

Usually, the ritual, economic and political determinants in caste ranking are positively correlated. But if castes improve their economic and political position, a status inconsistency arises. Faced with such an inconsistency, castes may start to claim a higher position in the ritual hierarchy by adopting the customs of locally dominant castes, which are considered to be more Sanskritized. These customs may include life-cycle rites, worship of the great Hindu deities, severe restrictions of the female sex, and abstinence from meat, liquor and many other things considered to be impure. More often than not, social and economic changes are at the root of Sanskritization movements. Material improvement, the acquisition of political power, education, leadership, and a desire to move up in the hierarchy, are all relevant factors in the Sanskritization as described by Srinivas, and each case of Sanskritization may show all or some of these factors mixed up in different measures.[14] Especially under colonial rule many political, economic and technological changes took place, which created new opportunities for groups to improve their position. However, Srinivas remains doubtful whether Sanskritization will ever enable untouchables to cross the barrier of untouchability.

Sanskritization is an attempt at upward mobility within the caste system. Mass conversion towards Christianity, on the other hand, implies a break away from Hinduism in favour of a new religion. Whereas Sanskritization, at its best, results in positional changes within the existing hierarchy, Christianization holds out a promise of more structural change by its adaptation to a more egalitarian Great Tradition, including achievement and individual responsibility. These are nice distinctions. But it remains to be seen,

[13] The concept of Sanskritization has been introduced first by M.N. Srinivas 1962, 1965 (1952) and 1969.

[14] Srinivas, 1962, p. 57.

whether the egalitarian aspects of Christianity did really change the converts' position in society and their relations with other communities. We may also ask to what extent the changes that did affect the converts' lives bore resemblance to the adoption of prominent Sanskrit values by other mobile Hindu castes.

This study is not the first attempt to describe the history of south Travancore's untouchables. Kusuman and Saradamoni have published valuable monographs on the history of slavery in Travancore and the emancipation of the slave castes, especially the *Pulayas*, in the nineteenth century. Their studies are mainly based on indigenous government sources and cover larger groups over the whole area. The well-known studies by Hardgrave and Jeffrey provide very interesting insights into the history of south Travancore's untouchables. But the chief emphasis in Hardgrave's work is on the *Shanars* or *Nadars* living in Madras territory, while Jeffrey is mainly occupied with analyzing the decline of the *Nayars*, one of the dominant castes in nineteenth century Travancore. Local historians have also shown interest in this field of study. Yesudas and Gladstone, to mention only the most prominent among them, have made extensive use of the missionary sources to reconstruct the nineteenth century history of their own Christian community. Yesudas' publication of documents, sometimes translated from local languages, and Gladstone's painstaking archival research were extremely useful to my own efforts in writing this book and I certainly owe them a great debt which I gladly acknowledge. But not being part of the communities under study, with all the obvious drawbacks it entails, also enabled me to maintain a more critical distance to the subject-matter of this study, especially in the appreciation of the European missionaries and the practical effects of their work.

Being a source-oriented study, this book will confine itself to the untouchables living in the LMS missionary districts in Travancore. But in spite of the fact that the LMS archival collections will merely be used as a source of historical information on the untouchables, this book almost inevitably tends also to become a history of missionary organization and practice. However, in line with the new trend in the study of Christianity in India, as expounded by David in his review of the six-volume *History of Christianity in India*, my intention is to give a key place not only to the western missionaries but also, if not more, to the common people organized within the church, to focus on their cultural, economic and political encounters, and to shift the emphasis from Christian theology to the persistent popular beliefs and practices, the line where established religion shadows off into popular piety. For too long the writing on mission and ecclesiastical history in India belonged more to the realm of hagiography than to history. Together with the often well-founded suspicion of Eurocentrism, this seems to be the main reason why academic historians have largely ignored ecclesiastical history, regarding it as unworthy of scholarly attention and as peripheral to the main stream of Indian history.[15] I can only hope that this book will serve to strengthen that new trend.

[15] David, pp. 5–13; Etherington, pp. 117–20.

II. A Short History of Travancore

II.1 Society and Religion

Travancore is situated in the south-west of India along the Malabar coast, more or less coinciding with the southern part of the present-day Kerala state. Geographically, this region consists of a long and narrow strip of land—174 miles in length with a medium breadth inland of 40 miles. According to myth, the land was reclaimed from the sea by the divine hero Parasurama, who offered it as a present to the Brahmins. It stretches from south to north and is locked in by the Arabian sea and a high mountain wall, the Western Ghats. The extreme southern tip is formed by Cape Comorin or Kanyakumari, named after another mythical deity, the daughter of one of the kings in the *Mahabharata* epos. Here in the south, the flattened mountains allow some communication with Madras territory to the East, for instance through the Aramboli pass, which forms the southern entrance into Travancore. From here, the chain of mountains rises steeply to the North, from the Mahindragherry (2000 feet above sea level) and the Ashambu (4000 feet) in the South to the Annamudi (8800 feet) in the northern part of Travancore.

It is because of this high mountain range, that contact and exchange between Kerala and the centre of peninsular India was always extremely difficult. The Chera empire, that had its base in present-day Tamilnadu, brought at least a semblance of unity in the region of Kerala, but after its dissolution about A.D. 1100, Kerala was left on its own and socio-political developments remained largely undisturbed by events in the rest of India. Within Kerala, internal communications were not without obstacle either, as numerous rivers flowed from the Ghats to the sea, crosscutting the area and complicating overland transport The Travancore coast alone was already intersected by no less than fourteen rivers, besides a great number of subsidiary streams and rivulets.[1] This territorial fragmentation contributed to a political system of many

[1] Horsley, p. 57.

small chiefs and petty rulers linked together by loose ties of vassalage to rivalling kings, all claiming succession to the last Chera emperor.[2]

Kerala, however, lay open to commercial contacts with seafaring nations such as the Phoenicians, Arabs, Chinese and, more recently, Europeans. Its most important towns were thus to be found on the coast and at the mouth of navigable rivers. The region behind this coastland was made up of low hills and fertile valleys, which formed the main area of traditional village settlement. Here, the cultivation of rice, spices, coconut palms and other crops was very much fostered by a usually abundant rainfall, which was especially heavy where the mountains were close to the sea. This abundance of water did not necessitate the people to reside closely together around a scarce number of wells, but permitted a dispersed settlement pattern, many families having their own well in their own family compound. The highlands of the Western Ghats represent a third socio-geographical category. Covered with rich forests, they were the traditional preserve of various tribal groups who in recent times had to face mounting pressure from coffee and tea plantations and timber companies.

Because of the existing trade connections overseas, Christianity and Islam could enter Kerala at a very early date. There is insufficient historical evidence for the apostle Thomas' alleged visit to India, but there is no doubt whatsoever that Christianity had a firm footing in Kerala from the beginning of our era and long before the Christianization of Europe had started. In the same way Islam had followed the channels of commerce to Kerala and became an established community long before the first Muslim empire had been founded in north India. Nevertheless, the 1875 Travancore census returned but a negligible proportion of Syrian Christians for the South of Travancore with the exception of Quilon and only about 50,000 Muslims for the same area. Numerically more important was the Roman Catholic fishermen population on the coast which had been converted by early Portuguese missionaries and numbered more than 65,000 in 1875 (see Appendix I). However, Hinduism unmistakably was the dominant religion.

One of the most fundamental problems in Hinduism is the question how the pure, i.e. that what represents life, can be

[2] Jeffrey, 1976, p. 1.

guaranteed against the impure, i.e. that what relates to death. The caste system with its specific rules with regard to food, marriage, rituals, etc., and its specialization in certain occupations appears to be pre-eminently suited for the purpose of avoiding or at least regulating contact with the impure. In Kerala, caste was a major consideration in the maintenance of social relations. Prevailing ecological conditions, like the already mentioned abundant rainfall and dispersed settlement pattern, may be hypothesized to have allowed the principal of ritual purity to achieve its maximal expression by the elaboration of distance pollution. Lower castes were permitted to approach the higher ones only up to a prescribed number of steps and the greater the ritual distance, the greater the spatial separation. Nowhere in India was the caste system as rigid as in Kerala.[3]

At the summit of the ritual hierarchy sat a small sprinkling of Brahmins who combined economic wealth as landholders with spiritual authority as temple priests. According to myth, Parasurama had peopled Kerala with Brahmins, at least with the most exclusive, Malayalam-speaking section among them, the *Nambudiris*. Behind this mythological story lies the historical truth that somewhere in Kerala's history Brahmins succeeded in gaining ascendancy over this region and in settling themselves as lords of the land. In Travancore, they paid no taxes but were subsidized by the state in the form of religious entertainments and ceremonies. Whereas sacred and official texts—usually emanating from the Brahmins themselves—described them as no less than God's representatives on earth, looked upon by their happy tenants as their royal liege and benefactor, missionary sources referred to them less respectfully as presumptuous, ignorant and exploitative.[4] The Malayali Brahmins never amounted to more than 1 per cent of the population. Very few of them resided in South Travancore, but the much more numerous Tamil Brahmins were also held in high esteem (see Appendix I).

Next in importance, apart from a small number of *Kshatriyas*, came the several subdivisions of the *Nayar* warriors, who were nominally *Sudras*. They numbered about 20 per cent of the population and were primarily involved in agriculture and administration

[3] Mencher, 1966a, p. 137 ff.; Miller.

[4] See for instance the Census of Travancore 1875, p. 191 versus Smith, p. 168.

although some lower sections worked as oilmongers, potters, barbers and washermen. As most Malayali Brahmins led a secluded life, leaving the management of their temporal affairs to *Nayar* agents, the *Nayars* were in fact ruling the country, dominating its political, economic and military affairs.

A very remarkable and widely studied peculiarity of this *Nayar* caste was its matrilineal kinship system. All *Nayars* who could trace descent matrilineally from a common ancestress lived together in one house and held their property in common (*taravad*). This matrilineal system should not be confused with matriarchy, as the leadership of the *taravad* was firmly vested in the eldest man, the *karanavan*. Before puberty, Nayar girls passed the *tali*-rite, inaugurating their marriageable life, and after that they could accept men as sexual partners in the so-called *sambandham*-union. But usually both partners remained in their own *taravad*. The women bore children for their own descent-group, and the men left their property not to their own but to their sisters' children, the so-called *marumakkathayam* law of inheritance. As only the eldest son of a *Nambudiri* family was permitted to marry within his own caste, several *Nambudiri* men also entered into a *sambandham*-union and became visiting husbands in the families of the more aristocratic *Nayars*, underlining again the Brahmin-*Nayar* condominium of society.[5]

About one-third of the population of Kerala as well as Travancore was made up of untouchable communities. Major groups among them were the *Shanars*, *Ezhavas* and slave castes like the *Pulayas* and *Pariahs*. One may contest that *Shanars* and *Ezhavas* belonged to the untouchables—as members of these communities are understandably inclined to do—but there is no doubt that in the nineteenth century they were treated as such by their social environment.

The main body of the *Shanar* caste lived across the border on Madras territory (present-day Tamilnadu). In Kerala they were a small Tamil-speaking minority group, exclusively to be found in the most southern *taluks* of Travancore (See Appendix 1). Traditionally, they used to tend the palmyra trees which they climbed with marvellous dexterity. From the flowering stem at the very top

[5] A detailed discussion of the *Nayar* matrilineal system can be found in Fuller, 1976.

of these tall, mastlike palms they extracted the sweet juice, which was made into jaggery, fermented into toddy or distilled into arrack.[6] Apart from that they worked as agriculturists and labourers. Most probably the impurity ascribed to them had to do with their toddy business—though most *Shanars* themselves abstained from alcohol—and with their tapping hammer which usually was made from the bone of a cow or bullock.

For a long time *Shanars* had had to suffer many social disabilities and harsh economic oppression. Because of these unfortunate circumstances, missionary sources claim, the *Shanars* had become "timid, deceitful and ignorant". But on the other hand, the same sources acknowledge that the *Shanars* were industrious, frugal and fairly enterprising, capable of development in a high degree.[7] Those *Shanars* who had managed to acquire at least some wealth and power formed a distinct subsection and were called *Nadans*; though important in Madras, they were not very numerous in Travancore.

More to the north and up to Cochin, the *Ezhavas* occupied a position similar to that of the *Shanars*. As tenders of the coconut palms they lived by toddy-drawing, rope making and weaving, worked as (sub)tenants or agricultural labourers, but also included several landowners, astrologers, teachers and *ayurvedic* physicians.[8] In the first part of the nineteenth century the *Ezhavas* like the *Shanars* were extremely poor and suffered from the same disabilities. While a *Nayar* might approach but not touch a Brahmin, a *Shanar* or *Ezhava* was supposed to pollute him within a distance of thirty-six paces. The main difference between both groups was their language and kinship system. The *Shanars* as a rule followed the pattern of patrilineal monogamous marriage, but the majority of the Malayalam-speaking *Ezhavas* shared the matrilineal customs of the *Nayars*, entering into sexual relationships with women of their caste by the simple expediency of "giving a cloth". Whereas among the *Shanars* inheritance was from father to children (the *makkathayam* law of inheritance),

[6] A useful description of the technique of toddy-tapping is given by Mateer in LMS Chronicle, 1882, pp. 297–8; and by K.B. Kurup, pp. 9, 16.

[7] Mateer, 1871, p. 41; Hacker, 1908, p. 16. No doubt the flattering comments by later missionaries were also influenced by the *Shanars'* willingness to embrace the Christian gospel in large number.

[8] Saradamoni, p. 130; Rajendran, pp. 25–6.

most *Ezhavas* left their property to their sisters' children (*marumakkathayam*). To the south of Quilon, the *Ezhavas* followed a mixed system of inheritance; the woman and her children were entitled to half of the man's self-acquired property, the other half passing to his nephews.

Undoubtedly the most wretched and downtrodden groups in Travancore were the slave castes, the *Pulayas* and the *Pariahs*. The *Pulayas* were primarily concentrated to the north of Trivandrum, whereas the *Pariahs*, found in every *taluk* of the country, were most numerous in the regions south of it (see Appendix I). Slavery in Travancore was not domestic, as all castes, the *Shanars* and *Ezhavas* included, considered themselves defiled if slaves approached them within too short a distance. Therefore, the slaves carried out the most arduous tasks in the rice fields, like pumping, hedging and digging, and were condemned to remain in the fields or to live on the banks of canals or the borders of the wilderness. Always exposed to dew and rain they were seldom free from rheumatism and fevers, and when not required for labour they were left to starvation, to live on wild roots and snails or to resort to theft. One missionary reported that they were:

> bought and sold like cattle, starved, flogged like buffaloes, made to work all day for a little rice, and kept at a distance as polluted ... suffering from ignorance and evil habits of drunkenness and vice, and devoted to demonism and sorcery'.[9]

In another letter written home we read about the slaves that

> [T]hose who reach maturity are doomed to work like beasts of burden, to live in wretched hovels, to eat the most offensive animals & reptiles, & to be treated as out-castes by their fellow-creatures. Their evidence is not admitted against their masters, if they meet a free person on the road, they are bound to run from him lest they pollute him .... By few are they comforted, pitied or relieved; none seek to remove their distresses, & no man cares for their souls.[10]

There was no agreement as to the relative status of these lowliest of the lowest. According to some contemporary observers, the

[9] Mateer, "The Pariah Caste ..." p. 7.

[10] Abbs, letter from Neyoor, 29.3.1841, in LMS Archives, Incoming Letters, Box 3.

Pulayas were considered to be slightly higher, as they, unlike the *Pariahs*, abstained from the flesh of bullocks and cows left dead by the roadside. But they used to eat fish which was cooked with arrack and in consequence of that *Pulayas*, especially the men, could be intoxicated for hours during broad daylight. As far as their marriage customs were concerned, *Pulayas* had much in common with Malayalam-speaking matrilineal castes, leaving inheritance partly to sons and partly to sisters' sons. The Tamil-speaking *Pariahs*, although also influenced by matrilineal patterns, especially in the Trivandrum area, mainly adhered to a law of inheritance by sons.

Even among themselves, these poor untouchables observed caste distinctions. *Pariahs* from one subdivision would not eat or intermarry with those of another. Generally, *Pariahs*, in the extreme south of Travancore, were socially less reduced than their caste-fellows further to the north. Speaking of the slave castes in general and of the *Pulayas* in particular, the missionary Mateer concluded that

> from lengthened acquaintance we have found them just like other men—under the power of many evils engrained in them from long-continued ignorance, superstition and oppression, but simple hearted, grateful for kindness, deeply attached to those who show themselves their friends, improving under instruction.[11]

The 1875 census called them "an extremely useful and hard-working race" and even praised their "rare character for truth and honour which their superiors in the caste scale might well emulate".[12]

It is very difficult to determine to what extent these untouchables belonged to the Hindu religious community. In state documents, like the census reports, they are reckoned to be Hindus. Influences of the Hindu Great Tradition are indeed clearly discernible in their deities and mythology, and some *Shanars* claimed to be *Saivites*. The prominent part played in their religious practices by blood sacrifice and spirit possession, however, seems to exclude the

[11] Mateer, 1883a, pp. 33–59, quotation from p. 43; further information on the slave castes has been obtained from Mateer 1871 pp. 45–8; idem, "The Pariah Caste ..."; report by Pattison in Jacob, Manuscript History, p. 112; Saradamoni and Kusuman.

[12] Census of Travancore 1875, p. 206.

untouchables from the ranks of the Hindu establishment. According to Caldwell "Demonism in one shape or the other may be said to rule the Shanars with undisputed authority", whereas Krishna Iyer spoke of animistic practices among *Pariahs* and *Pulayas*, modified in the direction of orthodox Hinduism.[13] We will come back to the religion of the untouchables in the last chapter of this book.

II.2 Political Events

As said before, somewhere in Kerala's history *Nambudiri* Brahmins succeeded in gaining ascendancy over this region. Most historians assume that these Brahmins were immigrants from the north and had settled in Kerala in the first millennium A.D.[14] In the same way, the *Ezhavas* are said to have been Buddhist settlers from Ceylon who established coconut farming in Kerala. Some historians even argue that all Malayalam-speaking castes, except the slaves, are immigrants.

The historian E.M.S. Namboodiripad has criticised these basic assumptions. Emphasizing fundamental similarities in social organization among the Malayalees and their manifest differences with comparable groups in northern India, he contends that all Malayalam-speaking caste Hindus in fact belong to the same ethnic stock. In substantiation of this thesis, he refers to the Syrian Christians and Muslims, who—as is generally accepted—settled in Kerala in very small numbers only, but influenced local society by numerous conversions. In the same way Namboodiripad holds that *Nambudiris* and *Ezhavas* were those sections of Malayalam society which were most deeply influenced by small groups of Brahmins from the north and Buddhists from Ceylon. Following this line of reasoning, the internal differences and contrasts found within Kerala are not to be attributed to waves of immigration, but to a process of socio-economic differentiation within the region itself.[15]

As far as politics are concerned, Kerala had no tradition to boast of. After the dissolution of the Tamilnadu-based Chera empire no power had been able to restore unity and Kerala remained divided

[13] Caldwell, quoted in Gladstone, 1984 p. 28, and Krishna Iyer, vol. III, p. 147.

[14] Mencher, 1966b, p. 185; E.K. Pillai, *Dark Periods of Kerala History*, Kottayam 1953, quoted by Mencher.

[15] Namboodiripad, pp. 20–5, 43 ff.; Pullapilly, pp. 25 ff.

in numerous petty kingdoms and principalities, engaged in seemingly endless warfare.

At the beginning of the eighteenth century, two major powers dominated the political map, i.e. the port-based kingdoms of Calicut in north Kerala (Malabar) and Cochin in central Kerala. In the south the region was politically fragmented into a number of fairly small and weak political chiefdoms.

One of these small powers was Travancore (Tiruvidamkod) in the extreme south. In 1729 a young *Nayar* prince by the name of Martanda Varma succeeded to the throne of Travancore. In a series of brilliant but ruthless military campaigns, he conquered all neighbouring principalities and, in contravention of the established rules of Kerala warfare, he disbanded their armies and annexed their lands. His no less ambitious successor, Rama Varma (1758–98) pushed Travancore's frontiers still further, controlling the whole of south Kerala from Cape Comorin or Kanyakumari in the south to the weakened but still significant state of Cochin in the centre.[16]

Travancore's emergence as the major single force in this region may be viewed in terms of military fiscalism, a process which occurred both in eighteenth century Indian regimes and under early Company rule. Military prowess and skilful leadership were important instruments in this process. But the main decisive element was the gradual shift in state income from tribute by local chieftains to general revenue collected by a body of state officials for the purpose of maintaining a centralized military system. This augmentation of military power enabled the state not only to eliminate its rivals but also to further increase its extractive capability.[17] A growing state control of the export trade was also part of Travancore's military fiscalism. The state even established a monopoly in the trade of pepper, the most lucrative export product, and constructed its own commercial outlet for it, Alleppey port (1762), to challenge the dominance of the European trading companies in this field.[18]

The eighteenth century *Rajas* also made the first attempts to improve internal communication and laid the foundations of a modern bureaucracy. Many *Nayars*, who after defeat by Travancore

[16] Jeffrey, 1976, pp. 3–4; Fuller, 1976, pp. 17 ff.

[17] Stein, 1985, pp. 391 ff.

[18] Schenk, pp. 31–2.

had been deprived of their military functions, silently found their way into the new state army or the expanding administrative services. But in these services and especially in the higher levels of the bureaucracy, they had to face strong competition from foreign personnel, viz. Tamil Brahmins. These Brahmins had been invited by the *Raja* for the very reason that he wanted to replace the old chiefs' families with politically loyal, non-martial and non-local officials.

In a certain sense, Travancore, starting from a tiny area near Nagercoil in the extreme south, can be seen as a Tamil incursion into Malayalee territory, resulting in a powerful and permanent kingdom. The southern part of this kingdom—the region that will be dealt with in this book—forms a borderland where Tamil and Malayalee influences co-existed and mutually penetrated.

Travancore's rise to power had been spectacular but its independent existence could not last for long. In the second part of the eighteenth century the emergence of the state of Mysore constituted a serious menace to the Kerala kingdoms. In 1766 the Mysoreans attacked Calicut for the first time and in 1784 Malabar was permanently occupied. In view of the impending danger on its northern frontiers, Travancore entered into a military alliance with the British East India Company, and a Company official was stationed in Trivandrum as political representative and liaison officer. After a fierce battle, the British troops invaded Mysore and forced its king, Tippu Sultan, to sue for peace. Malabar was ceded to the Company and became a directly administered British district.

Travancore survived but had to pay dearly for it. It had to defray the entire expenses of war against Mysore—partly in pepper—and had to pay a substantial annual subsidy in exchange for continued military protection by the Company (1795). Henceforth it had to recognize the British paramount power. In 1800 Major Macaulay—uncle of the famous historian—became the first Resident in Travancore with supervisory powers over Cochin that had concluded a similar treaty.

An insurrection by discontented *Nayar* warriors who had become redundant due to British military protection failed and a new treaty was forced upon Travancore, "binding on the contracting parties as long as the sun and moon shall endure" (1805). The annual subsidy was raised to no less than Rs 8 *lakhs* and the *Raja* had to promise "to pay at all times the utmost attention to such advice as the English Government shall occasionally judge it necessary to offer to him"[19] through the kind services of the Resident.

The 1805 treaty placed a heavy burden on the state's finance and soon the payment of subsidy fell in arrears. The *Raja* resented the increase of tribute as an act of extortion, but Resident Macaulay, "haughty and overbearing" as one Kerala historian has called him,[20] remained indifferent to all entreaties for reduction. In this situation another attempt was made to drive the Europeans out of Travancore.

This second insurrection was led by the *dewan*, Velu Thampi, who tried to rouse the people into revolt by appealing to their sense of loyalty to the throne and above all to their religious feelings. His surprise attack on the Residency, however, failed and the British response was prompt and swift. The Government of Madras issued a proclamation, declaring it to be their sole intention to rescue the *Raja* from the evil influence of the *dewan*, and assuring the people that there would be no interference in their religious institutions. At the same time, British troops moved into Travancore from different directions and marched on Trivandrum. In the south, the Aramboli pass was taken and in the neighbourhood of Nagercoil the remaining forces of the *Raja* were routed and dispersed.[21] Within months, the revolt was suppressed (1809).

In 1810, a new Resident was appointed for Travancore and Cochin, Colonel John Munro. Shortly after his arrival, the *Raja* of Travancore died and Munro managed to have him succeeded by his personal choice, the young and inexperienced *Rani* Lakshmi Bai. She could do nothing else than place herself and her country under the guidance and protection of the East India Company and on the day of her accession to the throne she declared the British Resident "as my own elder brother",[22] i.e. the *karanavan* of the *Nayar* matrilineal system.

This assignment perfectly suited Munro's own preferences. In 1811 he also took over the position of *dewan* and he used his power

[19] Text of the 1795 and 1805 treaties in Regional Records Survey Committee, vol. I, pp. 106–09, 112–5.

[20] A.K. Panikkar, 1969, p. 162. For a similar comment, see Regional Records Survey Committee, vol. I, p. 26.

[21] Caldwell, pp. 266–8; Nagam Aiya, vol. I, p. 440.

[22] Nagam Aiya, vol. I, p. 457.

to introduce several reforms. "No description", he reported to Madras, "can produce an adequate impression of the tyranny, corruption and abuses", prevalent in Travancore, where for the oppressed and exploited people, "complaint was useless, redress hopeless."[23] To change this situation Munro drastically curtailed the judicial powers of local officials, instituted *Zillah* courts and a Court of Appeal, reduced the expenditure on religious institutions, abolished several vexatious taxes and improved the system of revenue collection. For revenue purposes, the state came later to be organized into four revenue divisions, from south to north the division of Padmanabhapuram (Pulpanabapuram), Trivandrum, Quilon and Sharetala (later Kottayam), each under a *dewan peishkar*, an officer subordinate only to the *dewan*. The state was further subdivided into 32 *taluks* or districts, each ruled by a *taluk* officer or *tahsildar*, exercising revenue, police and to a small extent magisterial powers.[24]

There is no doubt that many descriptions tend to overestimate Munro as the man who laid the foundation of modern Travancore.[25] But from the British point of view, his main and decisive achievement undoubtedly was, that in less than three years, Travancore was able to pay off not only the arrears in subsidy but also all the outstanding debts to the Company to the extent of Rs. 18 *lakhs*.

The threat of annexation and incorporation into Madras Presidency was averted. Travancore as well as Cochin were allowed to carry on a quasi-autonomous existence as Native States. The whole administration of the state remained vested in the *dewan*, who was responsible to the *Raja* (in 1866 honoured with promotion to the title of *Maharaja*) and resided in Trivandrum the capital. But all important measures of legislation and finance, the appointment of higher officials and even the succession to the *musnud* or throne had to be submitted to the British political representative. Economically, Travancore was integrated into the British imperial system. In consequence of that, the total value of exports and imports showed a remarkable increase. To control this external trade, a British Commercial Agent was placed in charge of the

[23] Col. Munro's report to Government of Madras, 7.3.1818, quoted in Nagam Aiya, vol. I, p. 461 and in Yesudas, 1975, pp. 15–16.

[24] Mateer, 1871, pp. 66 ff.; Nagam Aiya, vol. I, pp. 461–2; Census of Travancore 1875, p. 99.

[25] Nagam Aiya, vol. I, pp. 461–8 and especially Yesudas 1977 passim.

state's Commercial Department and stationed in Alleppey. Coconut and coconut products, plantation crops like coffee and tea, and various spices constituted the main export articles. Under colonial paramountcy the Travancore economy was converted into an export oriented primary producer. But the reverse of this agrarian commercialization was that in the second half of the nineteenth century Travancore had to import a major part of its food requirements in rice and paddy.[26] As far as defence was concerned, the Travancore army, apart from a Royal bodyguard and escort, was placed under the direct command of British military officers with headquarters in Quilon. Travancore's independence, therefore, was purely nominal.

TABLE I. POPULATION OF TRAVANCORE 1816–1901[27]

Year	Number of People
1816/20	906,587
1836	1,280,668
1854	1,262,647
1875	2,311,379
1881	2,401,158
1891	2,557,736
1901	2,952,157

This political situation remained largely unchanged during the colonial period. After Independence Travancore and Cochin were amalgamated and in 1956 they were reunited with Malabar to form the state of Kerala. The Tamil-speaking southern part of former Travancore state was then ceded to Tamilnadu and forms what is now known as the Kanyakumari district.

[26] Isaac & Tharakan, pp. 2–7.

[27] Census of Travancore 1875, p. 102 and 1931, Part I, p. 331. The pre-1875 census enumerations are generally not considered to be very reliable.

III. Colonialism and Missionary Activity

III.1 The Company's Charters

Many authors tend to treat Christian missions as part and parcel of western colonialism. Studies made from this perspective argue that missionary bodies were hand in glove with the expansion of European economic and political interests and in fact served as the cultural arm of western imperialism. At the beginning of this century young Chinese intellectuals started to accuse foreign governments of using the mission as an excuse for military intervention. To substantiate their charge, they could refer to the recent past, when Christianity and opium entered China about the same time. For India, Panikkar has pointed at the dubious association of Christian missionary work with aggressive imperialism, and Jawaharlal Nehru has shown his amazement that "the gospel of Jesus, the gentle but relentless rebel against untruth and injustices" could so easily be made a tool of imperialism, capitalism and political domination.[1]

Not seldom do missionary sources themselves confirm this view. In the seventeenth century, the Dutch East India Company permitted missionaries to work among the native population "so that the name of Christ may be spread and the advantage of the Company furthered."[2] Two centuries later, the Church Missionary Society in Travancore concurred with official opinion that "the diffusion of genuine Christianity in India" was "a measure equally important to the interests of humanity and to the stability of our power."[3] And even in this century, missionaries in the Assam tea plantations prided themselves on their influence "in promoting order and discipline and in keeping the coolies contented and hard working."[4]

Nevertheless, a more searching inquiry reveals that the "mission as handmaiden of imperialism theory" presents too simple a version

[1] K.M. Panikkar, p. 297; Nehru, pp. 50–1.
[2] Quoted in van den End, p. 87.
[3] Annual Report CMS 1816–1817, p. 54.
[4] Becker, p. 63.

of reality. The English East India Company, to confine ourselves to that case, employed chaplains—normally Church of England clergy—but only for the benefit of its own servants, soldiers and merchants in Asia. And it took no less than eighty years before a Christian church for Company servants was built in India.[5] The Company proved still more reluctant to permit Christian missionaries to enter India, and before the nineteenth century, missionaries were allowed to operate only on the fringes of the Company's territories. These early missionaries were not British but came from Lutheran and Pietist churches in northern Europe and Germany, who had started to operate from small enclaves like Tranquebar and Serampore under the Danish flag. As Frykenberg recently reminded us, these missionaries never shared the political ambitions of the adventurers who at the same time launched the English and French Companies and their influence on for instance the Tanjore kingdom was free from any design of political nature. Occasionally, the local congregations of their converts and followers even had to suffer persecution from Company officials, and appeals for redress to London were met with stony rebuffs.[6]

Instead of being welcomed, the growing number of chaplains and, also, British missionaries in India had to face cold indifference, if not open opposition from most Company officials. There were several reasons for this non-cooperative attitude. First of all, the Company as a commercial organization could rule over the destinies of so many people in India only by profound accommodation to existing institutions, religion not excluded. Therefore, large sums were granted for the maintenance of Hindu temples and priests, and Government officials attended the more famous religious festivals with a view to showing them respect. An EIC, however, propitiating local deities and participating in Hindu ceremonies, provoked irksome questions from missionaries on the spot who, through their parent societies at home complained that the Company was behaving like the heathen kings of old, and criticized what they saw as the unchristian behaviour of individual Company servants.

Another reason for the Company's refusal to tolerate missionary activity was the suspicion that the Christian missionaries held

[5] Richter, p. 97.

[6] Frykenberg, 1985, p. 322.

radical political views and were actually seditious. These suspicions were not entirely unfounded, as Alter reminds us. Some Baptists in England had openly expressed sympathy for the ideas of the French Revolution, and American Presbyterians had played a prominent part in the American Independence Movement.[7] But most important of all, it was widely feared that the idol breaking inclinations of the early missionaries, who often evangelized in front of temples and mosques, might stir hostile and even violent reactions from indigenous society and upset a delicate balance of power. The resulting political instability could endanger profitable commercial relationships and thus threaten the Company's most vital interests.[8]

Missionary sources complain that the Company, in spite of its profession of religious neutrality, tended to unbounded favouritism towards the native religions and unjust slighting of Christianity.[9] Nevertheless, the number of Christian missionaries steadily increased, especially in the course of the nineteenth century, and official attitudes and policies changed. An important part in this change was played by Charles Grant, a Bengal civil servant of high rank who after twenty-two years of service returned to England in 1790, and became Chairman of the EIC's Court of Directors and Member of Parliament.

In 1787 Grant had already published a "Proposal for Establishing a Protestant Mission in Bengal and Berar", aimed at winning Government patronage for mission work in India. In 1792, he repeated his proposals in a more extensive document entitled "Observations on the State of Society among the Asiatic Subjects of Great Britain." In this document he argued that the prevalent disorder in India was largely attributable to the existing religious values and superstitions, apart from Company mismanagement in the past. As he saw a thorough reform of a degenerate Indian society as the sole justification for a continuation of British rule in India, the inevitable conclusion was that Christian religion and Western learning had to be introduced on a large scale. "The true cure of darkness is the introduction of light." For that purpose,

[7] Alter, p. 18; see also Forrester, 1980, p. 24.

[8] Frykenberg, 1978; Sen Gupta, p. 14; Manickam, 1977, p. 42. Thomas Twining, who had large interests in the tea trade, demanded in an open letter, published in *The Times* (1807), that all missionaries should be instantly dismissed from India, see Witz, p. 72.

[9] Richter, p. 185.

Grant requested the Government not only to permit Christian mission and education but also to support it.[10]

As the EIC's Charter was due for renewal the next year, Grant's friend William Wilberforce, the leader of the anti-slavery movement in British parliament, attempted to insert a clause in the new Charter, empowering and requiring the Company's Directors "to send out, from time to time ... fit and proper persons ... as schoolmasters, missionaries, or otherwise ... and to give directions to the governments ... in India to settle the destination and to provide for the necessary and decent maintenance of the persons so to be sent out".[11] This so-called "Pious Clause" aroused such vehement criticism that it was withdrawn before the third reading of the Bill in the House of Commons. According to Silvester Horne, the Company's Court of Directors thanked God that the conversion of India was finally considered to be impracticable.[12]

However, the 1793 Charter did not close the matter, but in fact initiated an extensive debate about the work of the Christian missions in India.[13] Many Company officials, who took an active part in this debate, held the opinion that the propagation of the Christian Gospel with Government support was a risky adventure, certain to alienate the Indian peoples from the British Government and likely to produce more serious repercussions. A retired civil servant protested that he "would rather save the lives of 30,000 fellow-countrymen in India than save the souls of all Hindus at so dreadful a price."[14] And if, contrary to all expectations, the missionary effort might prove to be successful, the objection was raised that a Christianized India would be less easy to govern and more inclined to claim independence from Britain.

Even within the churches, the advocates of mission work in India had to deal with strong opposition. The General Assembly of the Church of Scotland declared the preaching of the Gospel "among barbarians ... to be highly preposterous in so far as it ... reverses the order of Nature" (1796).[15] And a High Church man

[10] Embree, pp. 141–6; quotation from Grant's "Observations ..." in Sen Gupta p. 66.

[11] Text of the clause in Embree, p. 152 and Laird, p. 61.

[12] Silvester Horne, p. 91.

[13] A first thorough and systematic analysis of this debate has been given by Witz.

[14] Mayhew, p. 101.

[15] Mayhew, p. 101.

with Whig principles like Sydney Smith actively Compaigned against the admission of missionaries to India who

> would deliberately and piously ... expose our whole Eastern Empire to destruction for the sake of converting half a dozen Brahmins, who after stuffing themselves with rum and rice ... would run away, and cover the Gospel ... with ridicule ... Thanks God, that we are not required to desert our domestic duties in order to give a remote chance of conferring greater benefits on strangers at a distance.[16]

In defence against these criticisms, Grant contended that the propagation of the Christian faith, far from being a danger to British rule in India, would actually produce more obedient citizens. He flatly rejected the suggestion that the Indians, if Christianized, would demand separation from the British Empire, as religion would supply a common bond of union and attachment between the Government and the governed. In its success would lie our safety, not our danger, he argued. It would serve the interests of commerce and, in the words of Wilberforce, greatly strengthen the foundations of empire.[17] As far as the Company's policy of religious non-interference was concerned, Grant and his friends stressed that the Company could not refuse to assist Christian missions while at the same time it used its authority to maintain Hindu religious institutions. These arguments, Sen Gupta has remarked, carried more weight with the manufacturers of Britain than with the Government. They may explain the growing middle class support for what came to be called the missionary enterprise.[18]

In the meantime, developments in India were following their own course. In 1793, the year that the "Pious Clause" had to be withdrawn, William Carey and a colleague arrived as missionaries in Calcutta. Their entrance was illegal but the Governor-General Sir John Shore was sufficiently moved by his evangelical sympathies to connive at their activities.[19] In 1799 they were followed by four other missionaries who, on the advice of Grant, went to Serampore to seek protection under the Danish flag. Whereas the Bombay Presidency remained effectively closed to missionary penetration,

[16] Quoted in Robinson. p. 188 and Mayhew, p. 27.
[17] Sen Gupta, pp. 57–8.
[18] Sen Gupta, p. 58; Embree, p. 247.
[19] Ingham, p. 6.

the Bengal Government was not always hostile to illegal missionaries. In Madras there were even friendly relations between the Company and the Danish mission in 1793. In return for the tactful friendliness shown to the EIC, the Madras authorities not only approved of this mission, but even prevailed on the Directors in London to grant free passage to some missionaries and free transport of their letters and stores. This accommodating attitude, however, depended on the authorities on the spot and had no recognized basis in official policy.

A change of policy occurred only after another renewal of the Company Charter in 1813. Mounting pressure from missionary bodies and returned Company officials, like the former Resident in Travancore and Cochin, Macaulay, resulted in a parliamentary resolution asking the Government not to support but at least to permit the work of Christian missions in India. This resolution was translated in a special clause, inserted in the new Charter Act, and was passed without difficulty. The clause laid down that, in view of the interests and happiness of the native inhabitants of British India

> such measures ought to be adopted as may tend to the introduction among them of useful knowledge, and of religious and moral improvement, and in furtherance of the above objects, sufficient facilities ought to be afforded by law to persons desirous of going to and remaining in India, for the purpose of accomplishing those benevolent designs.[20]

Although the missionaries were not explicitly mentioned, they were definitely included among the "persons desirous of going". Henceforth they were permitted to enter and remain in India, provided only that they were in the possession of a valid official licence as prescribed for all British subjects by the India Act of 1784. The only financial obligation that was laid on the Company was the support of a small church establishment, primarily meant for British personnel in India.

During the first years after 1813, the British *raj* adopted a cautious policy towards the missionaries. After the arrival of Lord Bentinck as Governor-General in 1828 and the growing influence of reform-minded Utilitarians in leading circles, Government policy definitely changed in favour of the Christian missions. The

[20] Duff, p. 424.

number of Protestant missionaries showed a sharp increase, approximating 339 men in 1851, and British personnel soon outnumbered their German colleagues. At the same time, these later missionaries were, at least to a certain extent, nationalistic in their Anglicanism or Scottish Presbyterianism, and a closer alliance emerged between the British-Indian Government and most missionary societies. But even then, the imperialist-cum-missionary tendency never became completely dominant and was always being challenged, especially by non-British missionaries and non-Anglican societies.[21]

The clause in the new Charter Act permitting missionaries to enter India applied to British territory only. The rulers of native states had retained the right to refuse entry and in several important kingdoms no missionary activity of any kind was permitted up to 1947. In Travancore, however, the first missionary had arrived in 1806. He belonged to the London Missionary Society and this early start of missionary work was largely due to the kind interference of the first British Residents in Trivandrum. The next chapter will describe the entrance and operational structure of the LMS in Travancore in more detail. Before that, we will discuss the emergence of the LMS and analyse the socio-economic background of its Travancore-based missionary personnel.

III.2 The London Missionaries' Background

Eighteenth century England showed a serious decline in moral standards and a great lack of spirituality and social involvement. As a reaction to this, a religious revival movement emerged, both inside and outside the Church of England. This revival movement was marked by a strong belief in "the saving power of the Christian Gospel and also in the necessity of personal conversion and an intense moral earnestness."[22] Apart from a new religious awakening, the movement also showed a deep concern for the underprivileged poor, which manifested itself in a large number of charitable activities, like the establishment of schools and hospitals. In social terms, the movement was very much middle class in character and it spread widely among the trading and professional classes.

[21] Frykenberg, 1985, p. 323.

[22] Sen Gupta, p. 7; see also Witz, pp. 37 ff.

As Sen Gupta has pointed out, the concern for the salvation of the neglected people in England gradually grew into a concern for the salvation of non-christians in other countries. It found practical expression in the growth of numerous missionary societies within a short period.

Long before the revival, the *Society for Promoting Christian Knowledge* (1698) and the *Society for the Propagation of the Gospel* (1701) had been formed within the Church of England. They had very limited objectives and fallen into a slumber, they were resuscitated to new life at the end of the eighteenth century. In 1792, mainly through the efforts of William Carey, the *Baptist Missionary Society* was established. In 1795 it was followed by the *London Missionary Society*, the main missionary body working in south Travancore. Shortly after that, the Evangelicals in the Church of England formed the *Church Missionary Society* (1799). Its chief promotors belonged to the so-called "Clapham Sect" which counted among its members people like Charles Grant, William Wilberforce and John Shore (later Lord Teignmouth) who from 1793–98 had served as Governor-General of India. At the beginning of the nineteenth century, the Methodists, who had already started missionary work among the negro slaves in the West Indies, established their *Wesleyan Methodist Missionary Society*. Some smaller societies were formed at about the same time,[23] and they all joined the campaign to open India for missionary work.

According to its official historiographer, the London Missionary Society (LMS) arose from an awareness that British responsibility towards the people of Asia and Africa could not be adequately discharged by serving them with British goods only. These people were equally entitled to share in "the hopes of the Christian Gospel and the resources of the Christian civilization."[24] Several preparatory meetings laid the necessary foundation and in September 1795 the LMS was formally established. The first treasurer was a prominent merchant and one of the secretaries worked on the Bank of England. These happy circumstances may have contributed to the successful raising of £3,000 within one month. The foundation meeting appointed a Board of thirty Directors, twenty of whom were ministers. The management of the LMS was placed

[23] Sen Gupta, pp. 8–9, 13 ff.

[24] Silvester Horne, p. 2, quotation from p. 3.

in their hands. They were to be elected annually from the members of the society and membership was open to anyone who paid an annual subscription.

The LMS was founded by people from different denominations. Therefore, one year later, the LMS accepted and ratified as its fundamental principle, that

> its design is not to send Presbyterianism, Independency, Episcopacy, or any other form of Church order and government ... but the glorious Gospel of the blessed God, to the heathen; and there it shall be left ... to the minds of the persons whom God may call into the fellowship of His son from among them to assume for themselves such form of Church government as to them shall appear most agreeable to the word of God.[25]

This principle was honourably observed, but the LMS came to draw its chief support from the Congregational Churches of Great Britain. Although the LMS was thus in fact predominantly a Congregational (or Independent) organization, it is not known that the denominational preferences of an applicant were ever made a barrier to acceptance.[26]

In 1796 the first LMS missionaries departed for Tahiti and the South Seas. The first LMS man in India was Nathanael Forsyth, 1798. When he found that the Government of Bengal would not allow him to do his work, he went to the Dutch settlement of Chinsurah, 20 miles to the north of Calcutta. In 1804 the first LMS missionaries landed in south India and one of them started a LMS station in Travancore in 1806. He was followed by many others and before the end of the century a total of 48 LMS men and two lady missionaries had started working in south Travancore.[27]

Who were these 50 people? A greater knowledge of their socio-educational background and personal motivation may help us in better understanding the modus operandi of the LMS in this part of India. It may also further our understanding of the specific ways

[25] Silvester Horne, p. 16.

[26] Congregationalists and Independents (i.e. independent of the Union of Congregational Churches) will be treated here as one category.

[27] George H. Ashton, an Eurasian engaged by the missionaries in Travancore as an assistant (1819–60), and Miss Bertha Blanchard, who sailed in November 1900, are not comprised in this list of 50 persons. But Arthur Parker, who arrived in Travancore in 1900, has been included, as he had been working in India since 1888.

in which different sections of Travancore society were affected by and responded to the missionary presence.

Information about these 50 people can be obtained from the Candidate Papers, the alphabetically ordered personal files of LMS servants. Unfortunately, the information from this source is defective. The application letters, printed questionnaires and personal correspondence in these files focus upon Christian doctrine and personal religious experience more than on professional and educational qualifications. Apart from that, some files contain only one or two letters or a medical report, and from prominent missionaries like Mead and Cox a personal file is completely lacking.[28] Thus, an investigation of these papers may suggest some trends, but does not yield a complete and clearcut picture.

Looking at their places of birth, our group of 50 missionaries came from all parts of Great Britain. There was some concentration on London (Mabbs, Pattison, Ramsay and A. Thompson) and its immediate surrounding districts (Crow, Edmonds, Fells, Fry, Hewett, Newport, Whitehouse). Scotland proved also to be a fertile recruiting ground, supplying at least ten missionaries for south Travancore (Allan, Duthie, Gillies, Harris, Leitch, Lowe, C. Miller, W. Miller, Russell and Thomson). Mateer and Miss MacDonnell came from northern Ireland.[29]

As we have seen, the LMS was predominantly an organization of the Congregationalist or Independent Churches. But its fundamental principle of unity in mission enabled several members of other denominations to join it. The first LMS missionary in south Travancore was a German Lutheran (Ringeltaube). A considerable number came from the Presbyterian Churches (Duthie, Leitch, Mateer, C. Miller, J.C. Thompson and Thomson) and at least three missionaries came from a Methodist background (Dennis, Knowles, Mead). Sometimes their mutual cooperation and acceptance bordered closely on cultural arrogance. A. Thompson, a Baptist, was ready to offer his services to the LMS and had no

[28] Additional information can be gathered from Sibree's Register, the Personal Papers in the LMS Archives (for instance on Cox, Box 2/mf.894), and from memoirs and biographies, like Robinson, Birrell, Smith and Hacker 1887; some bio-data were also obtained from the always helpful archivist of the Council for World Mission (formerly the LMS), Rev. J.T. Hardyman. (See also Appendix III).

[29] All information is derived from the Candidate Papers or from Sibree's Register, unless otherwise stated.

desire to push his own views to the point of controversy, as long as "my sphere of work be among the unenlightened or heathen."[30]

The personal files contain many references to the candidates' motives to look for missionary employment. They all amount to the same overriding, ultimate aim that can be summarized as "the great commission of our Lord 'Go ye', which I take to mean me" (Osborne). As Warren has pointed out, these nineteenth century missionaries were "inner-directed men", knowing an overwhelming compulsion to follow some course of action which to others may seem wildly inopportune or extremely dangerous. The nineteenth century, with its expanding horizons, was full of that kind of men.[31]

As one candidate wrote, it was not an easy thing "to leave one's native country, to give up numerous and exalted privileges and in exchange become a stranger among Barbarians" (Smith). Another one said he realized very well that he was leaving fair prospects of worldly comfort for privation, annoyance and fatigue (Mateer). As he anticipated a hard life in rough conditions, Foster went even so far as to camp out on the moors in Yorkshire for several weeks "to harden myself somewhat." But all of them expressed their willingness to face these hardships, as they believed that God had called them and that it was their duty "to serve the salvation of heathen souls" and "to turn sinners from darkness to light" (Baylis, Abbs). Subordinate to this a few of them also mentioned a desire to improve the temporal conditions of the Indian people and to look after their material needs (Baylis, Parker).

Previous to their acceptance by the LMS, most of the candidates, their wives or fiancées, had been engaged in Sunday school teaching. Many of them had gained experience in open air preaching or the temperance movement, visiting the Norwich poor houses (Abbs) or the slums of Whitechapel (Hewett). Gillies had worked as a missionary in Ireland and Duthie was one of those who had served as tract distributor of a Christian Instruction Society, "to warn the neglected outcastes in our own lanes and courts." As has been explained above, the concern of these young men for the less

[30] The same Thompson was also of opinion that "the ideal Christian missionary should be—first and foremost—a man. Physical and morally he should exhibit manly qualities ..." (1887). Five years later, the first two lady missionaries of the LMS arrived in Travancore.

[31] Warren, p. 44.

privileged in their own society could easily turn into a concern for the salvation of non-christian peoples in Asia and Africa. The inner-directed men wanted to go outwards. "I long to go Osborne told the LMS Directors and Wills wrote that he so strongly believed in his calling that he should go on his own account, in case the LMS was not willing to accept him.

According to Warren, the missionary movement, as far as Britain was concerned, "was in part an expression of a wider development— the social emancipation of the underprivileged classes." The great majority of the nineteenth century missionaries belonged to a distinctive and emerging class, shortly summarized as that of "the skilled mechanic", comprising artisans, small traders, schoolmasters and so on. It was the same class that provided the pioneers of the trade-union movement which drew its early inspiration largely from the same source.[32]

The LMS missionaries in Travancore seem to conform to this more general picture of the nineteenth century British missionary movement. From the Candidate Papers the occupational background of at least 38 of our group of 50 men and women can with some certainty be ascertained; the remainder, most probably, went straight to college. Eight of these 38 people belonged to the category of skilled artisans and had been working as shoemaker, carpenter, stonemason, gasfitter, tailor or draughtsman (Addis, Abbs, Edmonds, Hewett, Knill, Mabbs, Parker and Smith). Ten other men had previously been engaged in trade or business, like assistant to a chemist, accountant to a bank, bookkeeper in a cotton manufacturing firm, printer or shop-assistant (Baylis, Dennis, Fry, Knowles, Lee, Leitch, Mateer, A. Thompson, Whitehouse, and Wills). When at college in London, Cox occasionally served the business of his father and brother who owned a wool mill in Gloucestershire.[33] Six of them had held a teaching position, either in a school or in a private capacity (Dennison, Miss Derry, Gannaway, C. Miller, W. Miller, Roberts), while six other men had been apprenticed to a butcher, stuff merchant, chemist or printer (Crow, Foster, Fells, Lowe, Mead, J.C. Thompson). Two candidates had previously worked as clerk in a solicitor's or an advocate's office (Bach, Duthie). Finally, three men had already

[32] Warren, pp. 37, 39, 42.

[33] LMS Archives, Personal Papers, Box 2/mf. 894.

served the ministry as missionary or clergymen (Gillies, Osborne, Russell). Ramsay had been employed as surgeon in a London hospital and Miss Macdonnell was working as a nurse. The agricultural occupations were conspicuous by their absence.

Warren and Oddie suggest that in the early nineteenth century, virtually all British missionaries in India came from a similar skilled working class background, whereas after 1844 candidates are said to have been drawn from a more representative cross-section of the population.[34] Our Travancore sample does not confirm this view. The occupational background of the 15 candidates that applied in the last quarter of the century does in no way differ from that of the whole group. Parker, the last man of our sample to arrive in Travancore (1900), came from a poor working class family. He had learnt his Greek, Latin and English grammars while in the workshop, had done his translation work in the same place at meal times, while he had managed to do his Euclid by studying early in the morning before going to work at six. This brings us to the question of education.

Some of the young men who offered their services to the LMS were already in college, usually following courses in Theology or Arts. Others made their application while still working as an artisan or tradesman, sometimes—like Parker—combining their daily labour with self-study. In both cases, but more in the latter, they used to ask for acceptance as a student of the Society which, if granted, meant that the LMS undertook to pay for their education.

At the beginning most LMS candidates went to Gosport Academy near Portsmouth (Crow, Knill, Mault, Mead, W. Miller, Smith, J.C. Thompson *c.* 1815–1825). There was no college building in Gosport, the students boarded with various families, and in the vestry of the local chapel they were daily lectured by Dr. Bogue who combined his pastoral duties with the task of educating young men for missionary labour. Many students received their first practical training by working with French prisoners of war on ships near Portsmouth.[35] Later on, more established colleges were attended by LMS candidates. In 1835/36 Cox, Lewis and Pattison studied at Highbury College in London. From 1855–60 no less than eight candidates for Travancore were at Bedford College

[34] Warren, pp. 39–49; Oddie 1979, pp. 11–12.

[35] Birrell, pp. 35 ff; Annual Report, LMS, 1812, p. 18.

(Dennis, Duthie, Gannaway, Lee, Lowe, Mabbs, Mateer, Wilkinson) and in 1890 Hewett and Osborne, who later worked together in Vakkam and Attingal, were class-mates at the Nottingham Congregational Institute. Most medical missionaries received their training at the Medical Mission Training Institute in Edinburgh (Fells, Fry, Leitch and Lowe).

A current theme in the candidates' correspondence with the Society was their wish to extend their college term, whereas the Directors showed an inclination to send them out as soon as possible. In view of this impatience, a well-wisher of the Society felt compelled to warn the LMS that its cause depended upon the educational qualifications of the missionary, "even tho savages or negroes are to be the object of his labors" (1816). In most cases missionaries were sent out immediately after their ordination. But the knowledge of their country of destination was very limited and fed mainly by reports and letters received from colleagues already in the field.[36] A study of the languages was started only after arrival in India.

The formal educational qualifications of the missionaries from different societies varied considerably. Compared to the LMS, missionaries of the Church Missionary Society (CMS) enjoyed a slightly higher status but their academic record was distinctly better. In Oddie's sample of missionaries in India for the 1844–1886 period about 40 per cent of the CMS agents were university graduates as against 20 per cent of the LMS. The Methodists, on the other hand, numbered only a handful of men in India with university degrees.[37] In the second half of the nineteenth century, Warren asserts, the educational standard of the British missionaries in India showed a marked improvement.[38]

Once again the LMS in south Travancore does not fit in this more general all-India pattern. University qualifications were extremely scarce among the Travancore missionaries and never reached the 20 per cent level. Leitch and Russell had followed university courses but held no degree. Harris and Wills were the

[36] *The Indian Missionary Manual—Hints to Young Missionaries in India*, compiled by John Murdoch, went through many reprints since the 1860s and consisted of numerous, topically arranged quotations and summaries from existing, mainly missionary works on India.

[37] Oddie, 1979, pp. 12–3.

[38] Warren, p. 50.

only graduates. Harris, M.A. in Theology from Glasgow, arrived in 1832 and Wills, M.A. in Science from Cambridge, arrived in 1892. The LMS also sent six medical men to south Travancore and they all had some medical qualification (MRCSE, LRCSE or MBCM). The fact that five of these six medical men arrived in the second half of the century was merely due to the late start of the medical mission in Travancore.

The conclusion must be, that it remains very difficult to ascertain whether later missionaries were more educated or better prepared on their arrival in Travancore. In 1827 Addis, who was in the business of selling leather, was sent to Travancore after a short course in Latin from his parish pastor and a nodding acquaintance with the Lancastrian system of education in his native place. He was no exception. In the second half of the century Dennis, a young printer and later foreman compositor in the Illustrated London News office, offered his services to the LMS and after a short course of study, he arrived in Nagercoil. Having little more than a basic knowledge of the Tamil alphabet but without proper pronunciation, he found himself in charge of a large district, that embraced many miles of country, thousands of converts, hundreds of schools, a great number of native agents, printing and binding establishments etc.[39] This spectacular career raises the question whether in some cases missionary employment may have served as an attractive avenue of social mobility to people who had few alternatives at home.

We have seen that in offering their services to the LMS, the candidates were actuated by spiritual motives and a strong sense of duty. There is no reason to doubt the sincerity of their statements. At the same time, other considerations may have been at work in a more unconscious or at least less explicit way. As an expression of a social emancipation movement the missionary society presented to members of the lower middle class career opportunities that were infinitely broader, carried more responsibility and entailed more influence than any conceivably open to them at home.[40] The LMS was perfectly aware of this as can be seen from the questionnaire that was used for the greater part of the century. One question (no. 7) asked whether the desire of improving his worldly

[39] Annual Report LMS, 1857, p. 80.
[40] Forrester, 1980, pp. 23–4.

circumstances entered into the candidate's motives of application; and a subsequent question (no. 12) asked him, seriously and sincerely, to state his motives "as there is too much reason to fear that some persons have become missionaries under the influence of improper principles."

In their written replies some candidates explained that if they were led by material considerations they would do better by applying somewhere else. Mabbs sacrificed a profitable career as draughtsman and engraver on wood to his missionary intentions, and Addis sold his leather business and offered the proceeds to the LMS treasurer. Nevertheless, many other instances indicate that missionary employment could bring considerable social and economic improvement.

As a youth, Baylis felt seriously hampered for want of a good education and the means to procure one. He only knew some apothecary's Latin, his "ordinary business" as a chemist's assistant. Neither had Duthie, an advocate's clerk, much education to boast of. Duthie's parents were very poor and his schooling remained confined to the usual branches taught in a Scottish parochial school. To them and many other young men of humble origin, acceptance by the LMS offered an unprecedented opportunity to develop their intellectual faculties and to raise their social status. In India Baylis became a prominent Tamil scholar, member of the Tamil Bible Revision Committee and Editor of the periodical *Desopakari*, right from its beginning in 1861. Duthie, who worked for more than fifty years in India (1856–1908), acted as principal of the Nagercoil Seminary and was awarded the degree of honorary doctor of divinity by the University of Aberdeen (1907).

Missionary employment could also serve as a stepping stone for a career at home. In their youth, Lowe and Fry had been apprentices to chemists. Their acceptance by the Edinburgh Medical Missionary Society enabled them to follow a course in medicine and the LMS sent them to Neyoor to staff its medical mission. After a short period of service Lowe had to return on account of ill-health of his wife. He was appointed as secretary and superintendent of the Medical Mission Training Institute in Edinburgh and after his death (1892) Fry came back from Neyoor to succeed him.

The first medical missionary in south Travancore, Dr. Ramsay, represents a different case. At the time of his application, he was already employed as surgeon in the hospital at Lambeth, London. According to the testimony of medical colleagues, his knowledge was sound but "not adequate to cases of capital importance" and it was even doubted whether he came up "to the standard at present required ... legally to entitle him to practice in England." These far from flattering comments did not prevent the LMS from accepting his application and Ramsay was asked to establish a medical mission in Neyoor. But after a few years, Ramsay preferred to enter the Travancore government and became the personal physician of the *Raja* (1842). His case resembled that of Mr. Roberts, a former army schoolmaster, who was engaged by the LMS to head its Seminary in Nagercoil. After four years of service Roberts accepted a lucrative appointment by the *Raja* as principal of the Government High School in Trivandrum.[41]

Jones may be seen as representative of the small number of missionaries who were able to capitalize on the economic opportunities that offered themselves in their field of labour. His background was poor and his education very defective, but on his return from India in 1877 he had considerable interests in several coffee estates, gardens and paddy fields in south Travancore.[42]

It is not argued here that the prospect of social advancement acted as the underlying motivating force which was only suppressed in the application papers because of official LMS disapproval. However, a critical evaluation of the candidates' papers and their later careers may help us to see that there was a connection between missionary employment and social mobility. Even though the social gains could not clearly be foreseen at the time of application, it may safely be concluded from this short investigation that mere spiritual motives do not exist, either in India or in England. The two clergymen who offered their services to the LMS may not have been prompted by material considerations, but their applications strongly suggest a wish to escape. The Rev. Osborne of Tutbury had strained relations with a group of parishioners; and the Rev. Russell of Rendall on the Isle of Orkney also had reason to prefer a fresh start somewhere else, as his

[41] Roberts' Malayalam letter of appointment (with English translation) in LMS Archives, Odds, Box 15/mf. 1102.

[42] Papers left by Mrs. Samuel Jones, LMS Archives, Personal Papers, Box 3/mf. 904. In 1875 Jones had been placed in charge of the Cooly Mission on the Travancore coffee plantations.

people complained bitterly of his "lack of zeal and devoteness to work."[43]

In view of their own social background, the missionaries might be expected to have much sympathy for the lower classes overseas and to work ardently for their emancipation. There were, however, two important impediments to any social engagement or political involvement. First, there was the fundamental belief that the mission had to work for the conversion of individuals and that only through its power to regenerate the individual, Christianity would surely regenerate society.[44] Secondly, as the mission was merely tolerated by the colonial government, missionaries had to undertake that they would offer all due respect to the civil authorities and abstain from all political interference. Nevertheless, even these constraints left the mission enough room to champion at least some of the interests of the lower classes.

Forrester emphasizes the difference in social background between the early missionaries and most of the Company's servants. He holds the opinion that the missionaries, who had found the class system of England impeding again and again their attempts at social improvement, could hardly be expected to look with affection upon the rigid caste structure in India. And Pandit adds that in view of the Evangelicals' revolt against the church hierarchy in their own country, it was only natural that they also raised serious objections to the caste hierarchy and high caste privileges.[45]

Oddie, on the other hand, does not think that the British missionaries were especially critical of the class system in Europe. Most of them had grown up in a society which stressed the value of worth rather than birth, enabling enterprising or talented individuals to rise through the class structure. Being in India, they only saw more clearly the shortcomings of the caste system which made them compare it unfavourably with the more flexible class system of Europe. Thus, Oddie contends that the principal reason for the missionaries' involvement in social and political protest cannot be found in their own social background or experience at home; "most of the pressure for intervention arose from the circumstances and developments within India itself."[46]

[43] Forrester 1980 p. 23 and Warren p. 51 acknowledge that at least in some cases missionary employment was sought as a way to social mobility.

[44] Oddie, 1979, pp. 17, 19.

[45] Forrester, 1980, p. 23; Pandit, p. 429.

[46] Oddie, 1979, pp. 7, 16, 66; quotation from p. 17.

As far as Travancore is concerned, the caste system here was exceptionally rigid and the treatment of the lower classes by their social superiors extremely harsh. But as the preceding discussion has shown, the LMS missionaries in Travancore—as compared to other missionaries elsewhere in India—had retained their skilled working class character throughout the nineteenth century. These two circumstances most probably influenced the missionaries' sympathy for Travancore's low and untouchable groups and stimulated their involvement in social protest, like low caste education, anti-slavery movement etc.

However, emphasis on individual conversion and respect to civil authorities were not the only impeding factors to a greater involvement in social change. A very important impediment was the missionaries' own built-in mental outlook and moral attitude. Although they were the propagators of the Gospel of Brotherhood, "they always and consciously wanted to maintain their distinct identity as the representatives of the ruling nation", an Indian church historian recently remarked.[47] Consequently, their fight against social inequality within Indian society could always cheerfully co-exist with a pronounced racial discrimination. And their support of social mobility movements from the lower rungs of Hindu caste hierarchy never made them receptive to the idea of a movement of national emancipation from the colonial power, not even within their own church organization, which remained strongly coloured by a benevolent paternalism. Attempts to cross the racial barrier provoked serious commotion, as the next section will show.

III.3 Personal Strains and Conflicts

The social order of the British in India resembled the caste system of the Hindus. At the top were the members of the senior government services. This ruling class was followed by British military officers and next in social order came different categories of businessmen, traders and planters. At the bottom of the scale ordinary British soldiers, domiciled Europeans and Eurasians were to be found.[48] A significant difference, however,

[47] Gladstone, 1984, p. 172.
[48] Allen, p. 45 ff.

was that in the social hierarchy of the *Raj*, religious specialists, such as missionaries and clergymen occupied a rather humble position on the periphery of fashionable European society.

Even among themselves, the missionaries were subdivided among several denominational subcastes with their own territorial sphere of influence. The relations between the LMS in the southern part of Travancore and the Church Missionary Society in the north were often strained and never free of rivalry. The arrival of the Salvation Army in southern Travancore in the 1880s was resented by the LMS as an intrusion in what it considered to be its own field and all cooperation was refused. Roman Catholics were regarded as heretics, even worse than heathen, and the fight against "bigoted popery" went along with hardly concealed attempts to take over its converts.

Internally, the 50 LMS missionaries and their families in south Travancore represented a fairly cohesive group, bound together by shared convictions, common origin and bonds of friendship, established at college or during a long sea-voyage. Not seldom family relationships further strengthened that cohesion. Mead and Mault, the founding fathers of the south Travancore mission, were brothers-in-law when they went out, and in England Dr. Fry married Miss Lowe, the daughter of his predecessor as medical missionary in Neyoor. More often, however, the family relationship was established after arrival in Travancore. Some young men went out single; others lost their wives at an early age, due to climate or lack of medical facilities. In 1866, for instance, Lizzie Mary Newport, wife of G.O. Newport of Pareychaley, died after four years of service at the age of 22 and was buried alongside two of her children. Incidentally, she illustrates the perseverance and self-sacrifice of many of these missionaries. Several of these young men or widowers married or remarried daughters of their older colleagues in the field. Whitehouse married a daughter of Mault (1849), Allan and Wills both married a daughter of Duthie (1892, 1896), Wilkinson married a daughter of Cox, the missionary of Trivandrum (1861), while Baylis, after losing his first wife, married another daughter of Cox (1865). After his death, his widow, Mrs. Cox-Baylis, married the widower Dr. Thomson, the medical missionary in Neyoor (1878) and a daughter of Baylis became the wife of Hacker (1887), after he had lost his first wife, etc.

At the end of the century the first lady missionaries arrived in India. Their presence widened the narrow boundaries of the missionary marriage network. The first lady missionary in Travancore, Miss Kate Derry, married Dennison (1898), while Gillies married a lady missionary from Calcutta (1895). The caste character of the mission also became manifest by sons and daughters assisting their parents in missionary labour. Cox and Duthie, for instance, received valuable help in their work from son and daughters, and later, Beatrice Jessie Duthie entered LMS-service herself (1901). Some candidates came from families which had already connections with the mission in general or the LMS in particular and medical missionaries, like Thomson, Fry and Fells were strongly influenced by their Edinburgh teacher and predecessor in Neyoor Dr. Lowe. Finally, Mrs. Ramsay, like Miss Lowe, had lived in Travancore before.

The close ties that bound many missionary families did not preclude internal strains and conflicts. When there were two missionaries in the same district, it was usually very difficult to settle satisfactorily the division of the work. In 1844 Pattison was even recalled by the Directors after his quarrel with J.C. Thompson had made the situation in Quilon unworkable. Occasionally, rivalry flared up between the wives of different missionaries about the division of subscriptions for female education, a branch of work many of them engaged in. But the most serious conflicts that shook the small LMS community had to do with the employment conditions of Dr. Ramsay and the remarriage of Mead and Cox with native Christian women.

The problem with Dr. Ramsay was that he was sent out (1838) without any instruments or medicines.[49] When he bought some surgical instruments on his own, the Directors charged them to his private account as the purchases were unauthorized. Also, it was decided that his estimate of medicines had to be agreed to every year. Ramsay complained bitterly of such treatment. He pressed the Directors for financial support to build a hospital and informed them that the only accommodation he could afford for surgical cases was an old stable.[50] Apart from that, his private accommoda-

[49] All information on the Ramsay Case is obtained from LMS Archives, Odds, Box 18, jacket 'Ramsay Case', unless otherwise stated.

[50] Ramsay, letter 2.12.1840, in LMS Archives, Incoming Letters, Box 3.

tion was far from satisfactory, as he considered his bungalow in Nagercoil to be situated at an unhealthy spot.

In marked contrast to this, stood the cordial way in which Ramsay was received by Dr. Brown, the *Raja's* court physician. Soon, Ramsay was also on friendly terms with the English military officers in south Travancore and rendered medical assistance at military stations, accepting *sirkar* money in return, as he thought his own travelling-allowance to be a mere pittance. Meanwhile Mrs. Ramsay, dissatisfied with her living conditions and bored with Nagercoil village, spent most of her time with the small European society in Trivandrum, where her daughter married a Captain Daly.

In these circumstances, Ramsay's relations with his fellow-missionaries became strained and gradually changed into open enmity. He was accused of neglect of duties, unwarranted absence from his station and refusal on various occasions to attend the sick before his travelling-expenses were paid. A meeting of the Travancore District Committee expressed its conviction, that Ramsay only used his situation in the LMS as a step to something better. Ramsay, on his part, felt slighted as he saw that complaints about his bungalow were not taken seriously. In 1841 he submitted his resignation and an acrimonious correspondence ensued about salary, instruments and furniture. Mead and Abbs, who had been able to remain on friendly terms with Ramsay, tried to save his services for their Neyoor station, but only roused the wrath of their brethren. The TDC meeting mentioned above accused Mead of a "general want of candour and straightforwardness" and concluded that "our confidence is completely shaken in being able satisfactorily to co-operate with Mr. Mead." Thereupon, Mead and Abbs called upon the Directors to transact the affairs and finance of Neyoor as a separate and independent station, as further cooperation with their fellow-missionaries, especially Mault and Russell, could only mean "renewal of strife and bad feeling."[51]

In this difficult and embarrassing situation the Directors in far-away London had to find a solution. After extensive correspondence and ample discussion, in December 1841 the Directors decided to accept Ramsay's resignation and to discontinue his services from midsummer 1842. In view of the deplorable want of harmony

[51] Mead and Abbs, letter from Neyoor, 14.9.1841, in LMS Archives, Incoming Letters, Box 3; Travancore District Committee Correspondence File 1841.

amongst the missionaries in south Travancore, it was also decided that the affairs of the several stations would henceforth be conducted by the resident missionaries of each station. This decision amounted to nothing less than a dissolution of the Travancore District Committee which was restored in 1858 only.

The English colony in Trivandrum, including Resident Cullen, was much incensed by the Ramsay case. His dismissal without a hearing was seen as shameful and unfounded, and the LMS was considered to be utterly undeserving of further countenance and support.[52] The local missionary, John Cox, seems to have been the man who had to suffer most for it. When shortly after that he dismissed a school-mistress, she went straight to Captain Daly and his wife (Ramsay's daughter) and told them stories implicating the honour of the Trivandrum missionary. The charges were made public and although investigations made by his brethren completely vindicated the missionary, feeling against him never disappeared, as later events would show. But before that a problem arose with Mead.

In 1850, after his second wife had died, Mead informed his colleagues of his intention to remarry Miss Lois Biddulph, the daughter of a LMS catechist. The LMS Directors do not seem to have disapproved, but vehement objections were raised by his fellow-missionaries in Travancore, as the woman in question was an Indian and a *Pariah* at that. Mault, Russell, Lewis and Whitehouse considered the proposed marriage to be "most injurious to the best interests of the cause of Christ in Travancore" and Lewis added that a *Pariah* or slave caste woman, however connected and well-educated, could never gain the esteem and command that were required of a missionary's wife.[53] This second objection may have been shared by a section of the local church which consisted chiefly of *Shanars*. But Mead's junior colleagues were his most bitter opponents and in a letter to the LMS Directors Mead expressed his surprise that there was "so much of caste spirit amongst Missionaries of our own and other societies."[54] The

[52] Mr. Caldecott of the Trivandrum Observatory, quoted in Cox, letter from Trivandrum, 19.4.1842, in LMS Archives, Incoming Letters, Box 3.

[53] Correspondence regarding Mr. Mead's marriage to a native woman in LMS Archives, Incoming Letters, Box 4. Also quoted in Gladstone, 1984, pp. 192–3.

[54] Mead, letter from Neyoor, 8.10.1851, in LMS Archives, Incoming Letters, Box 4.

Directors in their reply advised Mead that in case he insisted on the intended marriage, he must be prepared to go and take charge of some other Tamil mission station. In 1851 Mead did marry and since he was not prepared to leave Travancore, he had to retire. With him his wife's relatives, among whom were some of the chief agents of the mission, left and the LMS never regained a substantial foothold among the *Pariah* community in the Neyoor neighbourhood.

Missionary sources claim that Mead remained on fraternal terms with his former colleagues. Their correspondence, especially about the thorny question of transfer of missionary property, speaks a different language. The LMS awarded him a life-long pension in gratitude to his manifold services. But the main one to come to his rescue was the *Raja* of Travancore, who appointed him as Superintendent of the Government Printing Office and later as Inspector of Government Schools. Mead served the government for many years and after his death (1873) his widow was granted a state-pension of Rs. 300 annually.[55]

In 1861 another case occurred, involving John Cox, the missionary of Trivandrum. In aftermath of the Ramsay case malicious rumours had affected his reputation and he felt excluded by leading circles in the state capital. Some years later Cox had to welcome his daughters on their return from Europe with the sad news of their mother's demise. In 1860 the missionary fell ill and he received medical advice to return to Europe, at least for a change, after 22 years of uninterrupted labour. However, he preferred to stay.

Next year he disclosed in a letter to his brethren that for some months he had privately been married to Amy, a former *ayah* and teacher of the Girls' Boarding School, adding that she was in a state of pregnancy by him. In a most humble way, he asked to be allowed to resign from the LMS and urged his colleagues not to condemn him "as destitute of all faith and feeling."[56]

His fellow-missionaries received this information with unconcealed aversion. However much they appreciated Cox's eminent services as a missionary, they considered his marriage, performed in private by a native catechist, as illegal and prejudicial to the missionary cause. They recommended to the Directors in London to

[55] Report on the Administration of Travancore 1873–74, p. 168.

[56] Cox, statement 18.7.1861 and letter 27.7.1861 to the members of the TDC, in LMS Archives, Incoming Letters, Box 5/mf. 2665.

accept Cox's resignation[57] and even stopped his salary before the Directors had been able to reply. In private letters they referred to Cox's "disgraceful conduct" and "lamentable fall", and Lewis went even so far as to insinuate "vile passion", adding that old inhabitants of Trivandrum had always been of the belief that he was guilty of the charges referred against him twenty years ago.[58] To a large extent their harsh criticism was provoked by what they saw as Cox's indiscretion to cross the racial barrier. Even Cox himself was not entirely free from some racial prejudice, when he defended his wife "as one superior in character to the other natives."[59]

Cox also stayed on in Travancore. After Resident Maltby had refused him a Government position the crown prince and the *dewan* of the state asked him to manage their coffee estate in the Ashambu Hills. Thus started Cox's career as a coffee planter and he was soon to be followed by several native Christians. Later reports acknowledge the valuable services Cox continued rendering to the cause of the LMS, but he was also instrumental in bringing the Salvation Army to Travancore (1889).[60] To the great annoyance of the missionaries, the Salvation Army settled in the midst of LMS congregations and tried to win over their converts.

Soon after this affair, complaints were made that the missionary Baylis held intimate relations with the *ayah* in his household, who was also teacher at the Female Boarding School in Neyoor. The complaints were serious enough to warrant the institution of an Investigation Committee, that consisted of three LMS missionaries in Travancore, reinforced by the SPG missionary of Tinnevelly, Robert Caldwell. Personal relations were further strained by the Committee's insistence to hear an important witness whom Baylis regarded as unreliable and wanted to see dismissed from LMS

[57] Special Meeting Travancore District Committee 31.7.1861, in LMS Archives, Incoming Letters, Box 5/mf. 2665.

[58] Lewis, letter from Santhapuram, 16.10.1861, in LMS Archives, Incoming Letters, Box 5/mf. 2665.

[59] Cox, letter from Trivandrum, 27.7.1861, to TDC, in LMS Archives, Incoming Letters, Box 5/mf. 2665.

[60] Hacker, 1908, p. 50.

service. At the same time Mead added fuel to the fire by addressing a personal letter to the LMS Directors on the Baylis case. In the end, the Investigation Committee, though not entirely approving of Baylis' conduct, concluded that the evidence had failed to prove the existence of any improper intimacy between Baylis and the lady teacher.[61]

[61] Duthie, letters from Nagercoil, 7.6.1862 and 21.6.1862, and Proceedings of the Committee of Investigation, in LMS Archives, Incoming Letters, Box 5/mf. 2673, 2674.

IV. Missionary Advance in Travancore

IV.1 Entering the State

As we have seen, the Protestant mission in India started in the eighteenth century under the auspices of the Danes and the Germans. The landmark usually referred to is the landing of Ziegenbalg and Plütschau at Danish Tranquebar (1706). The first CMS missionaries in Tinnevelly, Rhenius and Schmid, were German clergymen and therefore, it comes as no surprise that the first LMS missionary to arrive in Travancore was also a German, named Ringeltaube. In 1796 he went to Calcutta on behalf of the *Society for Promoting Christian Knowledge*, but disappointed in his expectations he had returned to England. In 1804 he came back to India and landed at Tranquebar. When still on the eastern coast to study Tamil, he was requested by people from Mayiladi, a small place in south Travancore, to come to their village where many people were said to be desirous of embracing Christianity. Ringeltaube complied with their request and in 1806—one hundred years after Ziegenbalg—he made his first visit to Mayiladi (litt.: Peacock's dance). His first impressions were far from encouraging and in his journal Ringeltaube noted: "I had expected to find hundreds eager to listen to the Word instead of which I had a difficulty to make a few families attend for an hour."[1] Nevertheless, Ringeltaube came back the next year to settle more permanently in south Travancore.

In this enterprise Ringeltaube received substantial support from the first British Residents at the court of Travancore state. But his most important assistant was Vedamanickam or Maharasan, a *Pariah* from Mayiladi, who later was burdened with the name of his British benefactor Samuel S. Greathead.

In cases of extreme oppression, *Pariahs* in these southern parts used to seek refuge across the nearest border. It is probably for that reason, that high castes have been less able to degrade them than in the more northern regions. In the extreme south of

Quoted in Robinson, p. 79.

Travancore several *Pariahs* mixed pretty freely with members of intermediate castes, and some of them even enjoyed ancestral properties including land. Vedamanickam must have belonged to this exceptional category. His forefathers came from Tanjore which they had left to escape oppression. He was reasonably educated, grew up as a devout Hindu, and built a pagoda to the family god which he endowed with land. Disappointed with Hinduism, he became a Christian under the influence of family members in Tanjore. It was this Vedamanickam, who persuaded Ringeltaube to settle in Mayiladi and who offered him land for the construction of a chapel and a parsonage. Apart from that, he enjoyed sufficient confidence among the local people to act as a local teacher.[2]

One of Ringeltaube's first actions was to wait upon the *dewan*, Velu Thampi, to ask his kind permission to build a church in Mayiladi. Questioned by the *dewan* of what religion he was, Ringeltaube begged to inform him that he was of the religion of Major Macaulay, the then British Resident. "I never knew there was such a religion", was the short reply of the *dewan* who turned down the request.[3]

Shortly after that the same *dewan* led an armed revolt in a desperate attempt to drive the British out of Travancore (1808–09). The bitterness and resentment, created by the continuing interference in Travancore's internal affairs, was passed on to the mission and in a public proclamation the *dewan* warned the people that the British intended to abolish all religious and charitable institutions, and wanted to

> put up crosses and christian flags in pagodas, compell intermarriage with Brahman women without reference to caste or creed, and practise all the unjust and unlawful things which characterize Kaliyuga.[4]

Ringeltaube happened to be in Palamcottah at that time. Vedamanickam, however, was suspected to be a British spy and with other Christians from Mayiladi he had to flee to the hills and hide in caves, as all passes were closely guarded. They

[2] Mateer, "The Pariah Caste ..." pp. 18–9; Excerpts from Ringeltaube's Journal, in LMS Archives, Odds, Box 15/mf. 1092; Robinson, p. 91 ff; Agur, p. 424 ff.

[3] Agur, p. 503.

[4] Text of this proclamation in Nagam Aiya, I, pp. 434–6.

returned only when they saw the white tents of the English attacking force on the west of the Aramboli pass. Their grateful welcome to the invading Company troops is a clear manifestation of the early identification of Protestant Christianity with British political power.[5]

As soon as the revolt was over Ringeltaube went to Quilon to see Major Macaulay. In the new political situation the Resident had no problem to get Ringeltaube *sirkar* permission to settle in Mayiladi and to build a chapel there. This building was inaugurated at the end of 1809 and the next year nine more chapels were under construction. The Resident himself made Rs. 1000 available for the purpose, as the LMS Directors had not yet made provisions for church building.

Still more important was the kind assistance rendered by the next Resident, Colonel Munro, in obtaining land. On Ringeltaube's request Munro, acting as the *dewan* of Travancore, persuaded the *Rani* to grant the LMS two *sirkar* paddy fields, one in Vailakulam and one in Thamarakulam (1814). These fields gave full employment to many people and yielded two crops of 1464 *cottahs* of paddy per annum worth 350 Star Pagodas or Rs. 1200. Ringeltaube first refused to accept the royal grant because of the heavy revenue burden, but then the *Rani* consented to reduce it to 100 *cottahs* of tax a year. Under Ringeltaube's successors it was further reduced to a nominal tax of one *cottah* only. These fields made the LMS more independent of financial support from England and Ringeltaube wrote in his journal that

> this grant firmly established the Protestant religion in Travancore as long as the British flag shall continue to fly in as much as it secures the salary for Native teachers and some charity for widows and orphans.[6]

Some income from land was an urgent necessity, as Ringeltaube in his letters frequently complained that missionary headquarters failed to supply him with sufficient means. In its first years the LMS mission in south Travancore received more support from the British Residents in Trivandrum than from the Directors in London. But the reverse side of this benevolent patronage was a

[5] Hacker, 1908, p. 24; Robinson, p. 97 ff.

[6] Ringeltaube's Journal, quoted in Parker, Manuscript History, p. 4; Agur, p. 601 ff.

strong official involvement in missionary affairs. In this, the first Residents were led by a mixture of religious conviction and political calculation. In a letter to the Madras Government, Munro—perfectly in line with the argument raised earlier by Grant in England—expressed his belief that "the support of a respectable body of Christian subjects would contribute to strengthen the British power."[7] He was confirmed in this belief by Ringeltaube who assured him that the Protestant Christians were the only faithful friends of the British Government, "knowing that their lives are bound up in one bundle with theirs."[8] For the same reason, Munro invited the CMS to north Travancore with the express purpose to purge the Syrian Church of its "many Popish superstitions and ceremonies", and to reform it along the lines of the English Anglican Church. The first CMS agents were sent in 1816 and Munro suggested to the parent-organization to place its missionaries at his personal disposal.[9]

Communication between Ringeltaube and LMS headquarters in London seems to have been very defective. In 1811 Ringeltaube wrote that he had not received a word from the LMS for three years. On the other hand, when he left his station on the first day of 1816 the LMS Directors were taken by surprise, since no information of his intended departure had reached them. We should bear in mind that regular communication was also hampered by the fact that in those days it took seven to nine months for letters to reach their destination.

Ringeltaube had reported his intended departure, not to the Directors in London but to Colonel Munro.[10] When no immediate successor became available, the British Resident showed great impatience. He had reserved to himself the liberty of accepting or refusing any missionary who might be sent from Europe, and a

[7] Col. J. Munro, letter to Government of Madras, 30.3.1818, quoted in Yesudas, 1980, p. 245; see also Paulose, p. 36.

[8] Ringeltaube, report to Col. Munro, 1813, quoted in Agur, p. 598.

[9] Annual Report CMS 1816/17 p. 453 ff. and 1818 p. 119; see also "Travancore Early History" in LMS Archives, Odds, Box 15/mf. 1100. At first all CMS efforts were directed at the Syrian Christians. The Syrians resented this outside interference in their customs and after a break-up of the association in the 1840s the CMS had to start on its own.

[10] At least he informed W.C. Loveless, LMS missionary in Madras, of his intention to do so; see letter from Loveless, Madras 22.2.1816, in LMS Archives, Odds, Box 15/mf. 1100.

LMS correspondent in Madras warned the Directors in London that Munro was so desirous of a missionary in south Travancore that he would "place the first Missionary in it who may arrive, if he be a Man of Character whatever society he may belong to."[11] For some time the LMS missionaries in Madras considered relinquishing their Travancore station altogether, as they had a poor opinion of the work done by Ringeltaube. The LMS Directors, however, decided otherwise. They first appointed James Dawson of Vizagapatnam as Ringeltaube's successor, but he refused. He had heard that Colonel Munro controlled the mission and "wished the natives to be made Christians from Political motives", and Dawson could not approve of that.[12] Interestingly, this indicates that even at that time some missionaries rejected too close an association with political power. In the meantime, a fresh party of missionaries had arrived from England and one of them was Charles Mead, the new man for south Travancore.

Mead had sailed for India on 20 April 1816 on board "the Earl of Moira" in the company of eight other missionary families, among them two LMS colleagues, Render and Knill. In his letters Knill dwelled on the delights of intelligent Christian fellowship on the wide Atlantic, and the LMS official report referred to the voyage as "remarkably pleasing".[13] But in actual fact relations on board "the Moira" among these "inner-directed and strong-minded men" were not all that cordial and pleasant. Mead and Render, to confine ourselves to the LMS missionaries, absolutely could not stand each other and both heaved a sigh of relief when after arrival in India the Directors decided to send them to different stations. Render had yet another reason to feel unhappy. Weakened by seasickness he had collapsed on the deck after strengthening himself with a little brandy and water, which gave rise to the charge of intemperance and exposed him to the mockery of the crew and many fellow-passengers. The most stormy incident was created by Mead. On the king's birthday, Mead and one or two other missionaries forgot to drink to the king's health after dinner. Accused by one of the ship's officers of being a Jacobin,

[11] W.C. Loveless, letter from Madras, 16.3.1816, in LMS Archives, Odds, Box 15/mf. 1100; see also Mead, letter from Madras, 17.9.1816. ibidem.

[12] James Dawson, letter from Vizagapatnam, 7.7.1817, in LMS Archives, Odds, Box 15/mf. 1099.

[13] Birrell, pp. 59–61; Annual Report LMS 1817, p. 16.

Mead replied that he considered it no proof of loyalty or disloyalty not to drink to the king's health. When the officer insisted, Mead gave in, observing uncautiously that he had no objection "to drink confusion to royalty."[14] Something similar had once happened to William Carey who, before leaving for India, was strongly republican in his political views and on one occasion was rebuked by a senior Baptist missionary for not drinking to the king's health.[15] Mead was no Jacobin, but this incident earned him the reputation of a disaffected missionary right upon his arrival in Madras. The local missionaries were hesitant whether or not to give him a letter of introduction to Colonel Munro, and the LMS Directors considered calling him back to London to account for his conduct.[16] In the end the LMS Directors decided to send him a stern letter, reminding him of

> the Solemn assurances ... given to the Directors of the East India Co. that our missionaries ... would abstain from all political and civil concerns and confine themselves to the spiritual duties of their office—and yet, in defiance of all this, and while yet on the way to the scenes of your labours, you avow, and on a festive day ... a most democratical and disloyal and we may say, traiterous sentiment ....[17]

Finally, to his great relief, Mead was sent to Travancore. But on his way to Quilon he had to suffer further grief when his wife died, leaving him with a small baby. In December 1817 he arrived in Quilon and from there he went straight to Mayiladi, the place that about two years before had been vacated by Ringeltaube.

On leaving Travancore Ringeltaube had entrusted the management of all missionary affairs to his local assistant Vedamanickam. Pending the appointment of a European successor, Vedamanickam was authorized by a deed of transfer to superintend the congregations and schools, and to manage the property of land and buildings as carefully recorded by Ringeltaube in his Mission

[14] Mead, letter from Madras, 17.9.1816, in LMS Archives, Odds, Box 15/mf. 1100; see also Loveless, letter from Madras, 25.9.1816 ibidem.

[15] Alter, p. 18.

[16] Minutes of LMS East India Committee, 6.2.1817, in LMS Archives, Incoming Letters, Box 1; Loveless, letter from Madras, 25.9.1816 in LMS Archives, Odds, Box 15/mf. 1100.

[17] Letter from LMS Directors to Mead, London, 11.2.1817, extract in LMS Archives, Odds, Box 15/mf. 1101.

Book. Vedamanickam seems to have discharged his duties quite well, since Mead after arrival reported with characteristic condescension that Vedamanickam had done "as well as could be expected."[18]

Mead took over the native assistants that still actively served the LMS. Also, like Ringeltaube before him, he received the most kind assistance from the British Resident and Travancore Government. Shortly after his arrival Resident Munro offered his own circuit bungalow at Nagercoil to the London Mission and the *Rani* followed suit by granting the piece of land around it. Nagercoil was centrally situated on the main road from Trivandrum to Tinnevelly and in April 1818 Mead transferred his headquarters from Mayiladi to this place. The land offered by the *Rani* was to be used for the establishment of a press, school buildings and a large church.

Apart from land, the LMS received handsome financial donations. In 1818 the *Rani* of Travancore as well as the *Raja* of Cochin placed Rs. 5000 at the disposal of the London Mission. This money was used partly for the purchase of paddy fields at Pattamkulam and Vellamadam and partly for church building.[19] In these crucial years Munro used his influence not only to procure royal grants but also to enable the missionaries to buy land and building materials on favourable terms. Owing to his benevolent exertions and the kind disposition of the local government the London Mission was placed on a firm footing. Self-support, however, could not be achieved, since the missionary establishment and its personnel grew much faster than local income allowed.

For a short time, Munro even championed the appointment of Christian judges at Travancore Courts. These appointments were meant to increase the respectability of the Christian community as well as to improve the legal protection of converts through what was assumed to be a more impartial dispensation of justice. In the first months of 1818 Mead, freshly arrived from England, informed the Directors that he was surprised to find that the *Rani*'s Government had appointed him judge at the Nagercoil Court. At the same time Norton of the CMS was appointed to the Civil Court at Alleppey. In 1819 Munro wanted Knill, the LMS missionary who

[18] Mead, File "Travancore Early History", in LMS Archives, Odds, Box 15/mf. 1100; copies of entries in Ringeltaube's Mission Book, ibidem mf. 1093.

[19] Mead, letter from Quilon 4.4.1818 and from Nagercoil 26.10.1818, in LMS Archives, Incoming Letters, Box 1; Jacob, Manuscript History, pp 64–5.

had arrived the previous September, to become judge at Padmanabhapuram, but then official authorities in Madras intimated that they preferred to see no missionaries on these posts. As the LMS Directors also did not approve of their missionaries assuming public office, the experiment was short-lived.[20]

More successful were Munro's efforts to remove burdensome taxes and *corvées* that especially affected the lower classes to which most Christian converts belonged. We shall return to that shortly.

IV.2 Districts and Agency

In September 1818 Richard Knill had come to join Mead in Nagercoil, and in May 1819 John Smith and Charles Mault arrived from England. More missionaries followed, sometimes "en groupe" like in 1838 when Mead went on leave to England and returned with five new fellow-workers, Abbs, Cox, Pattison, Ramsay and Russell. The steady growth of LMS activity led to a continued expansion of the mission field and in the course of the nineteenth century the whole region between Quilon and Cape Comorin was organized in LMS districts and dotted with stations.

Nagercoil (litt.: temple of the serpent) became the first permanent station and developed into the centre of a large district. In the past, Nagercoil had occasionally been the residence of former *Raja's* and it still held some importance, having a *Zillah* court of law and a public bungalow for travellers. Its strategic location on the highroad to Trivandrum had earned the village one of the first post-offices in the 1850s—for a long time the only one within 40 miles.[21] One should not infer from this that south Travancore could boast of a good road system at that time. In the middle of the century travel from Nagercoil to Trivandrum was still very troublesome; conveyance was by *palanqin* and carts could pass only with great difficulty.[22]

[20] Annual Report CMS 1316–1817 p. 455; Munro, letter 18.1.1819, in LMS Archives, Odds, Box 15/mf. 1101; Mead, letter from Quilon, 4.4.1818, idem, Incoming Letters, Box 1. The appointment and maintenance of Christian attorneys was already suggested by Ringeltaube in a letter to Munro, quoted in Agur, p. 597.

[21] Whitehouse, letter 3.8.1855, in LMS Archives, Odds, Box 18, File Travancore & Education.

[22] Duthie, 1906, p. 11.

Round the missionary centre in Nagercoil, consisting of a church, bungalows and school buildings, grew a Christian settlement, independent of the original village. In 1901 the whole place had 25,782 inhabitants and within Travancore it was second only to Trivandrum in terms of population. Not far away lay the town of Kottar, the principal market of south Travancore, with public buildings like a government warehouse and a Catholic chapel. Still farther to the south lay Agasteesvaram, the old religious centre of the *Shanar* community. Nagercoil district was densely populated. The larger villages were primarily inhabited by *Nayars* and Muslims, but in the more numerous smaller villages *Shanars* dominated. Some inhabitants were employed in traffic or weaving, a small number worked as braziers or smiths, but the great majority lived off paddy cultivation and palmyra tree climbing.[23]

The second district organized by the LMS was Quilon. Quilon City, numbering about 8000 inhabitants in 1820s and more than 15,000 in 1901, formed the headquarters of a British regiment and contained a small European community, chiefly military. In 1821 Smith was sent to this northern place, more than 80 miles away from Nagercoil, with the express purpose to keep the Church Missionary Society out. The CMS with its centre in Kottayam had assumed language to be the most suitable line of demarcation between its field of operation and that of the LMS. Since Malayalam language dominated north of Trivandrum, the CMS had a church in Quilon cantonment, and a small number of congregations and schools in the vicinity of the town.[24] By sending a missionary the LMS more or less occupied the city. Faced with what it regarded as an encroachment upon its own field, the CMS preferred withdrawal to confrontation, but occasionally quarrels flared up over the question who was rightfully entitled to lay claim upon local converts. As a result the LMS region was divided in a Tamil- and a Malayalam-speaking area, which later caused serious problems in the set-up of central institutions.

In the first few years, the LMS mission in Quilon leaned heavily on the local military. The schools opened by Smith and his

[23] Annual Report Travancore District Committee, Nagercoil, 1858, p. 6 and 1867, p. 18; Horsley, pp. 21–2; Abbs, 1870, p. 238.

[24] Smith, letter from Quilon, 10.4.1821, in LMS Archives, Incoming Letters, Box 1.

successors were largely paid for by contributions from British officers, causing their closure during the Burma war (1825) when most units were transferred. Later, the LMS tried to keep more distance from the military and Thompson, the local missionary, called it unfortunate, that Christianity had entered Travancore in military uniform. But when Thompson died (1850), his funeral by the wish of the commanding officer was attended by all the officers of the regiment.[25]

Despite considerable efforts, Quilon never became a flourishing station. In contrast to the region south of Trivandrum, Quilon district proved to be "unusually barren soil", as the missionaries phrased it. Local response was virtually absent and the standard of instruction remained far from satisfactory, partly for want of qualified Malayalam-speaking agents. In 1850 Quilon numbered 200 native adherents which in the last decennia of the century rose to 3000.[26]

As Nagercoil witnessed a rapid expansion of activities and a steady increase of adherents, in 1827 it was decided to divide the district. The eastern division, with 34 congregations, remained under Nagercoil and was led by Mault. The western division, with 28 congregations, became a new district with a head station in Neyoor (litt.: butter village) led by Mead. Surrounded by a well-plastered wall this Neyoor missionary settlement looked like a small fortress. It was built on land that Mead had been able to buy very cheap. *Nayars* used to burn their dead on that place and therefore, many people did not dare to approach it lest evil should befall them.[27]

The whole district covered about 200 square miles and in the 1870s the missionaries estimated the population at about 126,000 people. A small number of local adherents came from the weaver,

[25] Thompson, letter from London, 9.8.1845, and Cox, letter from Trivandrum, 17.8.1850, in LMS Archives, Odds, Box 16/mf. 1106 and 1108. In 1886 Knowles reported that the Colonel in charge of the two companies was "an earnest Christian and has preached for us", letter from Quilon, 28.1.1886, ibidem, Incoming Letters, Box 11.

[26] Thompson comforted himself by the thought that there were enough people ready to be baptized, "but to me the purity of Christ's Church appears of greater importance than the number of Baptisms", report from Quilon, 23.11.1829, in LMS Archives, Odds, Box 16. Most information on Quilon has been derived from the "History of Quilon" File, ibidem, Box 18.

[27] Hacker, in LMS Chronicle 1889, p. 253.

fisher and slave castes. But mostly they were *Shanars*, some being respectable cultivators, others carrying on trade in jaggery, tamarind, paddy or cotton. A good number kept to their original employment of palmyra climbing.[28] Simultaneous with the establishment of Neyoor district, Travancore was made independent of the LMS in Madras and organized into the Travancore District Committee (TDC).

Right from the beginning, the LMS had wished to establish a station in the capital—Trivandrum. In 1827 Addis was appointed for Trivandrum. But Resident Morrison thought it was not prudent to apply to the state government for the necessary permission and Addis, after three years of waiting, left for Coimbatore. In 1838 Trivandrum was finally opened to the LMS thanks to the good offices of the British Resident General Fraser. The *Raja* even offered a piece of waste land for the purpose. Trivandrum (litt.: the city of the sacred snake) was important first of all as the centre of administration. It was built around a walled fort containing the *Raja's* palace, a pagoda of the royal family's household deity, and the *dewan's cutcherry*. The population within the fort was almost exclusively Brahmin. Two miles to the east on an elevated spot stood the British Residency. Spread around these centres were *bazars*, residential quarters and a small European cantonment. According to Horsley's description of 1839, the city numbered also several educational and scientific institutions, courts, palaces, a hospital and a printing press. In 1839 its population was estimated at 12,000 which in 1901 had risen to more than 57,000 inhabitants.[29] The LMS welcomed the opening of this station, as its presence in the capital offered an opportunity to exert more influence on the state's chief authorities, the *dewan* and the Resident.

Trivandrum became the centre of a fourth LMS district, covering an area about 33 miles long from north to south and holding a great variety of people. John Cox became its first missionary and he worked there for 23 years, having his residence in Kannamoola near Trivandrum. Later, Samuel Mateer shifted the mission premises to cantonment area. The LMS adherents chiefly came from the *Shanar* and *Ezhava* community. The first congregations were formed south of the high road and consisted mainly of *Shanars*;

[28] Annual Report Travancore District Committee 1858, Neyoor, p. 4; Hacker, 1887, p. 52.

[29] For an early description of Trivandrum, see Horsley, p. 24 ff.

from the 1860s new congregations were assembled to the north of the same road, dominated by *Pariahs* and *Pulayas*.[30]

About 25 miles south of Trivandrum and close to the high road to Nagercoil lay Pareychaley (Parassala), the centre of the fifth LMS district. The etymology of the name is unclear but probably it means "a place for *Pariahs*". Started in 1845 as a section of the Neyoor mission, it soon developed into a separate district (1854), that soon far surpassed the others in number of adherents (about 19,000 in 1900). Four miles to the east and on the bank of the Tambraparni river lay Kulitura. Kulitura was a large *Nayar* town with a *tahsildar* office, a small palace for the *Raja*, an *uttupura* and a bungalow for European travellers.[31]

The southern districts remained the most fertile recruiting ground for the LMS. Therefore, in 1846, Nagercoil district was further divided into three sections: a western section with its main centre in Santhapuram, half-way between Nagercoil and Neyoor, under Lewis; an eastern section, a flat and sandy area close to Cape Comorin with numerous palmyra trees and extensive rice fields, under James Russel with headquarters in Jamestown; and a central section, based in Nagercoil village and led by Mault. From 1860, Santhapuram and Jamestown appeared in the annual reports as separate districts, but in 1866 they were dissolved. Nagercoil district was reconstituted and the most northern congregations were organized on a separate basis as Tittuvilei district, one of the largest rice plains of Travancore and close to the hills. The former Jamestown was reorganized as Kottaram district but after a short time it was dissolved.

Finally, at the end of the century, a new district was opened midway between Trivandrum and Quilon. It was first headed by Hewett and Osborne who established their main station in Vakkam (1893) but later shifted to Attingal (1899). The district drew its adherents chiefly from the ex-slave communities in that region, although the congregations at Vakkam and Attingal were composed of *Ezhavas*.

Most descriptions of missionary history focus on the role of the

[30] Wilkinson, report from Trivandrum, 1881, in LMS Archives, Reports, Box 2/mf. 3317.

[31] Further information on Pareychaley district can be obtained from Abbs, 1870, p. 137; Horsley, p. 23; and Emlyn, report from Pareychaley, 1881, in LMS Archives, Reports, Box 2/mf. 3317.

European personnel. Here, we have even devoted a separate paragraph to it. Nevertheless, the most important though often underrated and neglected element in the organization of the LMS was the category of so-called "native agents". From the beginning, missionaries employed local people who had at least some education, and sent them to the villages to speak about Christianity and to read portions from the Bible. These people, called readers or catechists, were usually stationed in one of the congregations they had formed and did their work under close supervision of the European missionaries. In 1827 their number in Nagercoil and Neyoor district was already 34. In 1861 the office of evangelist was instituted, ranking above reader or catechist, and in 1866 the first native ministers were ordained, C. Yesudian, N. Devadasan, C. Masillamani and S. Zacharia.

Yesudian (1815–85) was a *Shanar* student of the Nagercoil Seminary, the educational institution that will be discussed in the next chapter. For many years he served as the Seminary's headmaster working in close cooperation with its principal Whitehouse. Duthie later acknowledged that "(i)ntellectually we had no native Christian in our Travancore mission at all his equal".[32] In 1861 he became assistant missionary and after his ordination in 1866 he was entrusted with the care of the new Tittuvilei district. His record as a preacher was poor, but he had an independent and original mind and could show much strength and persuasiveness in arguments with non-Christians. His great day came in 1878 when he was kindly received by the *Maharaja* in person. After his death, Tittuvilei district ceased to be a separate district and his family had to beg the LMS for financial support.

Devadasan (1815–74) had also worked as a teacher in the Seminary. He came from Tinnevelly and was one of the very few converts from the Brahmin caste. After a failed pilgrimage to Benares, Mault employed him as a village school teacher. In 1841 he publicly broke his sacred thread and was baptized a Christian. As a youth, Devadasan had been married to Lakshmi, a girl five years old, but because of his conversion her parents cancelled the marriage. Instead of her he married Santhai, a pupil of Mrs. Mault's boarding school and granddaughter of Vedamanickam,

[32] Duthie, letter from Nagercoil, 31.7.1885, in LMS Archives, Incoming Letters, Box 10; Jacob, Manuscript History, p. 152.

Ringeltaube's first assistant. But when Santhai died, Devadasan married his former betrothed and her parents consented, because she was a widow in their estimation and a burden at that. Lakshmi became a Christian on that occasion. After his ordination Devadasan was placed in charge of the Nagercoil Home Church.[33]

Masillamani was a grandson of Vedamanickam. Emlyn considered him "undoubtedly one of the ablest that have risen in our mission", a good speaker and writer endowed with an industrious spirit.[34] His industriousness was apparent from his active involvement in the nascent coffee plantation industry, but the depression that soon set in left him deeply in debt and humiliated before the public. From 1866 he had been pastor of Dennispuram, but his local creditors and *Pariah* background made it impossible to find him a suitable place somewhere else. In 1886 he took refuge in more remunerative employment in Madras, from where he hoped to pay off his debts and to raise a dowry for his marriageable daughters. His respectable career in LMS service ended in a disgracing quarrel over a house in Nagercoil that belonged to the mission but was occupied by Masillamani's son-in-law.

The number of native ordained ministers remained small, standing at 20 in 1900. The total number of Indian agents, i.e. pastors, evangelists and catechists, however, had risen to 371 in the same year.

Schoolteachers, male and female, represented the other important branch within the native agency. Usually, the forming of congregations went hand in hand with the establishment of schools, the same building serving for worship and education. In 1828 the LMS employed 95 schoolteachers, in 1860 200 and in 1900 511, bringing the total native agency to no less than 882 people.

In view of this large number of agents, in charge of hundreds of congregations and schools, spread over a wide area, it was both natural and inevitable that the European missionaries gradually receded in the background and assumed the position of administrator and coordinator. They were perfectly aware of this change in their role and a TDC meeting recorded in 1880 that the European "(m)issionaries being overburdened with District business, account

[33] Typed extract in LMS Archives, Odds, Box 17/mf. 1117, 1124; Jacob, Manuscript History, p. 152.

[34] See Travancore District Committee Correspondence re Masillamani, 1887, in LMS Archives, Incoming Letters, Box 11.

keeping &c. cannot engage in preaching and direct spiritual work".[35] The work among the people had to be done by the agents, who served as the vital link between the European missionary and the local community. These agents, as Gladstone has brought out so clearly, went around to preach the Gospel, formed most of the congregations, arranged the missionary's visit to the village, and did the follow-up work after he had left. Without an agent on the spot, local congregations would soon relapse.[36] For his own information, the missionary had increasingly to rely on the reports and diaries sent to him by the local catechist or itinerant preacher. And during times of crisis, it was the Indian agents that bore the brunt of local opposition and had to suffer both mentally and physically from Hindu retaliation.

In spite of this valuable and in fact indispensable contribution to the LMS effort, the Indian agents were treated as subordinate servants more than as fellow-workers. Duthie once acknowledged that the native agency and not the European missionaries were "the soul of the mission".[37] But this appreciation was never reflected in the LMS wage policy. In 1870 the European missionaries earned Rs. 2600 per year plus Rs. 100 per child, travelling allowances, bungalow maintenance and repair etc. On the other hand, the highest paid Indian agent at that time, C. Yesudian, earned Rs. 360 per year with few allowances, and all other agents received considerably less, from Rs. 16 to Rs. 180. Since the LMS as a rule paid its agents no pension or retirement benefit, many evangelists and catechists and even some pastors tried to provide for old age themselves by investing in land or trees. This desire to acquire property, "so very characteristic of Natives" according to the same Duthie,[38] was strongly disapproved of and even forbidden by the TDC, as it was feared it would lead to a neglect of the congregations. But whereas on several occasions the European missionaries

[35] TDC Meeting 3–5 August 1880, in LMS Archives, Incoming Letters, Box 9, quoted in Gladstone, 1984, p. 179. In 1879 Allan wrote: "The work in Nagercoil is a work much more of superintending than of evangelizing. I am plodding away at its regular routine ...", quoted in LMS Chronicle 1880, p. 89.

[36] Gladstone, 1984, p. 180; see also in comparison Luke and Carman, pp. 80–1.

[37] Duthie in Missionary Magazine and Chronicle January 1861, quoted in LMS Archives, Odds, Box 17/mf. 1117; the same opinion can be found in the Travancore District Minute Book, 1881, Annual Meeting Nagercoil.

[38] Duthie, letter from Nagercoil, 20.2.1872, in LMS Archives, Odds, Box 17/mf. 1123.

requested the Directors in London to increase their salary, similar requests from the agents were received with much dissatisfaction.[39] Whenever the missionaries considered raising their agents' scale of wages, they were chiefly motivated by a concern that they might lose their English educated servants to rival institutions like public works or coffee plantations.

As far as the financial status of their agents was concerned, the missionaries could in extenuation refer to their perennial problem of scarce resources. However, the same excuse could not apply to their extreme reluctance to share administrative responsibility with the Indian agents. As a step towards some measure of self-government a South Travancore Church Council was established in 1872, including among its members Indian ministers and local representatives apart from European missionaries. The authority transferred to this body was insignificant.[40] And when the Directors suggested to include one Indian minister in the Travancore District Committee (1895), the missionaries dismissed the suggestion as impracticable, as they knew of no Indian minister "of such acknowledged outstanding abilities (and) character" as to qualify for the post.[41] Yesudas holds the view that the LMS missionaries were ready to accept the idea of entrusting the responsibilities of the churches in local hands. But from the sources quoted by him it is clear that the LMS, worried by shrinking funds, was mainly interested in self-support, and even that idea was made conditional to the creation of "a deeper sense of individual responsibility among our people", which as yet was thought to be lacking.[42] There was no concept of an increasing association of agents in the LMS organization with a view to the progressive realization of church self-government. Instead the missionaries, to follow Gladstone's conclusion, could only think of creating a team of workers who would work loyally under European supervision.[43]

The internal conflicts that did not fail to erupt in the course of the century both highlighted and sharpened the hierarchical

[39] Gladstone, 1984, pp. 182–3.

[40] Membership, Rules etc. of South Travancore Church Council in LMS Archives, Odds, Box 17/mf. 1123 (TDC Meeting Pareychaley 1872). A preliminary meeting of the Church Council was held in Neyoor 1874; see Yesudas, 1980, p. 88.

[41] Duthie, letter from Nagercoil, 21.4.(1895?), in LMS Archives, Odds, Box 17.

[42] Yesudas, 1980, pp. 85–7, and sources quoted by him in the notes 2) and 4).

[43] Gladstone, 1984, p. 184–5.

distinction between European supervisors and Indian assistants. On several occasions, the Indian Christians criticized the authoritarian and often derogatory dealings of the missionaries in unmistakable terms. But their requests for greater participation in church affairs were met with arguments which clearly indicated imperialist attitudes. The missionaries complained of their agents' lack of initiative and their tendency to settle down and to do next to nothing. Therefore, to quote Duthie once again, "it will never do to allow these Native Brethren to be independent".[44] It was also alleged that many Indian Christians were unwilling to entrust their interests wholly to Indian leaders and preferred the European missionaries who were impartial and above considerations of family and caste. Real steps towards self-government of the south Travancore church had to wait till the twentieth century.

From 1867, deacons were appointed in the local churches. It was their task to collect the subscriptions, to maintain the buildings and generally to make the congregations self-supporting. The three first deacons in the Nagercoil Home Church were P.D. Devasagayam, Daniel Paramanandam and N.R. Nathaniel (Chettiar), "influential and leading landowners and proprietors", according to Jacob.[45] Devasagayam was a successful coffee planter and benefactor of the local church. We will make his acquaintance more extensively in one of the following chapters. Paramanandam was a cousin of Vedamanickam and may also have been associated with the coffee growing business. At least, the name of his family can be found on the list of Nagercoil estate owners. A short life-history of Nathaniel was found in his house after his death.

Nathaniel (1818–1887) belonged to a respectable silk weavers community from central India that had settled in Kottar, close to Nagercoil, for purposes of trade. Their language was a mixture of Tamil and Telegu. In 1835 he went with his widowed mother to Trivandrum to sell coloured jackets to Muslim women. His talent for singing and the quality of his silk and silver thread drew the attention of the royal palace. He was introduced to the *Raja* who was so much pleased with him that he ordered the expense connected with his investiture with the sacred thread to be paid from the royal treasury. Three years later Nathaniel received a contract

[44] Duthie, letter from Nagercoil, 20.2.1872, in LMS Archives, Odds, Box 17/mf. 1123.

[45] Jacob, Manuscript History, pp. 154–5.

to furnish the palace with supplies of silk cloth every month, which yielded him a large income. In 1841 he came into contact with Devadasan, the later pastor of Nagercoil, and he started to associate privately with Christians in Kottar. According to Nathaniel's own life-history, these Christian contacts were reported to Trivandrum by jealous relatives and neighbours and in 1847 he lost his lucrative trade with the palace. Then he invested his money in rice fields and in 1853 he became a Christian and was baptized by Mault. He was a pillar of the local church and bore the entire expense of a new, substantial building in Kottar, meant as a place of worship and schoolroom. The LMS hoped through Nathaniel to have found an opening among this wealthy and very exclusive caste of silk weavers, but although hopes were often raised, only one or two families went over to Christianity.[46]

The large number of Indian agents employed in numerous schools and congregations stands in marked contrast to the handful of European missionaries on the spot: eight in 1850 (one of whom died that year) and twelve in 1900. This striking imbalance may be seen as illustrative of another important aspect: though the European element controlled the vital positions at the top and—most important of all—pulled the financial strings, by its sheer weight and number, not to speak of its aspiration, the Travancore Christian community gained a momentum of its own. Native Christians lived and worked under the aegis of a largely Indian-run missionary organization, they supported it and benefited from it, and although their adherence might involve hardship, many of them held on to it. The Christian religion was not imposed on an ignorant and passive population, but it was adopted by certain groups for a variety of reasons. This leads us to the question which groups were most eager to embrace Christianity and for what motives.

IV.3 The local Response

Ringeltaube's baptismal registers of Mayiladi and adjoining congregations record the names of south Travancore's first Protestant Christians. Unfortunately, these registers do not give much

[46] Life-history of Nathaniel in LMS Archives, Odds, Box 17 (1887); see also Annual Report Travancore District Committee, Nagercoil 1867, p. 10, and idem., Seminary Report 1883, p. 10.

information apart from lists of names and short comments like "One marked Naden", "a girl belonging to a Madras Lascar", "a Nair from Trivandrum who left again", "a slave girl", "one described as a madman" etc. We know however, that the people who persuaded Ringeltaube to come over to south Travancore were *Pariahs*, and later missionary reports confirm that these first congregations consisted mainly, if not exclusively, of *Pariahs*. In 1815 Ringeltaube reported to have baptized 1019 people since 1809, of whom 747 had remained.[47]

Soon after their arrival, Mead and Mault succeeded in placing 3000 *Shanars* under Christian instruction, and in 1822 their number had risen to 5000.[48] There was a slight decline in the following years, but the dress disturbances of 1828/29, that will be discussed later, are said to have caused a fresh wave of conversions. The statistical evidence in the LMS archives is too defective and fragmentary to confirm this trend. But there must have been a steady progress, especially in Neyoor, and in 1840 the annual report of the LMS recorded 13,233 LMS Christians in the Nagercoil, Neyoor and Trivandrum districts.[49]

New mass movements started after 1860, when new waves of converts joined the LMS. But whereas up-till then the mass movement had remained largely confined to *Shanars*, south of the Neyyar river, from 1860 *Pariahs* and *Pulayas* more to the north "literally crowded the mission".[50] The ex-slave communities approached the mission with requests to send them teachers, and showed great readiness to build places of worship and, where possible, to support their own catechists.

In 1868 the LMS numbered 33,729 Indian adherents. The following years saw a slight fall in numbers, but in the 1870s the mass movement among *Pariahs* and *Pulayas* resumed momentum and was further strengthened by the entrance of a new group, the *Kuravars*. These *Kuravars* were said to originate from Tinnevelly, but many of them lived in Travancore with a large concentration in the Quilon and Trivandrum district. They claimed to have ruled these lands in the past, but in the nineteenth century their

[47] Ringeltaube's Register and Statistics in LMS Archives, Odds, Box 15.

[48] Mead and Mault, letter from Nagercoil, 3.1.1820, in LMS Archives, Odds, Box 15/mf. 1101; Jacob, Manuscript History, p. 71.

[49] Annual Report LMS 1840, pp. 64–7.

[50] Hacker, 1908 p. 52.

descendents followed less honourable professions as musicians, snake-charmers, basket-makers, cultivators or robbers. A trifle superior to *Pariahs* and *Pulayas*, they proved eager to learn and contributed to the spectacular growth of the LMS in the 1870s and the 1880s. In many areas these *Kuravars* were the only people associated with the LMS, which gave Christianity the name of "*Kurava* Vetham" or the religion of the *Kuravars*.[51]

From modest beginnings in 1806 the LMS had succeeded in enlarging its flock to 17,000 in 1850, 40,000 in 1875 and 63,000 in 1900 which amounted to 5 per cent or 6 per cent of the local population.

TABLE II: LMS CHRISTIANS IN ABSOLUTE NUMBERS AND AS PERCENTAGE OF THE SOUTH TRAVANCORE POPULATION IN CENSUS YEARS[52]

	1875	1881	1891	1901
Census Reports	58224 (7.3%)	47283 (5.8%)	35867 (4.2%)	47051 (4.8%)
LMS Sources	40449 (5.1%)	40453 (5%)	49267 (5.8%)	57500 (5.9%)

As may be clear from the foregoing, this adherence was chiefly made up of *Shanars, Pariahs, Pulayas*, and *Kuravars*. Many other groups supplied converts at one time or another but in much smaller numbers. The LMS worked hard to gain a foothold among the *Ezhavas*, but although congregations of *Ezhavas* were formed in Trivandrum and Quilon, they never joined the mission in the same way as the *Shanars*.

[51] Reports from Quilon by Mateer, 1877 and 1880, and by Wilkinson, 1881, in LMS Archives, Reports, Box 2/mf. 3309, 3313 and 3317; Lee in LMS Chronicle 1885, p. 317; Knowles in Travancore District Committee Minute Book August 1886; Gladstone, 1984, pp. 150–1.

[52] Data for this table have been derived from the Census of Travancore and the Annual Reports of the LMS for the years mentioned. The south Travancore region includes the *taluks* Tovala, Agasteesvaram, Eranial, Kalkulam, Vilavankodu (Padmanabhapuram division), Neyattankara, Trivandrum, Nedumangadu, Sirayinkil (Trivandrum division) and Quilon (Quilon division). Together these administrative units, listed from south to north, represent the closest approximate to the LMS area.

The Census reports show remarkable variations in the number of people belonging to the different Christian denominations. Most probably, the LMS missionaries, who were more familiar with the denominational niceties, were in a better position to determine the number of their adherents. In 1900 the LMS statistics give the number of adherents as 63,152, which in 1901 has fallen to 57,500.

Occasionally there was mention of movements among the weavers of the *Saliar* caste, especially in Neyoor.[53] Continuous efforts were also made to win over the *Mukkavar* fishermen on the coast, many of whom had joined the Roman Catholic church centuries ago. These efforts never led to a substantial extension of the LMS support base. Neither was the mission able to convert people from the high castes. The rare Brahmin or *Ṇāyar* who did come over to the LMS was an outcaste or became one shortly, and the ranks of the caste Hindus remained effectively closed to all outside penetration.

The reports by Ringeltaube clearly testify to the material considerations that were at work among his converts. The years 1810–12 were very bad because of famine and Ringeltaube was perfectly aware that many new adherents were driven in by the distress of the time. With funds raised from affluent European families, he tried to organize long-term relief by planting trees and digging tanks and canals. These efforts did not remain unnoticed and when in addition the *Rani* granted his mission two paddy fields, the local population began to flock to his church. Ringeltaube however, waiting for the appearance of "pure" converts, rejected their motives and scornfully wrote home that he got "a vast number of cunning rogues for converts", burdening his congregations with what he called "hypocritical and worthless members".[54]

The question of vaccination may serve as another colourful example of what money could do in a situation of poverty. In 1814 small-pox was raging and the government created facilities to vaccinate people, especially children, as a preventive measure. But people proved unwilling to get vaccinated and even after Ringeltaube had undergone this treatment himself in their presence, his local Christians remained reluctant.

> At last I offered to every child a small bounty and in a moment 50 little black withered arms were stretched out and very cheerfully submitted to the operation.

The missionary came to the conclusion that "In India gentle persuasion is good, if accompanied by a little money"; but in the

[53] Jacob, Manuscript History, pp. 99, 161, 185, 188; Mead, report from Neyoor, 1850, in LMS Archives, Odds, Box 16/mf. 1108.

[54] Ringeltaube, reports for 1813 and 1814, and Journal 25.8.1814 and 8.11.1814 in LMS Archives, Odds, Box 15(/mf. 1093).

same report he had to admit that "(t)he heathen ... were not to be persuaded by any means".[55]

Some months later, Ringeltaube was requested by the *dewan* to submit a complete list of Christians in order to get them exempted from the capitation or poll tax. This tax, levied from the time that Martanda Varma started building his empire, placed a heavy burden on low caste communities like *Shanars* and *Ezhavas*. Ringeltaube had not asked for exemption, but did not dare to refuse the *dewan's* request:

> My people knew of the circumstances and would have forsaken me as their enemy had I obstructed this great blessing. I therefore proposed to give them regular certificates by means of which they were to be exempted.

But thereupon happened, what he had already feared: more than a thousand families asked for certificates. Ringeltaube felt greatly embarrassed, as he could not turn them away. To his great relief, however, very soon the message came that this favour would be extended to Hindus as well as Christians. After this news had spread, the great majority of these candidate members dropped out through the back-door and only 20 families remained with the congregations.[56]

Ringeltaube was pressed very hard for material help. His converts referred to Tinnevelly and Tanjore, where much charity had been given and even intimated, the missionary wrote, "that I purloined what was sent to me for their use." Others left his congregation, as they found him unable to give sufficient relief or any relief at all. Ringeltaube did not blame them. He knew their bitter distress and his small salary was completely spent on his poor fellow-Christians in the form of wages or little charities to the sick, orphans, etc. Contemporaries described him as an eccentric, who cared little for personal comfort and the customs of civilized society, and many years later people still told with vast amusement, how the utterly ragged missionary, on his visits to the British Resident, used to create great consternation by his mere appearance. His conversation however, according to a contemporary, was most fascinating.[57] Apart from sympathizing and comprehending, his experiences also made him bitter and scornful. In a letter to his brother he called the native Christians

[55] Ringeltaube, report for 1814, in LMS Archives, Odds, Box 15.
[56] Ringeltaube, report for 1814, in LMS Archives, Odds, Box 15.
[57] Robinson, pp. 109–10; Silvester Horne, p. 97.

great rogues; the poorest of them consent to be made proselytes for money and good words, and afterwards they cleave to you like leeches. I have about 600 of them (adults), and therefore I am quite poor.[58]

The same ambivalence was evident in Ringeltaube's letters to the LMS Directors. He urgently requested an enlargement of his meagre financial resources, and even suggested—like many missionaries after him—an arithmetical connection between the amount of investment and the number of converts. But at the same time, he cautioned the Directors not to jump for joy at the news of baptisms, as he had strong reasons to suppose that the motives of his converts were far from purely spiritual. He baptized about 1100 people in Travancore, but in one of his last letters, he confided to his sister: "If you read mission reports from India, you must think that they contain much humbug and little reality."[59]

Depressed and severely weakened, Ringeltaube left Mayiladi on New Year's Day 1816. Next September he reported from Malacca that he was embarking for Batavia. He never arrived there and most probably was buried at sea, his most faithful adherents in Travancore believing that God had taken him away like Enoch (Genesis 5: 24).[60]

The experiences of later missionaries were not materially different from those of Ringeltaube, though most of his British successors showed more wariness in formulating their views. As Mead and Mault discovered, the mere expectation that a missionary connection might yield official favour or government protection could induce many people to change their religion. When Mead was appointed civil judge at Nagercoil in 1818, more than 3000 *Shanars* from the neighbourhood came over to join the LMS and were received on profession as catechumens. The *Shanars* and other low caste communities suffered many forms of injustice and hoped to receive better treatment at the court by adopting the faith taught by the judge. After Mead had relinquished his judicial

[58] Ringeltaube, letter to his brother, 27.8.1814, in Robinson, p. 116.

[59] Ringeltaube, letter to his sister, 24.4.1816, in Robinson, p. 124; see also his annual reports and especially his letter to the LMS from Colombo, 9.4.1816, in LMS Archives, Odds, Box 15.

[60] Ringeltaube, letter from Malacca, 24.9.1816, in LMS Archives, Odds, Box 15; last letter to his sister, 27.9.1816, in Robinson, p. 128. We have to conclude that Hardgrave's dating of Ringeltaube's activities is incorrect, see Hardgrave, pp. 35, 45.

office, most of these people quickly gave up their profession of Christianity and returned to their old religion. This was the background of the first *Shanar* mass movement in south Travancore.[61]

Several years later Mault had a similar experience, when his Nagercoil station was granted the exceptional honour of a visit by the Travancore *Raja*, the *dewan*, and the British Resident. The distinguished visitors were shown round the schoolbuildings, the church and the printing office, which seemed to have greatly aroused their interest. At the end of his visit the *Raja* offered the mission Rs. 2000 and 20 teak trees in appreciation of their educational efforts. Mault, in a proud report to the LMS Directors, was clearly impressed by this royal favour. But still greater was the impression made upon the local population. Many people came to Mault and expressed their eagerness to receive Christian instruction. They were prompted by the belief that Mault was able through his influential connections to redress their grievances. When Mault made clear that it was not his intention to interfere with government policies, the growth of interest soon subsided.[62]

A form of oppression that weighed heavily on the poorer communities was *uliyam* or *corvée*, i.e. free labour services exacted by the state, and the obligation to furnish provisions to *uttupuras* and temples. Through the influence of Resident Munro, Christians had been exempted from these services, at least on Sundays and as far as they were meant for the performance of Hindu religious ceremonies and festivals. Although this measure offered only partial relief, its result was, as Whitehouse reported in 1851, that in those months of the year when government exactions in preparation of Hindu festivals were most burdensome the number of people eager to embrace Christianity showed a marked increase. In case government officials were inclined to ignore the exemption measure, the missionaries were asked to interfere. But as soon as the threat of *uliyam* had passed or protection had been obtained, many of these people went back to their old religion, only to return if similar need arose.[63]

In the course of the century the missionaries became increasingly

[61] LMS Archives, Odds, Box 18 (Ramsay Case File).

[62] Mault, report of the royal visit, Nagercoil, 16.1.1835, in LMS Archives, Odds, Box 16.

[63] Whitehouse, letter from Nagercoil, 5.3.1851, in LMS Archives, Odds, Box 16/mf. 1108.

successful in protecting professing Christians against unjust *uliyam* demands. Through their easy access to government offices and courts, where the lower castes did not dare to tread, the missionaries could represent the interests of their people in a very wide sense, and get at least part of their grievances redressed. The militant Cox fought a case in court against *Nayars* who had compelled a Christian to carry a burden on Sunday. In spite of much delay and obstruction Cox won the case and the chief assailants were put in prison. Some years later, Wilkinson submitted a petition to a sub-magistrate on behalf of *Kuravar* converts, who had complained about cruel treatment at the hands of their *Nayar* landlords. The landlords were forced to seek pardon from the complaints in order to escape punishment, which meant an unprecedented victory for the underprivileged classes.[64] These successes could not fail to make a deep impression on the low caste communities who came to see the missionary as their trusted friend and ally. The missionary assistance in the fight against one of the most glaring disabilities, that with regard to the dress of women, will be discussed in a later chapter.

The missionaries were also very much involved in the social concerns of their converts. Agur writes that the first spectacle that would often strike Ringeltaube when returning home from his visits was the numerous long *cadjan* petitions the people used to hang on the low roof of his small bungalow. And on their visits to the village congregations the missionaries were overburdened with all sorts of litigations, from cases of theft to problems about property and marriage, making them virtual leaders and arbiters of the community.[65] With a sense of despair some missionaries wrote home, that they had to settle so many temporal affairs of their people that there was hardly time left to explain the Gospel.

Most of the case material presented thus far pertains to the first fifty years of the mission and—apart from the Ringeltaube period—mainly bears upon *Shanars*. These *Shanars*, as contemporary observers recorded, based their social ambition on many proud references to a more glorious past. After 1860 *Pariahs* and *Pulayas* started joining the LMS in great numbers. The circumstances of their conversion do not seem to have been radically

[64] Wilkinson, report of Quilon, 1881, in LMS Archives, Reports, Box 2/mf. 3317.

[65] Agur, p. 572; Gladstone, 1986 pp. 32–3.

different. Steeped in abject poverty and subjected to many degrading disabilities, the (ex-)slave castes belonged to the most wretched communities of Travancore. Yet, even these lowest of the low were not completely devoid of social ambition. The *Pariahs*, Mateer wrote, delighted to speak copiously about their former free and elevated position and claimed in the past to have produced kings, saints and even gods. According to their own tradition, they were once a division of the Brahmins who had fallen from that proud position through the intrigues of the latter who had entrapped them into eating beef. In substantiation of these claims they could refer to some curious privileges—like the conspicuous role played by *Pariahs* along with Brahmins in some Hindu religious festivals—which might be seen as surviving vestiges of ancient *Pariah* prominence. In the same way, *Pulayas* used to cherish the memory of a dominant position in the past, when they claimed to have ruled the country as the original owners of the soil. In the suburbs of Trivandrum *Pulaya* chiefs or kings were said to have had a fort and many legends refer to a *Pulaya* woman in connection with the origin of the famous Padmanabha Swami Temple in that capital. All these claims may be seen as a typical blend of surviving historical consciousness and social pretentions, explaining the enslavement of these communities and justifying their ardent desire for improvement.[66]

In the nineteenth century, however, the slave castes had no economic resources to add any force to their pretentions and generally they remained unaffected by the far-reaching economic changes of the time. But as mentioned earlier, the second half of the century witnessed a growing association of these (ex-)slave castes with the mission, and the CMS reported a similar run on its stations in the north of Travancore.[67] Many of these new converts, as missionaries wrote with satisfaction, were remarkable for the liberality of their contributions compared with the scarcity of their means.

It is too much to say that the European missionaries came to Travancore with the express purpose of uplifting the poorest

[66] Mateer, "The Pariah Caste ...", pp. 1–7; Mateer 1883 pp. 34, 38, 299; Krishna Iyer Vol. II, pp. 84, 119,; Paulose, p. 34; Ayrookuzhiel, p. 111 ff; Saradamoni, p. 45 ff.

[67] Travancore and Cochin Mission, in CMS Archives, G2 I.5/0 for the years 1880–1882.

sections of society. The prevailing percolation theory did not make the mission feel much inclined to start the work of conversion at the very bottom of society. Slave caste Christians lowered the prestige of the mission and involved the risk of offending and estranging converts from more respectable castes. Some missionaries even seemed to share the general contempt for these people and denounced them as "superstitious drunkards", having "even less intelligence than the beasts of the field".[68] As this condition however, was understood to have been determined by age-long oppression, most missionaries took a much kinder view and, in course of time, the LMS came to identify itself closely with the *Pariahs* and *Pulayas*, and actively championed their cause. In fact, the mission had taken up a very early interest in the condition of the agrestic slaves. In the girls' schools, established by Mrs. Mead and Mrs. Mault, little slave girls were instructed to make lace and embroidery and by their earnings to purchase their freedom. This approach, however laudable, was not very successful, as the few girls who were able to gain their freedom but lost their identity. They could not be reabsorbed in their community and consequently had to be settled on mission compounds.[69]

In the 1840s the LMS and CMS started a campaign for the liberation of all slaves. In 1847 they presented a joint memorial to the Travancore *Raja*, referring to the abolition of slavery throughout the Company's territories in India and urging the introduction of similar legislation in Travancore.[70] In this campaign, the missionaries had to face strong opposition from slave holders and government officials. These dominant classes feared that abolition of slavery might upset the existing economic and political power structure in society. Slaves who had sought the help of the mission were beaten up, threatened with loss of work and driven from their masters' compounds. The association of conversion with slave emancipation only heightened hostility towards the Christian religion. But the LMS held on and did not shirk its own responsibility. The few slave-holding Christians, though a valuable asset to the mission because of their wealth, were struck off the list of

[68] Russell from Jamestown, 24.1.1856, in LMS Archives, Odds, Box 18/mf. 1147, and Newport from Pareychaley, 1865, ibidem Box 17.

[69] Mrs. Mault, letter from Nagercoil, 10.2.1826, in LMS Archives, Incoming Letters, Box 1; Hacker, 1908, pp. 42–3; Gladstone, 1976, p. 59.

[70] Complete text of memorial in Kusuman, pp. 78–80; see also Cox, p. xiii ff.

adherents, if they did not abandon all interests in the property of slaves.[71] Slavery was finally abolished in 1853 and 1855, and the *History of the Freedom Movement in Kerala* attributed their liberation chiefly to the "untiring labour, sincere devotion and great influence" of the Christian missionaries.[72] These legislative measures, however, granted legal freedom only. The majority of the ex-slaves remained with their old masters and saw hardly any change in social and economic status. According to missionary reports, agrestic slavery was still common after World War I.[73] In this respect, it should be borne in mind that abolition was not the result of a movement among the slaves themselves. The reforms were imposed by British rulers, who were pressed not only by missionary societies, but also by anti-slavery groups in England and capitalist planters in India, who may have hoped to profit by a free labour market.

IV.4 Material and Immaterial Considerations

After 1860, efforts to improve the temporal circumstances of the *Pariahs* and *Pulayas* were continued with renewed vigour, though with modest results. Education was offered, but not made much use of, and eagerly sought employment opportunities could be provided only to a limited extent. The mission lacked the financial means to organize material aid on a large scale and both the LMS and the CMS had to cope with reduced grants-in-aid from their parent-bodies. Nevertheless, some missionaries maintained that these people did improve economically, and Masillamani, the native pastor of Dennispuram, recorded in 1880 that many ex-slaves now lived by the cultivation of their own lands and built houses and cattle sheds on places where formerly stood their shrines.[74] Others, however, contended that the position of the ex-slaves had not materially changed and even that they were better fed and looked after in the days prior to their emancipation.[75]

[71] Leitch, letter 22.11.1853, in Smith, p. 91; Abbs, letter from Neyoor, 29.3.1841, in Incoming Letters, Box 3.

[72] Regional Records Survey Committee, Vol. I, p. 57.

[73] "Report of the Mass Movement ...", in IMC/CBMS Archives.

[74] Masillamani, report of Nagercoil district, 1880 in LMS Archives, Reports, Box 2/mf. 3316.

[75] Krishna Iyer, Vol. II, p. 191.

Christians among them seem to have fared still worse. Instead of yielding material improvement, conversion could involve considerable loss. The commandment not to work on Sunday, if strictly enforced, would mean a severe reduction of the ex-slaves' already meagre earnings. Apart from that, the missionaries were very keen on fighting theft. A catechist from Quilon reported that the *Pulaya* Christians in his congregation were not paid enough for their work in the rice fields to buy proper food. Formerly, in times of scarcity these people used to steal their master's property. But after conversion they had to give up that habit on penalty of being struck off the congregational list, making it still harder for them to survive.[76] Most probably, the strict discipline that the missionaries tried to maintain among their flock made the landholders more kindly disposed to the mission. Several landholders had used force to withhold their (ex-)slaves from visiting a church. But at the end of the century the missionaries could record that many (ex-)slave masters were encouraging their people to associate with the LMS. These landholders said that they discovered that Christianity made their *Pulayas* better and less intemperate servants. Some *Nayar* landholders asked the LMS to supply them Christian families to work their uncultivated lands; others offered support in building a chapel for their land labourers, if they became Christians.[77] This growing understanding between landholders and the LMS, however, could only serve to make the mission a less obvious ally for the ex-slave communities.

Many observers are inclined to establish a connection between a period of famine and the start of a mass movement. In many cases early converts to Christianity were indeed famine orphans. Forrester offers the suggestion that the spiritual, social and material aspirations which expressed themselves in a mass movement were best able to surface and become effective in times of social and economic dislocation, of which famine and drought represented an extreme case. Indian authors are more reluctant to relate the mass movement to subsistence crises. Gladstone, referring to the severe famine in south Travancore in 1860/61, contends that in spite of the missionary relief operations, there were no conver-

[76] Noah, report Quilon, 1884, in LMS Archives, Odds, Box 17.

[77] Wilkinson, report for Quilon, 1875; report Pareychaley, 1898; and Edmonds, report from Quilon, 1899, in LMS Archives, Odds, Box 17; Mateer 1883, p. 314.

sions to Christianity. Only after the famine and cholera had disappeared, the mass movement resumed its momentum.[78]

When we take a look at the LMS statistics for the famine years 1860/61, we see a spectacular increase in the number of Christian adherents, from 18,624 (1860) to 22,688 (1861) (See Appendix IV). This increase cannot be explained by the breast cloth disturbances, as the missionary historiography will make us believe.[79] The dress riots, that will be discussed in more detail in a later chapter, were over in the summer of 1859, and apart from this chronological factor, it were *Shanars* who benefited from this struggle, whereas after 1860 *Pariahs* and *Pulayas* crowded the mission. During the famine the LMS was actively involved in official relief operations like a food for work programme and it is much more likely that this involvement induced many people to become Christians. Also, the great mortality among the people, in spite of abundant offerings, raised doubts as to the use of traditional worship and many temple sheds were reportedly destroyed.

Another serious famine occurred in 1870. After the crops had failed for want of rains, cholera swept through the country. This famine was much more localized in character. Nagercoil and Neyoor were sadly afflicted, but more northern districts like Trivandrum suffered much less. Now the remarkable fact is that the famine-stricken districts, after many years of steady growth, recorded a substantial loss in adherence, whereas Trivandrum noted an increase. These losses, as can be seen from the local statistics, were much higher than the number of reported victims. One explanation might be that in the situation of 1870 many people were able to survive without the help of the mission, as large-scale employment was offered by the Public Works Department and the coffee estates in the neighbouring hills. Nevertheless, we can also glean from the missionary reports that during this famine many LMS Christians decided to go back to their ancestral belief. Fearing that famine and disease were a punishment from demons and ancestor spirits for abandoning their worship, they returned to their old shrines and offered sacrifices as before.

When we look at still another severe famine, the one of 1881, we

[78] Forrester, 1977, pp. 42–3; Gladstone, 1984, pp. 97–8.

[79] Jacob, p. 119; Hacker, 1908, p. 51; Gladstone, 1984, p. 96; Yesudas, 1980, p. 197.

find that the steady growth of previous years continued without interruption in all districts. That does not mean however, that this famine had no effect on the mass movement. The standstill proposition, applied by Gladstone to the 1860 famine, is superficial and misleading. Below the surface of plain numbers something more fundamental was at work. What appears to be a standstill was in fact a more or less even balance between converts coming and going.

The unpublished missionary sources almost unwillingly disclose a continuing border crossing between Hinduism and Christianity. Emlyn observed that "oodles return every year" and Newport sighed in 1867 that half his district (11,000 people) consisted of Christians of only five years standing,

> those that were formerly Christians being now hardened Heathens, and those that were then Heathens being now the only worshippers of the true God.[80]

The conclusion must be that famines and epidemics merely created a kind of rush hour in an already existing religious boundary traffic.[81] Yet, we should be careful not to be misled by the missionary perception attributing to the people only one religious identity at the same time. In fact, most people could easily combine their old religion with Christianity, and change of religion often amounted to a change of emphasis from one trend to another within a larger religious complex.

From this short investigation, we may conclude that for the untouchables of south Travancore material advantage was an important but not the sole consideration in the decision to adopt another religion. What the *Shanars, Pariahs* and similar groups wanted was not only material improvement but also social reform and a rise in social rank. I think Duthie phrased it extremely well when he wrote

[80] Emlyn, enclosure in Wilkinson, letter 23.5.1870, in LMS Archives, Incoming Letters, Box 7/mf. 2739; Newport in Annual Report Travancore District Committee, Pareychaley, 1867, p. 3.

[81] The relation between mass movement and famine has been dealt with more extensively in Kooiman, 1988.

> Change of religion is contemplated not so much from a sense of spiritual needs, as from a growing [consciousness] that it is only in connection with Christianity that the desired social goal can be effected.[82]

Duthie and other missionaries used to comfort themselves with the thought that a spiritual need was also discernible or would sooner or later manifest itself as a result of the Christian instruction imparted. Faith in the message of God's universal love for all mankind should indeed not be underrated as insignificant. There was also much fear of demons and ancestor spirits which Christianity could do away with. But the available evidence, however scanty in this respect, strongly suggests that Christian beliefs were understood in terms of direct local interests and concerns. Deliverance from evil sounded promising enough to people who had to cope with so many kinds of evil in their daily existence. The call to start a new, more dignified life perfectly suited the aspirations of those untouchables who cherished the hope of a better future. And the assurance that all human beings possessed their own, inalienable worth as creatures of God was a kind of revelation to those who had always been despised and rejected.

At the beginning of the century, Ringeltaube had dismissed many potential converts as "great rogues", who were driven by "impure motives". Throughout the century most missionaries remained convinced that expectations of material help, mediation and leadership were totally wrong conceptions of the missionaries' real duties. Suffice it to refer to their application papers, quoted in the previous chapter. But latter on other voices were also to be heard, although as yet weak and hesitant. In 1896 Osborne and Hewett, who worked among the ex-slave communities in Vakkam agreed with a colleague from Madras that conversions among the untouchables were "not caused by a deep conviction of sin and a strong desire to be saved", but more by the wish to better their worldly conditions, to emancipate themselves from their social misery, and to be freed from the tyranny of the higher classes. "They want friends and guides and they find them in the Missionaries. Are we to despise them on account of their motives? By no means. Let us do all we can to elevate them."[83]

[82] Duthie, Seminary report 1892, in LMS Archives, Odds, Box 17; Duthie is referring to *Pariahs* only, but his statement has in fact a much wider application.

[83] Osborne and Hewett, report for Vakkam, 1896, in LMS Archives, Odds, Box 17.

To the *Shanars* a close connection with the mission could be useful for the realization of their own social aspirations. For a similar group like the *Ezhavas*, however, the situation seems to have been quite different. Acquaintance with missionaries was fairly common among ambitious *Ezhavas*, and both LMS and CMS were frequently requested to establish separate *Ezhava* schools. But although the mission did offer education and protection, the *Ezhavas* were much more reluctant to become Christians than the *Shanars* in the south.[84]

First of all, the matrilineal *Ezhavas*, who were used to loose and flexible marriage ties, did not easily comply with the missionaries' more rigorous view of matrimonial relations. We will come back to that in the last chapter of this book. Apart from that, prosperous *Ezhavas* and similar groups which held property in common were deterred from Christianity by the prospect of forfeiting their inheritance rights. In its directly administered territories, the East India Company had enacted "that no one should suffer by loss of property or in any way on account of a change of religion" (Act XXI 1850). However, this law was not introduced in Travancore. The missionaries had petitioned the *Maharaja* to pass the same law in Travancore and also to guarantee the parental rights of children against the authority of the maternal uncle, but in vain. They also fought against the community of property which was thought to discourage individual activity and independence of spirit, and the inheritance through sisters' children (*marumakkathayam*), which was regarded as a serious obstacle to the spread of Christianity.[85] Fresh memorials were submitted in 1888 and 1893[86], but the *dewan* was advised by his legal counsellors that introduction of Act XXI (1850) was highly inexpedient and would result in ruinous litigation

[84] The 1931 census, the only one to enumerate Christians by caste origin, returned 2,311 Christian *Ezhavas* as against 168,573 Christian *Shanars* (all denominations), Census of Travancore 1931, Part I, p. 382–4.

[85] Petition to *Maharaja* on Disabilities of Christians, 1861, full text in LMS Archives, Odds, Box 17/mf. 1117; see also Lee, report of Nagercoil, 1880, ibidem, Reports, Box 2/mf. 3316 and Mateer, 1883[b], pp. 301, 304. Yesudas, 1977, p. 54 states that in 1815 the children of Christian fathers in Travancore had been allowed to inherit the property of the latter, but that proclamation, also quoted in Agur, Appendix XVIII, 1, had remained a dead letter.

[86] In protest to a court decision of 1885 which reaffirmed that converts had no inheritance rights, LMS, CMS and Syrian Christian leaders sent a joint memorial in 1893, text in LMS Archives, Odds, Box 17.

among followers of the dominant *marumakkathayam* law of inheritance.[87] The real problem, according to the Chief Justice of Travancore, was that the Christian communities had no common civil law, which created many complicated questions at the courts.[88]

Next, Christianity did not hold out much hope of an improvement in social status. It had become clear to the *Ezhavas* that conversion would not gain them access to the ranks of the Syrian Christians. North of Trivandrum the Syrian Christians occupied a position equal to that of the *Nayars*, and they were equally anxious to keep the lower castes at a distance, whether they were Christian or not.

But the most important reason why the *Ezhavas* had no need for the mission was their own improved economic conditions. In the second half of the century, the exports of coconut products like coir and copra sharply increased, especially in the north. Although most of these profits were pocketed by native landlords who owned the trees and foreign merchants who controlled the trade, *Ezhavas* had a sizable share. By 1900 a few *Ezhavas* even owned coir factories or weaving-establishments. All these developments put money into *Ezhava* hands and, to quote Jeffrey, "money brought education and social ambitions".[89] In these circumstances an increased respectability within caste society became a more desirable goal than a dubious position between contemptuous Syrians and polluting *Pulaya* converts. Thus, there was a clearly discernible trend among the *Ezhavas* to adopt the customs of the *Nayars* as was evident by their dress and jewellery, the style of their newly-built houses and the cremation of their dead. This Sanskritization and a growing self-confidence were the main factors behind the formation of the *Ezhava* caste association, the SNDPY.[90] One of the main pioneers of this association, P.T. Palpu, owed part of his education to the missionaries.

Nevertheless, a threat of mass conversion was to remain a useful

[87] Memorandum by legal advisory committee, Trivandrum 13.3.1889, in Crown Representative's Records, R/2(879/33).

[88] Memorandum by K. Krishnaswamy Row, Chief Justice Trivandrum, 30.3.1894, in Crown Representative's Records, R/2(879/33). At least for the nineteenth century there seems to be little ground for Gladstone's conclusion, that people from different castes and sects found a new unity in the socio-religious order of the Christian church, Gladstone, 1984, p. 178.

[89] Jeffrey, 1974, p. 45.

[90] Here, I closely follow Jeffrey's argument in Jeffrey, 1974.

political weapon for the *Ezhavas*. On different occasions it was seized upon to press for wider admission to state-sponsored schools and more employment in government service. As Christian *Ezhavas* received a better treatment from the state in these matters, the weapon was excellently suited for the purpose and educated *Ezhavas* did not hesitate to wield it, as for instance in their memorial to the *Maharaja* (1896).[91] In the political situation of the twentieth century, it was going to acquire a new relevance.

[91] Saradamoni, 1980, pp. 134–6; Rajendran, pp. 67–75.

V. Education and Employment

V.1 Village Schools

The socio-cultural and economic impact of the Christian mission is the topic of a long and much debated controversy. Several orthodox Hindus and ardent nationalists take the extreme position to deny all missionary influence in the reform and development of Hindu religion and society. They consider that influence to have been only harmful to India's interests, and ascribe the social reform movement entirely to the regenerating spirit of India's own culture. On the other hand, the claim is made by some writers that the work and the ideas of the Christian missionaries were the major stimulus to social reform in the nineteenth century.[1] That point of view is strongly supported by some missionaries, who in the absence of an impressive number of converts seem naturally inclined to overemphasize their agencies' contribution to social change. This may serve to warn us that an assessment of the impact of the Christian mission does not lend itself very easily to a more detached evaluation.

There seems to be more agreement that the fear of losing all untouchables to Christianity had prompted many caste Hindus to remove at least some of the most glaring caste disabilities. Manickam, after studying the Methodist mission in the Trichy-Tanjore area among untouchable communities (1820–1947), concludes that the various reform movements which have sprung up since the last quarter of the nineteenth century were but the direct result of the missionary activities, and Patwardhan, in her book on change among the *Mahars*, largely argues along similar lines.[2] The Hindu Mission Societies that were set up to elevate the untouchables and other weaker sections of society were not only inspired by but also closely patterned after the example of the Christian mission. The Deccan Education Society had its membership rules drawn up

[1] Heimsath, 1964, p. 51; Sen Gupta, pp. 168/69, 191, 194; K.M. Panikkar, p. 290.

[2] Manickam, 1977, p. 257; Patwardhan, p. 112.

specifically on the lines of two Christian missionary associations, and many of the reforms introduced by Shri Narayana Guru among the *Ezhavas* were derived from Christian models. "The fear of the Christian missionary (and his conversions) has been the beginning of much social wisdom among us", was Chandavarkar's well-known comment.[3]

Education has always been one of the main fields of missionary activity and in Travancore the LMS missionaries may rightly be called the pioneers of English education. Congregations were established in close association with the opening of schools, the same building often serving both for worship and teaching. Ringeltaube and Mault took pride in the fact that they had schools attached to all their congregations, not only for Christian children but open to all castes and creeds, and at the end of the century Mateer observed, that where there were no schools, spiritual progress had been but small, "Intelligence is the basis of our work."[4]

In their letters and reports, the missionaries tell us that they were approached with numerous requests for schools and teachers. All groups of people were said to manifest a strong desire to obtain education for their children and many applications for schools were received from villages where as yet no Christian was to be found. In response to these requests the LMS opened a large number of day schools in the villages and several boarding schools in central stations. The village schools were generally conducted according to a uniform plan, four classes learning the alphabet, spelling and reading alongside catechism lessons and, in the 4th class, the reading of the Bible. Apart from these four classes, there was usually a 5th and 6th class, composed of children of the 3rd and 4th class, the former for writing and the latter for arithmetic. The children stood in their places in their respective classes according to their progress.[5]

In the course of the century, the number of LMS schools and

[3] N.G. Chandavarkar, *Speeches and Writings*, Bombay, 1911, quoted in Mazumdar, p. 47.

[4] Mault, letter from Nagercoil, 6.10.1820, in LMS Archives, Incoming Letters, Box 1; Mateer in Annual Report, Trivandrum District (printed), 1884, p. 22, in idem., Odds, Box 17.

[5] Report of Nagercoil, July 1832, in LMS Archives, Odds, Box 16.

children under instruction showed a remarkable increase. In 1830 the LMS numbered about 100 schools with more than 3,000 scholars; in 1860 the number had risen to 200 schools and 6,700 scholars and around 1890 it had reached 300 and 14,000 respectively.[6] An important innovation was the stress on female education and on an average one quarter of the children attending mission schools were girls. Still more significant was the fact that these children chiefly came from the poor and untouchable communities which till then had been deprived of all opportunities for intellectual development. Under the influence of this missionary education, several congregations, composed of people from these communities, had a large number of members able to read the Scriptures, and in the 1850s congregational literacy rates of 30 per cent were no exception.[7] The results of their work strengthened the missionaries in their conviction that caste distinctions were not founded on any difference in natural ability and that low caste people could equal or even excel those considered their superior. There can be no doubt that the educational efforts of the LMS and other missionary societies have substantially contributed in making Kerala the most literate state of India.

This apparent success of the LMS educational department should not make us lose sight of the many problems the mission had to cope with. In spite of the many requests for schools, the missionary sources, especially from the first part of the century, disclose a great lack of interest among many people and a terrible shortage of means. The government, at first indifferent, acknowledged the mission's educational endeavour by granting support, but at the end of the century it imposed various restrictions in an attempt to gain control of this important field.

Many missionaries reported an extreme indifference on the part of parents with regard to their children's education. They did not care to send their children to school and when the master came to collect them—which was usually the case where he was paid by the number present—he was frequently insulted or ridiculed. Attendance was irregular and children were easily taken away from school before they were able to read or kept at home if they could assist in earning some money. Although there were compelling economic

[6] For more detailed figures see the Annual Reports of the LMS, appendix IV.

[7] Guestimates based on statistics of the South Travancore Mission for 1855–1859, in LMS Archives, Odds, Box 16/mf. 1111–1113.

reasons for this behaviour, some missionaries spoke contemptuously of "the mercenary disposition" of these parents and their neglect of parental authority.[8]

Especially in the field of female education, the LMS had to face strong prejudice. As the Directors were unable to render financial help, many missionaries' wives started boarding schools for girls on their own responsibility, supported by friends at home. In one of her letters, Mrs. Mault wrote that in spite of the offer of board and clothing she had great difficulty in keeping her girls at school. Children collected one week, were frequently drawn away the next, and she had only some hold on those children whose parents depended upon the mission; but "even those were no sooner brought under discipline, than they ran away, and in some instances were encouraged to do so by their parents."[9] If remaining in school, most parents preferred their daughters to learn sewing or needle-work rather than reading and writing.

Another problem was the quality of the teachers the LMS had to employ. There were bitter complaints about the apathy of the schoolmasters, who were said to be "mere hirelings" knowing very little and finding it difficult to impart what knowledge they had to the children. We should bear in mind, however, that the quality of the teachers undoubtedly improved in the course of the century and that the poor opinion of the local schoolmaster which the missionaries so bluntly ventilated does not easily fit in with the educational progress they were so eager to boast off. Caste considerations were not altogether absent. Whitehouse reported that some schools must always be conducted by high caste masters as they would be instantly deserted if low caste men were appointed to that office.[10]

As a matter of course, the great number of schools and teachers placed a heavy burden on the LMS budget. When in the 1860s the financial position of the LMS forced the Directors to drastically cut their expenditure, that burden became too heavy for the Travancore missionaries. Many schools had to close due to lack of

[8] Mault, report of Nagercoil, 10.6.1828, in LMS Archives, Incoming Letters, Box 1; Mault and Miller, half-year report of Nagercoil, 24.7.1832, idem., Box 2; Whitehouse, letters 17.8.1851 and 30.8.1852, idem., Odds, Box 16/mf. 1108 and Box 18.

[9] Mrs. Mault, letter 2.6.1830, in LMS Archives, Incoming Letters, Box 1.

[10] Whitehouse, letter 30.8.1852, in LMS Archives, Odds, Box 18.

funds and Mateer wrote that the small grants of the LMS enabled him to support only a handful of teachers. Most of the children in his congregations grew up without education, though they urgently needed it as a protection against fraud and oppression. At the same time, the Government under the administration of *dewan* Sir T. Madhava Rao embarked upon a fairly ambitious policy of educational expansion.[11] But since the village schools opened by the *sirkar* remained closed to the untouchables, there was no alternative for the local Christians and thus lagged behind.[12]

In this situation an important group of Christians expressed its growing desire for the education of their children. In 1871 they sent a petition to the British Resident, signed by 200 householders, pointing out that the LMS through want of funds had suspended schools and reduced the salaries of schoolmasters. As the petitioners were not allowed to send their children to *sirkar* schools and were too poor to maintain their own schools unaided, they asked the Government to help the mission schools by grants-in-aid, similar to the system operative in British India.[13] There the principle of grants-in-aid for private education had been established by Wood's 1854 despatch and the missionary societies had not failed to make extensive use of that opportunity to get their schools subsidized.

It is not clear from the sources whether this petition was prompted by the European missionaries and how many schoolmasters belonged to the group of 200 householders. In any case, the LMS fully agreed with it and decided to submit a similar petition to the *Maharaja* two years later. In that petition, the European missionaries reminded His Majesty that in eleven of the sixteen English District Schools and twenty-three of the twenty-seven Vernacular Schools Protestant Christians were refused admission solely on caste grounds, while from the numerous village schools recently opened in many parts of the country they were absolutely and universally excluded. The Christians were said to feel their disadvantages very much, the more so as they had risen in social scale and in several cases contributed more to the funds of

[11] Tharakan, pp. 40 ff.

[12] Duthie, report of Nagercoil, 1872, in LMS Archives, Odds, Box 17/mf. 1123; Mateer, report of Trivandurm, 1874, idem., mf. 1125.

[13] Text of Petition (1871) in LMS Archives, Odds, Box 17/mf. 1123.

the state than their neighbours of higher castes who were allowed access to the *sirkar* schools.

> We, therefore, very respectfully and very earnestly beg Your Highness to issue orders for the admission of all cleanly decently dressed and well behaved children into all the schools supported at the public expense.[14]

As the LMS missionaries had spent large sums and devoted much effort to the introduction of popular education in Travancore, they felt confident also to ask the Government to allow some kind of grants-in-aid towards the secular instruction afforded in their village schools.

The petitions and personal entreaties by the missionaries were not in vain, though there were also other forces at work, like a more enlightened policy in Trivandrum and some gentle pressure from Madras.[15] In 1875, the Travancore Government announced that it had decided to allot Rs. 15,000 annually for grants-in-aid to primary schools under whatever management which taught vernacular up to a certain standard and adopted the same course of instruction as followed in government schools. The grants, amounting to Rs. 50 for schools with an average daily attendance of 25–40 children and Rs. 75 for schools with a higher attendance, were to be paid every half year on the report of government inspectors.[16]

Acceptance of grant-in-aid meant governmental supervision and curtailment of religious instruction. Nevertheless, the LMS being desperately short of money, much more so than the CMS, was quick to respond to this scheme. The first grant-in-aid school was

[14] Text of LMS petition to *Maharaja* re education (1873) in LMS Archives, Odds, Box 17/mf. 1125.

[15] Tharakan, p. 45; Gladstone, 1984, p. 271. Jones discussed the urgent need of grants-in-aid for education with the *dewan* Madhava Rao personally, when both were in the Ashambu hills, LMS Archives, Personal Papers, Box 3/mf. 904 Baylis wrote home that Mr. Ballard, the then British Resident with whom he was in communication, must have brought the subject of the remaining disadvantages of the untouchables before Lord Napier, the Governor of Madras, and that on the late visit of the *Maharaja* and the *dewan* to Madras, "they were given to understand very plainly by Lord Napier what ought to be done", Baylis, letter from Neyoor, 19.5.1870, in LMS Archives, Odds, Box 17/mf. 1123.

[16] Report on the Administration of Travancore 1875–76, p. 54; Nagam Aiya, vol. I, p. 571; Wilkinson, report of Quilon, 1875, in LMS Archives, Odds, Box 17/mf. 1125. Tharakan, p. 47, suggests that mission schools could already in 1868–69 benefit from official grants-in-aid, but LMS sources contain no reference to that.

in Vadasagary, the grant having been procured by the *Nayar* chief magistrate there, who was educated by the LMS in Nagercoil.[17] Of the 218 schools receiving grants in the first year no less than 104 were managed by the LMS, the remainder belonging to CMS, Roman Catholics, Syrian Christians and a small number of *Nayar* agencies. The next year, the LMS drew Rs. 5,378 for 117 schools out of a total disbursement of Rs. 10,982. The reports of LMS schools were generally favourable and contained only some complaints about irregular attendance.[18]

Apparently, the Government preferred grants-in-aid to admitting untouchables to its own schools with all the concomitant social tension. The LMS clearly benefited from this scheme as the annual reports made abundantly clear. In 1870, when the financial difficulties of the mission were making themselves felt, the number of schools had dropped to 161 and in 1872 it even fell to 124 with about 4,000 children attending. In 1875, when official support became available, the number of schools immediately rose to 146 with 7,000 children and in 1882 the level of 200 was reached again, just as in 1860, but now with considerably more scholars, almost 11,000 boys and girls. Also, the general standard of mission schools, both in terms of subjects covered and books used seems to have improved.

In spite of this substantial governmental support, acknowledged in many district reports, the missionaries were not fully contented. In Pareychaley district, for instance, education was decidedly of a low standard when the grant-in-aid scheme was introduced. Several congregations had schools with less then 25 children or no school at all, and teachers were poorly qualified. Therefore, Pareychaley could benefit from the government scheme only to a limited extent. After the situation had improved, it turned out to be almost impossible to increase the low grants obtained in the beginning and almost as difficult to get any increase in the number of schools receiving grants. One of the conditions was that a school should be in existence for at least six months. Emlyn had opened many new schools in Pareychaley after 1875, but he had to wait so long for a reply to his applications that lack of money forced him to close a number of them. Mateer also had to close several newly opened

[17] Duthie, 1906, p. 14.

[18] Report on the Administration of Travancore 1875–76, p. 54 ff; 1876–77, p. 52; 1877–78, p. 94–5.

schools, as to his great disappointment the government granted him less than 1/4 of what he had applied for.[19] But there was worse to come.

In 1894, after the Madras Government had announced a number of concessions to the untouchables in the field of education, the Travancore Government issued a new grant-in-aid scheme. Henceforth, all grants-in-aid were to be given on the principle of strict religious neutrality to all schools imparting sound secular instruction according to recognized methods. Certain castes, like *Shanars, Pulayas*, etc., were declared backward and special grants were sanctioned to schools opened for such castes.[20] According to the *dewan* the code was not less liberal than the Madras one and all private bodies were fully satisfied with the working of the system. On behalf of the LMS, however, Knowles vehemently protested against the new scheme. He pointed out in a letter (1897), that 296 of the 351 LMS schools had received grants-in-aid under the old system, whereas under the new one the number of schools receiving grants was only 147. As new applications took much time and the amount of grants was much lower than expected, the LMS had to close schools and to dismiss some of its teachers who had been trained at great expense to come up to the official requirements. Other objections were the official control over the choice of text books which might result in the exclusion of the Bible in grant-in-aid schools, and the uncertainty whether Christians were included in the backward class category. The LMS had always insisted on the Christians' separate identity free from caste society, but now exclusion would make them ineligible to the special grants sanctioned to the backward castes category.[21]

Further restrictions were imposed in the following years, and after Independence governmental control over state-aided, private schools became a very controversial political issue. Suffice here to say that in the nineteenth century the LMS was able, partly with official support, to introduce a system of education that strongly emphasized primary and vernacular instruction at the village level. The proud centre of this educational network was formed by an English College at Nagercoil, to which we will turn now.

[19] Travancore District Committee Minute Book, 1886, Annual Meeting Pareychaley, and idem., 1888 Neyoor.

[20] Text of Grant-in-aid Notification 10.12.1894 and all related correspondence in Crown Representative's Records, R/2 (879/43).

[21] Gladstone, 1984, pp. 71, 187; Yesudas, 1980, pp. 145–47.

V.2 The Nagercoil Seminary

Right from the beginning in 1806, Ringeltaube had considered the feasibility of establishing an English Seminary as an educational centre of the south Travancore mission. Most probably, the Central English School in Mayiladi, mentioned by Jacob,[22] was meant to serve that purpose. In 1818, his successors Mead and Knill, encouraged by Resident Munro,[23] took up the idea and transferred the remnants of this Central School to Nagercoil, where it was continued under the name of the Nagercoil Seminary. From modest beginnings this Seminary emerged as the crown of the LMS mission in south Travancore.

Initially, Mead had promoted "the communication of religious and useful knowledge" with a view to elevating his toddy-tapping Christians who—in his own words—"never had their minds occupied by anything higher than the extraction of the juice of a tree."[24] But very soon, the Seminary became the backbone of the missionary enterprise itself, its design being to train a native agency to meet the urgent demand for catechists, readers and schoolmasters. About the same time the Church Missionary Society started its own College in Kottayam in north Travancore.

The first teachers of the Seminary had to be transferred from established missionary centres such as Tanjore and Tranquebar. Mead, who had remarried a daughter of a Tanjore missionary, was the chief means of enlisting support from that place. Later instructors were recruited from amongst the Travancore Christians who had been educated at the Seminary, like Yesudian who for many years acted as the headmaster. More incidental was the appointment of a well educated *Nambudiri* who, outcast after his conversion, became the Seimnary's teacher of Malayalam.[25] In 1827 a LMS deputation reported favourably on the qualifications and devoted labours of these teachers, but some years later Whitehouse complained that it was hard to get good teachers and that he was obliged to employ teachers who themselves needed to be taught.[26]

[22] Jacob, Manuscript History, pp. 51, 65, 68.

[23] Munro, letter to Knill, Quilon 11.1.1819, in LMS Archives, Odds, Box 15/mf. 1101.

[24] Mead, letter from Nagercoil, 10.8.1819, in LMS Archives, Incoming Letters, Box 1.

[25] Duthie, Seminary Report 1866, in LMS Archives, Odds, Box 17/mf. 1121.

[26] Yesudas, 1980, pp. 142–3; Whitehouse, letter from Nagercoil, 17.2.1846, in LMS Archives, Odds, Box 16/mf. 1106 and letter 30.8.1852, ibidem., Box 18; from 1880 Duthie received assistance from his son who had returned from England.

In 1829 the Seminary was temporarily closed. However, with the engagement of John Roberts, a former army schoolmaster, the institute received a fresh impetus. When the *Raja* visited the LMS establishments in 1834, he was sufficiently impressed by the achievements of the seminarists to invite Roberts to take charge of the Government High School in Trivandrum that opened the same year.[27] Roberts, who after a promising start soon quarrelled with his brethren, accepted the invitation on the condition that he should be allowed to give Bible lessons in Trivandrum.[28]

At the same time, some co-workers of the LMS Printing Press moved from Nagercoil to Trivandrum to start the Government Printing Press. In 1820, Mead had introduced the first printing press in Travancore from Tanjore. One year later, it started working with Indian personnel trained at Tranquebar and paper imported from England free of duty. In 1831, a press for printing tracts and books in Malayalam was installed in Quilon by Thompson, and Mead established a third press in Neyoor sent by the Directors in London. For some time a separate School of Industry was maintained where students of the Seminary were taught printing and bookbinding. Later, the three printing establishments were amalgamated into one LMS Printing Press (1855), located in Nagercoil and first led by Dennis, who made his own paper and tanned his own leather.[29] As we have seen in a previous chapter, Mead and Thompson had been printer apprentices, and Dennis was a printing expert and photographer. As skilled workmen these missionaries made an important contribution to the introduction and spread of printing presses in this part of India.

After Roberts had left, the Seminary was temporarily removed to Neyoor, where Charles Miller became its first principal. In 1842, it returned to Nagercoil, where it was placed on a new footing by Whitehouse who had received some training as a teacher. Whitehouse introduced fixed times for admission and settled standards of qualification and seems to have pushed the institute

[27] Saradamoni, p. 119 and Nagam Aiya, I, p. 488 suggest that the opening of this High School, also called the *Sircar* Free School, inaugurated the beginning of English education in Travancore, but they overlook the earlier start made at Mayiladi and Nagercoil.

[28] Roberts' Malayalam letter of appointment—with English translation—in LMS Archives, Odds, Box 15/mf. 1102; in 1855 Roberts retired to Birmingham with a generous pension from the *Raja*.

[29] Press File in LMS Archives, Odds, Box 18; see also ibidem., Box 15/mf. 1101; Goodall, p. 44; Hacker, 1908, p. 35; Jacob, Manuscript History, p. 68.

to a higher level of efficiency and educational quality. Only boys of promise, who were 12 to 14 years of age and had learned to read Tamil easily in the LMS village schools, were accepted in the Seminary. After six months of probation they could be fully received and were to remain in the Seminary till the age of 18. A theological class, meant to prepare students of suitable disposition for ministerial office, was repeatedly considered but remained at an experimental stage. For the greater part of the nineteenth century, seminarists were directly employed by the mission or found situations elsewhere.[30]

The Seminary consisted of a boarding school as well as a day school which both offered the same courses. In 1818 it started with about 30 boys and a few girls, but soon the girls were placed in a separate boarding school and the Seminary became an exclusive male province.[31] From the 1830s to the 1860s the number of students in the boarding school increased from an yearly average of 40 to 70, numbering to more than 100 at the end of the century. At first, the number of day-scholars was more or less equal to that of the boarders, but after 1870 the day school started to grow very rapidly and the number of its day-scholars doubled that of the boarders, bringing the total number of students in the 1890s to more than 300.

As against the boarding school, the day-school could be attended by children of all religions. Usually, half the number was LMS Christians with always one or two Roman Catholics, and half was Hindu, but no Muslims. As the Nagercoil Seminary offered much sought after English education, many caste Hindu parents shed their doubts and sent their children to this institute. In 1844 Whitehouse reported that three young Brahmins had joined the English day-school and that all boys from the Brahmin to the *Pariah* were sitting together in school without the slightest objection.[32] If this observation is correct, it may be called exceptional, as

[30] Educational program by Whitehouse, Nagercoil Seminary Report 1844, in LMS Archives, Odds, Box 16/mf. 1105; Hacker 1908, pp. 71 ff.

[31] Mead and Mault, letter from Nagercoil, 3.1.1820, in LMS Archives, Odds, Box 15/mf. 1101; see also 'Outline History of Nagercoil Seminary', ibidem., Box 18, and Annual Report LMS 1819, p. 55.

[32] Whitehouse, report of Nagercoil Seminary, 1844, in LMS Archives, Box 16/mf. 1105; the same is told of the Medical Mission Dispensaries, see Smith, p. 182.

most missionaries kept reporting about recurrent caste rivalries within their congregations. In the 1860s and 1870s when more *Sirkar* English Schools were opened in the neighbourhood, the number of non-Christian day-scholars showed a sharp decrease and remained confined to a small number of local youth.

Boarding students of the Seminary were boarded, fed, clothed and educated at the expense of the mission. This policy implied that the LMS had to spend substantial resources on the maintenance of this institute. To a large extent these resources were produced by the rice lands or "Mission Fields" that the LMS had received as a gift from the royal family at an early date.[33] In accordance with local custom, these lands had been parcelled out to tenants at a rent varying from 50 to 60 per cent of the produce, depending on the quality of the soil. In the 1840s these Seminary lands yielded crops to the tune of Rs. 800 a year and in 1866 this income had increased to Rs. 1546. Seasons of drought or destructive floods, however, could seriously imperil the Seminary's agrarian base, forcing it to reduce its number of boarders. Therefore, the institute remained also dependent on donations from friends in England and in 1866 this source of income amounted to Rs. 1,198.[34]

Other sources of income were, for instance, a scholarship fund, raised in commemoration of Mault, the yearly interest of which was used to support two boys in the Seminary. Sometimes voluntary contributions were made by students who, in 1863, were kind enough to pay for the new furniture. And when in 1881 there was no rice for the boarders because of crop failure, the Seminary was helped by a donation of Rs. 500 by an unknown friend, whose name was later disclosed as that of the *Maharaja*.[35]

The missionaries had not the slightest doubt about "the immense

[33] In the same way, an endowment in land, equal to the support of 40 or 50 students, had been given to the Church Missionary Society College in Kottayam; Munro, letter 19.7.1816, in Annual Report CMS 1816–17, p. 455; Yesudas 1977, p. 5.

[34] Lands & Income 1841–1845, report in LMS Archives, Odds, Box 16/mf. 1106; Duthie, Seminary Accounts 1866, ibidem., Box 17/mf. 1121. Total expenses in 1866 amounted to about Rs. 2850. Donations in 1866 included fees, but this source was as yet negligible, see Local Income 1861–1865, report in ibidem., Odds, Box 17/mf. 1120.

[35] Annual Report Travancore District Committee, Nagercoil Seminary 1860, p. 9; Dennis, report of Nagercoil, 1863, in LMS Archives, Odds, Box 17/mf. 1118; Duthie, Seminary report, 1881, ibidem, Box 17.

scope of self improvement arising from a knowledge of English".[36] Therefore, although the instruction in theology and in many other subjects was given in Tamil and Malayalam, the teaching of English was given a very prominent place right from the beginning. Desirous of learning that language, in 1835 the first *Nayar* boys, no less than 14 in number, started to attend the Seminary as day-scholars. Nevertheless, in 1828 and again in 1851 the teaching of English was suspended. One of the reasons was that at that time the demand of the *Raja's* semi-autonomous government was yet mainly for personnel educated in Malayalam, and English did not present a way to wealth in Travancore, "though the Baboos in Calcutta think it to be such there".[37] Very soon, however, along with the commercialization of the Travancorean economy, English was reintroduced, as we will shortly see.

Other languages taught were Sanskrit and Greek. No reasons were given for the teaching of Sanskrit, but it is very likely that, just as in Bengal, this course was introduced to give the Indian Christians a more respected position in their own society.[38] In 1841, a visitor was struck by the boys' ability to read Homer and the Greek New Testament in the original text.[39] The study of Greek was thought to offer a useful training in parsing and accuracy. In 1844 it was given up, "as the time [could] more usefully be employed in other studies",[40] but its teaching was resumed some years later. Other main subjects were Arithmetic, Algebra, Euclid, Natural Philosophy, Geography and History, whereas Scripture lessons figured prominently in the curriculum of all classes.

In 1860, Duthie took over the Seminary. Oral and written examinations were conducted by the English missionaries, whereas the lower classes were examined by the headmaster or senior teachers. No students were as yet presented for public examinations, as that would mean elimination of much theological and even Scriptural teaching and increased expenditure. In view of the

[36] Whitehouse, letter from Nagercoil, 15.3.1845, in LMS Archives, Odds, Box 16/mf. 1106; see also Manuscript History, Nagercoil Seminary.

[37] Whitehouse, letter 17.8.1851, in File "Travancore and Education", in LMS Archives, Odds, Box 18.

[38] Cf. Sen Gupta, pp. 113–4.

[39] The visitor, the Bishop of Madras, is quoted in Yesudas, 1980, p. 139.

[40] Whitehouse, report of the Nagercoil Seminary, 18.9.1843 and (quotation from) idem., Nagercoil, 11.9.1844, in LMS Archives, Odds, Box 16/mf. 1105.

pressure of the local Christians, however, a first matriculation class was reluctantly begun in 1868, and from 1878 Nagercoil seminarists appeared at the Entrance Examinations of Madras University, though initially with modest results. In 1887 about 500 people from all districts submitted a petition to raise the Seminary to a second grade college and expressed their willingness to contribute financially to achieve that end. Applications for affiliation to Madras University were as yet rejected, but lack of money forbade improvement of the teaching staff. Finally, however, funds became available from England, the Madras University gave its sanction, and in 1893 the College started in Nagercoil with nine students, later to be called Scott Christian College.[41]

V.3 Employment Opportunities

At this point, the question should be raised: what happened to the students who completed their education in the Seminary? Did they live up to expectations by offering their services to the mission as catechists and schoolmasters? And if they sought employment elsewhere, to what extent did their missionary education further their employment opportunities and material prospects?

As the Seminary was set up for the training and recruitment of Indian assistants to the LMS, its principal did not fail to report every year the number of boys that did indeed enter missionary service after leaving the Seminary. From the registers, Whitehouse concluded that in the 1842–56 period 41 seminarists had left the institute to become agents of the mission.[42] In other words, an average of less than three a year. Deducting deaths and dismissals on account of improper conduct, this average of three a year leaves a substantial number of students that apparently found employment elsewhere. Now, the problem in dealing with this "elsewhere" is, that in their correspondence the missionaries treated this category more or less as a lost cause. They hardly mentioned this accidental by-product of their educational

[41] Outline History of Nagercoil Seminary, typescript, in LMS Archives, Odds, Box 18; Duthie, report of Seminary, 1878, ibidem., Box 17/mf. 1126; Travancore District Committee Minute Book, 1887, Annual Meeting Quilon; Yesudas, 1980, pp. 141–42. In 1870 the Government High School in Trivandrum had been affiliated to Madras University.

[42] Whitehouse, report of Seminary, Nagercoil 5.8.1856, in LMS Archives, Odds, Box 16/mf. 1111.

endeavour. A patient scrutiny of the files of correspondence, however, may yield at least some indications.

In the second part of the nineteenth century, the *Raja's* Government opened several English schools in Travancore, especially when Sir Madhava Rao held the office of *dewan* (1857–72).[43] But in the beginning of the century, English higher education was possible mainly in the *Raja's* High School in Trivandrum, the CMS College in Kottayam and the LMS Seminary in Nagercoil. Matriculation from one of these institutes became an important stepping stone to *sirkar* employment and several high caste parents sent their children to Nagercoil to be trained for that purpose. Especially *Nayar* families, which lost much land and privileges in the nineteenth century, turned to this new type of education as a key to jobs, which offered them security without affecting their rank and status. Students from these families successfully applied for government situations and Whitehouse recorded that some of them were in the *Sirkar Anchal* (Postal Service), the Medical and Engineering Departments or worked as clerks in government offices.[44] The most famous alumni, of course, were N. Nanu Pillai, the first *Nayar* of the country ever to become *dewan* (1877–80) and T. Rama Rao, a disciple of Whitehouse, who attained the same office (1887–92); they both honoured the Seminary by the grant of financial donations and annual prizes. Another ex-seminarist who rose to prominence in government service was Vedathirithasa Mudaliar, who became a High Court Judge.

In 1860, just to give one example, nine students left. One boy, after completing his terms, started a study of medicine under the direction of Dr. Waring, the *Raja's* physician, with a view to being employed by the government; another boy left on request of his family and contrary to the wishes of his teachers to become a Time Keeper in the Martanda Varma Canal Works that were started at that time; one boy died of cholera; four boarders were dismissed for improper conduct; one boy was employed by Duthie as a Tamil teacher, and another one started working as a teacher in Neyoor.[45]

[43] Nagam Aiya, vol. I, p. 548; Jeffrey, 1976, p. 75 ff.

[44] Whitehouse, Seminary report, Nagercoil 5.8.1856, in LMS Archives, Odds, Box 16/mf. 1111; also in Annual Report LMS 1857, p. 79; Saradamoni, p. 119.

[45] Annual Report Travancore District Committee, Seminary, 1860, p. 9. In 1867, 16 ex-seminarists accepted employment in the mission, an exceptionally high number for that time, Duthie, Seminary report 1867, in LMS Archives, Odds, Box 17/mf. 1122.

As most of the Christian students came from the lower strata of society, they had great difficulty in getting government situations in nineteenth century, caste dominated Travancore. One of the reasons why the missionaries pleaded for annexation of Travancore by the East India Company was their hope, that direct rule would give the lower castes a better chance to attain higher positions that up-till then had remained effectively closed to them.[46] After the 1857/58 disturbances were over and annexation was no longer likely, the missionaries submitted a new petition to the *Raja*, asking him to remove all caste disabilities of their converts, like the exclusion from *sirkar* employment.[47] Nevertheless, Christian converts, in spite of their educational qualifications, had to fight their way into government service against strong opposition. The higher castes were thus in a much better position to use the Seminary as a preliminary to the better-paid government situations, whereas the lower caste Christians had to be content with missionary employment, reinforcing prevailing conception of Christianity as "the religion of the poor."[48]

Yet, the Christians were not as bad off as missionary sources tend to suggest, especially if we compare them to groups of similar standing. In 1891 *Nambudiris, Nayars, Ezhavas* and Syrian Christians submitted a memorial to the *Maharaja*, complaining that the Malayalam-speaking people of Travancore were denied a fair share in the government of their own country due to a preponderance of foreign, i.e. Tamil and Marathi Brahmins in the higher grades of service. Although the memorialists had been able to obtain the signature of one or two native Christians, the LMS Christians, led by ex-seminarist P.C. Joseph, supported a counter memorial, expressing satisfaction at what the government had already done for its subjects. These Christians seem to have had good reasons to feel satisfied. In the medium grade appointments carrying Rs. 10 p.m. or more, 272 of the 3,366 posts were held by Christians of whom only 76 were Syrians. More striking was the distribution at the top: of the 246 top officials of Rs 50 p. m. or more (Europeans

[46] Baylis, letter from Neyoor, 18.11.1857, in LMS Archives, Odds, Box 16/mf. 1112.

[47] Text of the petition (1861) in LMS Archives, Odds, Box 17/mf. 1117.

[48] An official enquiry in 1888 disclosed that in twelve leading Protestant Missionary Colleges in Madras Presidency the percentage of Christian students was only 10 per cent as against Brahmins 60 per cent, Manickam, 1977, p. 225.

not included) Christians numbered 65 (16 of whom were Syrians), as against 61 Malayali and 120 foreign Hindus.[49] Unfortunately, these non-Syrian Christians were not further specified, but we may be certain that LMS Christians were among them. That means that, at the end of the century, higher education and official patronage had enabled the LMS Christians to gain a foothold in the government services. At the same time, university degrees made these Christians over-qualified and too expensive to work as missionary agents.

Commenting on these memorials an *Ezhava* protested in a letter to the *Madras Mail* that there was not a single *Ezhava* holding any Government appointment on a monthly salary of Rs. 5 or above, though educated and intelligent men were not lacking among them. In contrast to that, he argued,

> The claims of the Shanars of South Travancore who have embraced Christianity, though they suffered from similar disabilities, have been recognised by the State owing to the pressure brought upon the Government by large-hearted Missionaries, but as the members of my community who contribute much to the revenue of the State have remained within the pale of Hinduism, our cause has not yet enlisted the sympathies of any influential men ....[50]

Official sources confirmed that this complaint was justified. In 1894, Chief Justice Krishnaswamy Row admitted that *Shanar* or *Ezhava* Christians were appointed to positions and had access to places from which their unconverted brothers were excluded.[51] Therefore, the decision of the LMS Christians to join forces with the counter memorialists was well-founded. But that stand could only make them more susceptible to the charge of belonging to the foreign influences in Travancore.

However, occupational opportunities did not remain restricted to Travancore. Elsewhere, developments took place offering

[49] The Travancore Memorials and Counter Memorials, pp. 1–4. In 1881, for instance, *dewan* Ramiengar visited the Seminary and offered a situation in his own office to a Christian student whom the local missionary might think qualified to fill the post. Duthie, Seminary report, 1881, in LMS Archives, Odds, Box 17/mf. 1126.

[50] Madras Mail, 19.2.1891, in The Travancore Memorials and Counter Memorials, p. 7.

[51] Memorandum by Chief Justice Krishnaswamy Row, Trivandrum, 30.3.1894, in Crown Representative's Records, R/2 (897/33).

alternative employment. In 1830s the first coffee estates opened in Ceylon and from that period onwards the coffee planting industry on the island experienced a sustained growth, reaching its heyday in the 1860s and 1870s. After that, the spread of leaf disease—a mischievous orange red blot on the underside of the leaf—ruined most enterprises and coffee was replaced by tea.

As local Sinhalese labour showed no interest in working on the estates and planters preferred an uprooted labour force easy to control, the needed workers were drawn from southern India. Systematic recruitment started in 1839 and labour migration to Ceylon was legalized in 1847. Population pressure, famines and lack of economic prospects in south India were the main factors behind this labour migration. In 1847 the number of emigrants was as yet small, but it was to increase considerably. In the 1850s, coffee estates absorbed at least from 70,000 to 80,000 labourers at crop time and in 1867 more than 1.5 million Indian emigrants had moved to Ceylon, of whom about 850,000 had returned.[52] According to Dharma Kumar, 90 per cent of this migrant labour force was from Madras.[53] The remainder, as far as I can see, came from Travancore and was largely *Shanar*.[54]

These so-called coffee coolies belonged to the lower classes of tenants, agricultural labourers and toddy-tappers. For the greater part, their migration to Ceylon was seasonal. Frequently, whole families moved since plantations offered work to women and children as well. Before we start to investigate the connection between missionary education and coffee plantations, a short introduction to the recruitment practices will be necessary.

In the beginning, Ceylon planters sent their own agents to India to recruit the necessary labour. Within a short time, the workers began to migrate on their own, forming a gang with one of them as the leader. This leader or *kangany* first of all conducted his gang on the hazardous journey from south India to Ceylon, mainly along the "North Road" via Mannar through the flat, malaria affected, densely forested lands, where many fell victim to fatal diseases or local robbers. On the estates, the *kangany* negotiated

[52] Roberts, pp. 1–3; Kumar, p. 129; Hobbs, quoting figures from the Colombo Observer, in Hobbs, Annual Letter 1859, in CMS Archives, Tamil Cooly Mission.

[53] Kumar, p. 129.

[54] Mateer, 1871, p. 116; see also the report by the Protector of Emigrants in Madras (1857), quoted in Tinker, pp. 54–5.

wages and other employment conditions, and eventually supervised his people at their daily work.

In the 1850s, a new and more enterprising class of *kanganies* emerged. Apart from being the leader of a gang, he became the agent of the planter. In the beginning he was despatched by the planter to procure hands from India. But now he was given substantial cash advances as a proportion of the wages of potential workers and as an incentive to recruitment. Placed in an ambiguous position between planter and estate labour, the *kangany* was able to build up a position of considerable power. Not seldom he misused his power by terrorizing his workers and by depriving them of their legitimate advances or gains. Nevertheless, his power was not unlimited and in cases of cruelty or injustice he could be deserted by his men.[55]

Even to the planters the *kangany* system was no unmixed blessing. There was always the risk that *kanganies*, after receiving their coast advances, would not return or move their workers to another estate offering better terms. Nevertheless, the planters preferred this free labour system, as their demand for labour was largely seasonal and the *kanganies* took over most of the functions of supervision and control. Consequently, they remained dependent on their *kanganies* and could not do without them.

At the instance of the Home authorities, the Governments in Colombo and Madras several times considered intervening in these labour recruiting practices by licensing the *kanganies* and making them responsible under heavy penalties for the welfare of their gang members. But nothing came out of it. As *kanganies* usually recruited from among their own relations, friends and co-villagers in south India and therefore, had a natural understanding of the immigrants' interests, customs and prejudices, no legislative protection of labour was thought to be required. It was this more permanent relationship that made the *kanganies* different from the professional contractors of labour, who recruited for countries like Mauritius and the West-Indies and whose dealings with labour ended with the first stage of recruitment.[56]

In the 1850s, it was especially Baylis in Neyoor who drew attention to a drain of intellect from the missionary educational

[55] Samaraweera, p. 138; Roberts, p. 12; Lewis, p. 55; de Silva, 1961, p. 133; Millie, Ch. III.

[56] Roberts, pp. 32–3, 112; Wesumperuma, pp. 11–2.

institutions towards Ceylon. In a letter to the British Resident Lt. Gen. Cullen, Baylis attributed the growing intelligence, wealth and influence of the Christian *Shanars* largely to the efforts that had been made to educate them. He continued to explain that many of them often went to Ceylon,

> where some are employed in situations of trust and responsibility, some of our people having situations of from 50 to 70 Rs. per mensem as Conductors &c [*kanganies*], and having a large number of coolies under them....[57]

Whitehouse, who registered 41 ex-seminarists as employed by the mission in 1856, reported that "many others ... are now superintendents of different grades on coffee plantations."[58] Apparently, work on the plantations, especially in some superior capacity, was very attractive from a financial point of view. On his way to Nagercoil in 1859, Duthie met several Indian assistants of Baylis in Neyoor and he was much pleased to find that

> the superior training of the Seminary had not had the effect of turning their minds towards mere money making speculations, though the temptations to young men knowing English held out in Ceylon and other places, have been too much for some of whom Mr. Baylis had hoped for better things.[59]

These and other letters clearly show, that from the 1840s missionary schooling in general and English education in particular could successfully be turned to commercial purposes. It may also be inferred, that this education enabled at least some low caste LMS adherents to obtain remunerative and influential positions in Travancore that had remained beyond their reach. When in 1856 Russell visited the Ceylon plantation area, he seems to have been much interested in establishing good relations with the planting community, and Jeffrey mentions that some of the migrant

[57] Baylis, letter to the Resident, Neyoor, 17.1.1859, in Yesudas, 1975, p. 188; see also Baylis, report of Neyoor, 18.11.1857, in LMS Archives, Odds, Box 16/mf. 1112.

[58] Whitehouse, Seminary report, Nagercoil, 5.8.1856, in LMS Archives, Odds, Box 16/mf. 1111; also in Annual Report LMS, 1857, p. 79.

[59] Duthie, letter from Nagercoil, 7.12.1859, in LMS Archives, Odds, Box 16/mf. 1113.

workers carried letters of introduction from their missionaries to English planters in Ceylon.[60] Even though there is no evidence that these planters were much in sympathy with the cause of the mission,[61] they must have realized that some knowledge of English could only increase the efficiency of their local assistants. As might be expected, the position of conductor or *kangany* was most eagerly sought after. Because of their basic knowledge of English, reading and arithmetic, the educated Christians were very well qualified for this mediating agency, whereas their Christian background may at least have raised an expectation of greater trustworthiness. The fight of the mission against theft, drunkenness and insubordination must also have served to make Christian migrants more suitable workers from the planters' point of view.[62] These circumstances may explain why many Indian Christians occupied *kangany* positions and seem to have done so in larger numbers than their proportional number warranted.

The occasional references to south Indian Christians performing as superintendents or managers of estates are more difficult to interpret. The management of the estates did gradually move from the European owners into the hands of paid superintendents. But it does not seem very likely, that at that time European owners were willing to entrust the management of their property to Indian hands. Yet, south Indians served as assistant superintendents or assistant managers, and sometimes *kanganies* were coffee estate owners in their own right. For enterprising individuals of that kind, some elementary education undoubtedly was a valuable asset. In the next chapter we will deal more extensively with the role of local enterprise in the production of coffee.

If Christians of south Travancore really had a large share in the *kangany*-system, it must have made itself felt in their place of

[60] Russell was also interested in extending the LMS operations to the Ceylon coffee plantations, Hobbs, Journal, June 1856, in CMS Archives, Tamil Cooly Mission; Jeffrey 1976, p. 51.

[61] Hobbs, missionary in Kandy, Ceylon, received help from some planters, but had to face much opposition from the majority whom he considered sad examples of European Christianity and "too delicate a subject to speak much of"; see his Annual Letters 1857–1862 in CMS Archives, Tamil Cooly Mission; de Silva 1965, pp. 270–71.

[62] In the same way Assam tea planters became more favourably disposed to the mission when they found that the influence of the missionaries in promoting order and discipline was considerable, cf. Becker, pp. 63–4.

origin. *Kanganies*, as we saw, used to recruit primarily, if not exclusively, from among their own family and village. Nagercoil village, where the LMS Seminary was situated, may serve as an illustrative case in point.

In 1844 Mault, commenting on a fall in number in the congregations in Nagercoil and surrounding places, attributed the decrease to cholera and to an extensive emigration of the people to Ceylon where labour was better remunerated than in Travancore. This piece of information, confirmed by subsequent letters, clearly indicates that labour migration from south Travancore to Ceylon had started at an early date and that local Christians had a large part in it.[63] In close relationship with the coffee cultivation Nagercoil developed from a simple hamlet into an increasingly wealthy, Christian village. In 1858, there were 239 persons, parents and children, on the Nagercoil congregational list. From that list 15 men and 6 women (9 per cent) had reportedly left for Ceylon, drawn there by the influence of estate labour.[64] This migration did not remain restricted to the southern parts of the LMS area. In the 1870s Mayanadu, a coastal congregation in Quilon district, numbered about 300 adherents, of whom about two-thirds of the male adults had left for Ceylon.[65]

The LMS was not represented on the Ceylon coffee plantations. But reports by Hobbs, the local CMS missionary, frequently refer to Christian conductors and *kanganies*, some of whom were actively engaged in pastoral or evangelistic work. Hobbs came across several labour gangs from south Travancore and in 1859 he informed the CMS authorities at home that "a large proportion of Tamil Christians on the Estates are connected with the London Mission and send their contributions in aid of it to Nagercoil." He was humble enough to regard his own presence on the estates as an imporant contribution to the stability of the mission in Tinnevelly and south Travancore.[66]

[63] Mault, letter from Nagercoil, 20.4.1844, in LMS Archives, Odds, Box 16/mf. 1106; see also Annual Report LMS, 1854, p. 85.

[64] Dennis, report of Nagercoil, 21.2.1859, in LMS Archives, Odds, Box 16/mf. 1112.

[65] Mateer, Report of Quilon, 1877, and Wilkinson, idem., 1881, in LMS Archives, Reports, Box 2/mf. 3309 and 3317.

[66] Hobbs, letters 29.12.1856, 29.8.1859, Annual Letter 1857 and 1859, quotation from letter 24.11.1859, in CMS Archives, Tamil Cooly Mission. Hobbs mentioned that some CMS catechists, paid by the planters, also served as labour recruiters, letter 22.1.1856 and Journal, January–March 1856.

An Outline of the Plan of the Protestant Mission in South Travancore.

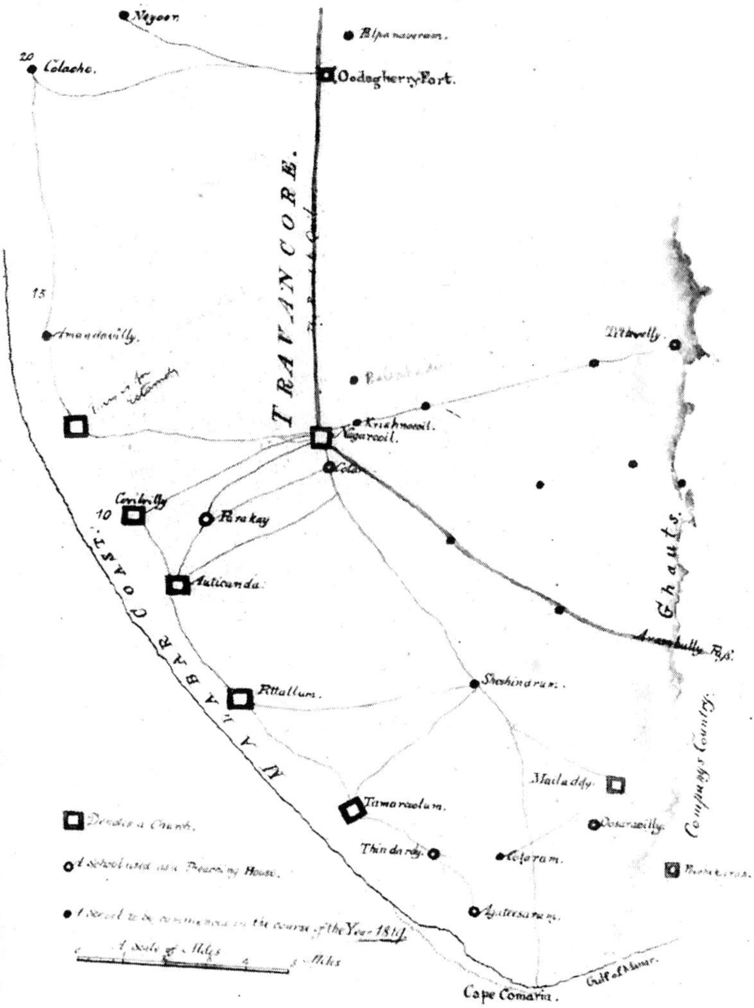

1. *Shanar* tree climbers, Travancore

2. Hill Tribes, Travancore

3. Charles Mead, LMS missionary in Nagercoil and Neyoor

4. John Cox, LMS Missionary in Trivandrum and Quilon

5. Nagercoil village school and seminary

6. Palanqin

7. Dancer in the folk-religious tradition, Travancore

8. Demolition of a temple shed, with unknown missionary

9. Lady missionary, Pareychaley district

10. Boarding school girls, Nagercoil, with their European teacher

11. Congregation of *Pariahs* and *Pulayas* before their place of worship central Travancore

12. Mannyakala congregation, Quilon district with (most probably) missionary Parker

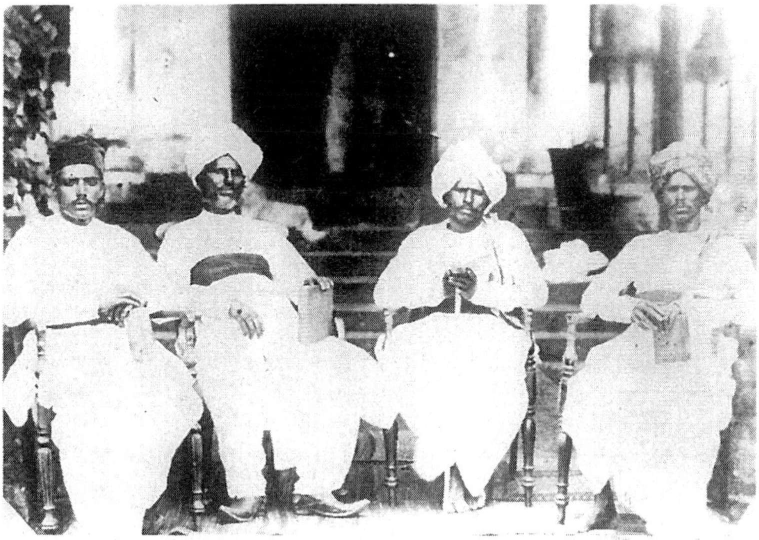

13. Group of first pastors, Nagercoil, from left to right Joshua (Nagercoil) C. Yesudian (Tittuvilei), C. Massilamani (Dennispuram) and unknown pastor

14. Travancore mission staff around 1900, from left to right A Parker J.D.D. Duthie, W.D. Osborn, A. Fells, I.H. Hacker. A.T. Foster, W.J. Edmonds and H. Hewett

The prosperity of several Christian *Shanars* was not due only to connections with the coffee culture in Ceylon. Coffee was known to Travancore and had already been grown there by the population of the low country, although not in exportable quantities. In the next chapter we will see that successful planters from Ceylon introduced large-scale coffee planting into Travancore and that local people, among whom many Christians, were actively involved in this commercial enterprise.

V.4 The Commercial Value of Language

Wage differentials played an important part in the labour migration to Ceylon. A comparative investigation will make this point clearer. In the 1860s some of the English educated catechists in charge of smaller congregations received less pay than an able bodied labourer working on the canal, road or other public works. And according to Duthie, manual labour in Travancore at that time was much cheaper than in Madras or neighbouring Tinnevelly district, not to speak of the coffee estates in Ceylon.[67] An indication of these wage differentials is given in the following table:

Table III: Comparative Statement of Wages[68]
(all wages in Rs. per month)

South Travancore (1860s)		Coffee Estates Ceylon (1860s)	
Eur. missionary	Rs. 200 + allow.	Superintendent	Rs. 100 or more
Assist. missionary	Rs. 16	*Kangany*	Rs. 50–70
Evangelist	Rs. 8	Worker (male)	Rs. 8–9
Catechist	Rs. 3–7.25	Worker (female)	Rs. 6–7
Schoolmaster	Rs. 2–5.5		
Schoolmistress	Rs. 1.5–4		
Manual labourer	Rs. 4–6		

[67] Duthie, letter from Nagercoil, 20.11.1861, in LMS Archives, Odds, Box 17/mf. 1117.

[68] This statement has been constructed from a survey of LMS agents' salaries by Duthie, 1864, in LMS Archives, Odds, Box 17/mf. 1119; Baylis, letter from Neyoor, 11.11.1864, ibidem., mf. 1120; Ferguson, 1868, pp. 123, 126; Mateer in LMS Chronicle 1869, p. 135; Mateer, 1871, p. 117; Annual Report Travancore District Committee, Neyoor, 1867, p. 12; Lewis, pp. 45, 56; Roberts; Jeffrey 1976, p. 91.

The variation in LMS salaries partly depended on regional divergences, an agent in Jamestown earning more than his colleague in Neyoor. I have not been able to trace, whether these divergences were due to differences in geographical distance from Ceylon or to differences in local costs of living.

Another observation to add is that wages as well as prices were constantly rising. An increasing demand for labour considerably raised the wage level, while from 1854 to 1864 the price of paddy doubled and that of clothing even trebled. This development has been attributed to the labour migration to Ceylon, the emergence of the coffee planting industry in Travancore and the large-scale public works undertaken by the Travancore government. To a large extent these factors were interconnected, as most of the roads built by the Public Works Department were designed to give ready access to the coffee plantations on the hills.

Finally, the comparative statement of wages does not include information about subsistence costs, which in Ceylon must have been higher than at home. In Ceylon, Roberts has computed the costs of subsistence per worker at Rs. 4 per month (1860s), leaving a margin of Rs. 2–4 for savings or extra spending.[69] Therefore, even if travelling expenses and interest on debts have to be deducted, the Ceylon plantation earned the migrant worker a very reasonable income.

At first sight, the LMS could only benefit from the increasing income which some of its adherents derived from the coffee culture. Christian *Shanars* who had made a successful career in commercialized coffee planting became prominent supporters of the mission and from the 1860s references to "Friends in Ceylon" or "Conductors from Nagercoil" became frequent in the LMS donation lists.[70] Jeffrey holds the view that the LMS encouraged its educated youth to seek work in Ceylon, as it realized that only prosperous Christians could make a prosperous mission.[71] However, I don't think this observation to be true; at least, it does not apply to the educated youth of the Nagercoil Seminary.

From the 1850s, missionaries started complaining that many boys who had received English education in the Seminary were

[69] Roberts, pp. 118–9.

[70] See, for example, the lists of donations for a chapel in Tittuvilei and for a reading room in Kottar (1867), in LMS Archives, Odds, Box 17/mf. 1122.

[71] Jeffrey, 1976, p. 51.

tempted away to Ceylon by the far higher salaries to be obtained there. It is unmistakably clear from the LMS correspondence, that most missionaries regarded this as a waste of the scarce resources invested in education. Baylis, one of the most vocal exponents of this point of view, informed the Directors in 1875:

> I have seen instances of late of lads coming out of the Seminary & at once getting 15 or 20 Rupees a month with Coffee planters when others who have left the Seminary for years & have been working steadily in the Mission, who are far their superiors in education & character are getting 6 or 7 Rs. only.[72]

Since the funds at their disposal were small, the missionaries had great difficulty in keeping their agents from going off to Ceylon, and Mateer and Wilkinson were unable to retain the few Malayalam-speaking seminarists who had been educated for service in Quilon. To counter this drift to the plantations, the missionaries passed a general rule which required all boarders to sign a document binding them to serve the LMS for a period of at least five years, starting from the time of leaving the Seminary. Those students who had already made up their minds to go in search of more lucrative posts on the coffee estates were greatly troubled and an agitation followed. Some boarders readily signed the bond, others did so after much hesitation, but a small number refused and left.[73]

Moral objections against migration were also raised. Mateer acknowledged that many migrants returned "independent, manly and enterprising", but most reports agree that the plantation workers had gained materially but lost spiritually. The higher wages and bad working conditions in Ceylon had led many workers into habits of drinking and they came back "greatly corrupted". Much money circulated in the LMS congregations because of the people's connection with the coffee business as clerk, *kangany*, worker or even planter. But however much the missionaries as representatives of an emerging middle class welcomed this economic development and their flock's share in it, their Puritan background made them highly critical of a "money-getting

[72] Baylis, letter 14.7.1875, in LMS Archives, Odds, Box 17/mf. 1126.

[73] Official address held at Centenary Meeting LMS, Travancore by Matthias, ex-seminarist, in Manuscript Histories, Ecclesiastical Archives, LMS 95; unfortunately, Matthias gives no information about the exact date and practical effect of this measure.

spirit" which was increasingly associated with what they saw as "worldliness and selfishness".[74]

There were also changes in the curriculum to indicate a resentment against English educated seminarists seeking employment in the coffee planting industry. Right from the beginning, studies in the Seminary had been carried on chiefly through the medium of the English language, no distinction being made between boarders intended for mission work and day-scholars pursuing their studies with a view to obtaining better paid secular employment for which English was becoming an important qualification. From 1860, however, greater emphasis was laid upon Tamil studies and the LMS expressed the view that English should be regarded as subordinate to the language of the country. In 1862, a decision was taken to stop gradually all teaching in English as far as those educated at the expense of the LMS were concerned. In support of this decision, the official reports referred to the availability of a sufficient number of Tamil language class books to pursue studies with advantage solely in the vernacular and to the need of mission workers to be trained in the language of their countrymen, amongst whom they would be sent for labour. In the day-school English was to be taught as before, the only change being the introduction of a small monthly fee.[75]

There were, however, other forces at work, more down to earth but not less powerful. The LMS did not have the resources to compete effectively with the coffee estates, and seminarists themselves questioned the utility of their studies when people with less education earned much better salaries as overseers on coffee estates. In their private correspondence, both Duthie and Baylis argued that a training for mission work in the vernacular only would ensure the LMS a greater number of agents who would prove immune to the financial attractions usually associated with

[74] Baylis, report of Neyoor, March 1856, in LMS Archives, Odds, Box 16/mf. 1111; letter from Neyoor, 14.7.1875, in idem., Box 17/mf. 1126; letter from Neyoor, 19.1.1861, in idem, Incoming Letters, Box 5/mf. 2666; Mateer, report of Trivandrum, 1874, idem., Odds, Box 17/mf. 1125; report of Quilon, 1877, in idem., Reports, Box 2/mf. 3309.

[75] Duthie in Annual Report Travancore District Committee, Seminary 1860, p. 7; Seminary reports 1862 and 1863 in LMS Archives, Odds, Box 17/mf. 1118; Minutes of TDC Meeting 29.1.1862, in idem., Incoming Letters, Box 5/mf. 2672; the official explanation of the curriculum change is faithfully followed by Yesudas, 1980, p. 141.

an English education. An education in the vernacular, according to these missionaries, would produce a class of people satisfied with the small salaries that the native congregations were able to raise and on the whole just as well adapted to the requirements of missionary service. In sum, Baylis commented tersely, we want native pastors and no reverends, "making them think they must change all their customs and ape equality with Europeans".[76]

The removal of English teaching from the Seminary's boarding school was only of short duration. In 1866 the decision was reversed and in 1867 English, including selections from Shakespeare, returned on the curriculum. Reasons for this new change of educational policy were not given. But there is some evidence to suggest that a re-introduction of English perfectly suited the LMS' own interests.

At home, the LMS Directors were hard-pressed for money and in 1867 they announced a reduction of the Travancore annual budget by at least Rs. 10,000. In order to avoid a serious deficit, the missionaries in Travancore were forced to make several adjustments and the Seminary was not going to escape the general retrenchment. An application for government grant-in-aid, which had saved so many village schools, was not considered. It would lower the prestige of the institution and, apart from that, the government, though more favourably disposed to the mission than formerly, was not likely to finance Christian education on a regular basis. Therefore, it was decided that henceforth students should pay some financial compensation for the benefit of their education. Seminary boarders were asked to contribute half a rupee per month towards the expense of their own board and in 1869 this fee was raised to one rupee, whereas day-scholars not preparing for mission work paid a fee of one rupee or more. The fees gradually increased in the following years.[77] In view of the lamentable plight of

[76] Baylis, letter from Neyoor, 29.4.1863, in LMS Archives, Odds, Box 17/mf. 1119; also, Baylis, letter 11.11.1864, ibidem., mf. 1120 and letter 7.9.1876, ibidem., mf. 1126; Duthie, letter from Nagercoil, 21.2.1862, ibidem., mf. 1118; Jones, Seminary report 1871, ibidem., mf. 1123. For the same reasons the CMS considered to eliminate English from the curriculum of the Kottayam College to make its students less employable elsewhere, Jeffrey 1976, p. 51.

[77] Duthie, 1906, p. 50 and Seminary reports for these years in LMS Archives, Odds, Box 17/mf. 1122 and 1123; see also Baylis, letter from Ooty, 22.10.1870, and Travancore District Committee Meeting, Neyoor 8.2.1872, in LMS Archives, Odds, Box 17/mf. 1123; Travancore District Committee Minute Book, 1876, Annual Meeting Quilon.

mission finances, the imposition of fees meant a substantial relief to the Seminary's funds, yielding Rs. 680 in 1873 and Rs. 1,196 in 1880. There was hardly any risk that this new arrangement would thin the college classes. The missionaries knew very well that the eagerness of many boys to hurry through an English Seminary was mainly inspired by a desire to put their services in the market at the earliest opportunity. These boys and their parents were not likely to shy away from the imposition of fees. Therefore, it seems that the LMS had also come to learn the commercial value of language.

The LMS finances improved, but the position of many boarders got worse. Henceforth, food was measured out according to the stature of the boys, and all grants, including those of clothes, were terminated. As a result, the students who used to wear colourful uniforms with handkerchiefs of Turkey-red dye hanging over the shoulder now presented the sorry spectacle of "a shabby, ragged, tattered, woe-be-gone collection of human creatures, clad in only the remnants of garments".[78] Yet, the Seminary survived this difficult period, not in the least because of the lasting demand for English education, also among Christian parents. But not all groups could afford to pay the charge for admission. Fees were reduced for those unable to pay, but this seems to have been a temporary measure with restricted application. Therefore, the main result was that the poorer Christians lost their easy access to the Seminary and started falling behind.

The feeling of being excluded was clearly expressed in the petition that Christians of south Travancore placed before the LMS home authorities in 1885. Referring to the paddy fields that were granted to the mission during Ringeltaube's time and Vedamanickam, the petitioners contended that the yields from this land were expressly meant for the education of the poor Christian children of south Travancore as well as for the support of widows and orphans. They had to conclude, however, that for the last 17 years neither orphans nor children of the poor had been admitted free of charge into the Seminary and the help rendered to the poor had been considerably reduced. Meanwhile the fee for boarding-students had risen to Rs. 2 or 3 per month, apart from the necessary

[78] History of Nagercoil Seminary, in Manuscript Histories, Ecclesiastical Archives, LMS 95; it is not clear from Duthie 1906, p. 47 at what time this uniform was introduced, but the context of his story suggests that it was before 1867.

books and clothing, and thus only the children of mission agents and more well-to-do Christians were in a position to receive education in the Seminary. From the Seminary reports the petitioners had learned that the funds received from the Home Society and the increased local contributions were quite sufficient for the support of the 95 boarders then on the rolls. Therefore, they were very anxious to know what was done with the large annual income from the paddy fields. The Home Secretary of the LMS was asked to make investigations and to ensure that the financial accounts of the paddy fields were made public together with the Seminary reports. Only a clear and public reply to these questions, the petition ended, would satisfy the poor Christians, most of whom did not dare to complain openly about these things, as they feared excommunication from the church or dismissal of their children from the schools.[79]

The petition, signed by about 170 people, was framed by Moses Jacob, a *Pariah* from Mayiladi connected with the early Christians in that village. Added was a copy of the deed by which Ringeltaube on his departure authorized Vedamanickam to manage all mission property including the fields. In January 1883, Jacob and others had already tried to submit a similar petition to the visiting LMS delegates Thompson & Spicer, but Duthie and Joshua, pastor of Nagercoil, had prevented it. In August of that year, Jacob had asked the same questions in a letter to the Travancore District Committee and receiving no reply, he finally placed the matter before the home authorities.

As far as the object of the royal grant was concerned, Jacob was definitely mistaken. The Seminary came into existence after the fields had been obtained and only in 1827 it was for the first time suggested, that the Nagercoil Seminary was to be supported from the proceeds of the landed property. Nevertheless, the idea that the fields were expressly meant to support poor students of the Seminary had gained very general currency, and Parker in his Manuscript History mentioned that several such statements were made after admission fees had been imposed.

On behalf of his brethren, Duthie wrote a very angry letter to ondon to inform the LMS Directors. In case the petition had

[79] The original petition with signatures, dated 10.10.1885, in LMS Archives, Incoming Letters, Box 10; text also in Parker, Manuscript History.

reached them, he strongly advised the Directors not to take any notice of it, as petitions should not be sent home directly but dealt with by the local missionaries. And if the petition happened to reach his own desk, Duthie saw only one way to deal with it and that was to throw it into the waste paper basket. He described Jacob as "a poor drunken fellow" who had been removed from the congregation and whose son was refused by the Seminary on account of lack of room and funds. The people around him were said to represent "the worst section of the *Pariah* Christians", desiring only to receive all sorts of advantages free of any costs to themselves. For that reason they had started an agitation and sent petitions, claiming rights to land that were absolutely baseless.[80] The pastor and deacons of the Nagercoil Home Church, who were converts from the *Shanar* community, also distanced themselves from the petition. They objected on formal grounds and accused Jacob of collecting signatures under false pretexts from relapsed Christians and from schoolboys whose names corresponded with those of respectable Christian families.[81]

The paddy fields had been granted to the mission at a time when most converts were from the *Pariah* caste. But claims to land were not at the root of the agitation. The basic problem was that the proceeds from these lands were used to support a Seminary from which the poorer Christians felt debarred by the imposition of high admission fees. The Nagercoil Seminary was the crown of the LMS educational effort. During the last decades of the century, however, that crown became increasingly associated with a more respectable class of Christians, able to pay for the advantages that might accrue from a good education.

[80] Duthie, letter 20.1.1884, in Parker, Manuscript History, and letter from Nagercoil, 17.10.1885, in LMS Archives, Incoming Letters, Box 10. The 1884 letter was written in anticipation of the petition that was sent to London later.

[81] Letter from pastor and deacons of Nagercoil Home Church, 31.10.1885, in LMS Archives, Incoming Letters, Box 10.

VI. Emergence of Coffee Plantations

VI.1 Policies of the Travancore Government

Coffee drinking had reached Europe through contacts with the Middle East. When coffee houses became popular in Europe in the seventeenth century, Mocha in Yemen was still the main source of the bean. To meet the rising demand, the Dutch started the planting of coffee shrubs in Java by 1712. This turned out to be a great commercial success and in the nineteenth century coffee had become the Dutch East Indies' major export crop. After 1880, leaf-disease hit the orchards and although the cultivation of coffee recovered, it was replaced by sugarcane as the main export crop.

At that time, Brazil dominated the world market as the largest producer of coffee. Started only one century before, it was able to supply three-quarters of the world's coffee by the end of the nineteenth century. Other centres of production were Mexico and Guatemala.[1]

Surprisingly, Eric Wolf, from whose excellent chapter on "The Movement of Commodities" this information has been derived, does not mention Ceylon as a centre of production, nor British India. Only under the heading "Tea" reference is made to Ceylon's past as a coffee producer. Yet, although small in comparison with Brazil, the growing of coffee held a prominent place in the economy of nineteenth century south Asia. In 1877 British India and Ceylon had 354,070 and 272,243 acres respectively under coffee cultivation. South Travancore's share in British India's total acreage under coffee cultivation was almost 6 per cent (see Table IV).

The first coffee plantation in Ceylon was opened in 1824. The real expansion began in the 1840s, when hundreds of coffee estates were laid out and in 1856 Ceylon numbered 404 and in 1877 1357 estates. In south India the commercialization of the coffee production started a bit later. The first plantations were laid out in Nilgiris (1838), in the Hassan and Kader districts of Mysore state (the 1840s) and in Coorg, where an English planter started

[1] Wolf, pp. 336–7.

TABLE IV COFFEE IN SOUTH ASIA 1877[2]

Area	Number of Estates (opened)	Total Acreage under Cultivation
British India	1388	354.070
South India	780 (56.2%)	110.081 (31.1%)
South Travancore	98 (7.1%)	20.884 (5.9%)
North Travancore	30 (2.1%)	4.046 (1.1%)
Ceylon	1357	272.243

commercial production of coffee near Mercara in 1854. Another important coffee region was Wynad, in Malabar district. Here, experimental growing of coffee had started in the 1840s, and in 1862 there were already 10,000 acres under cultivation. In Travancore, large-scale and commercial production of coffee began about 1860.

Shortly after that, in 1868, leaf disease made its first appearance in Ceylon. In the 1870s, the fungus spread over a wider area and in the course of a few years most of the Ceylon enterprises were ruined or switched to tea. After 1870, the volume of the Ceylon coffee-export went down but for some time its value increased, partly because Brazilean coffee was considered to be of inferior quality.[3] At the end of the 1870s, leaf disease had the same devastating effect on Travancore and about 1890 most planters shifted to tea.[4] The disease seems gradually to have moved to the north. At the beginning of the twentieth century, all British-owned plantations in Malabar were still growing only coffee when the fungus attacked the shrubs and destroyed many of the enterprises.[5]

In this chapter, we will discuss the circumstances under which the coffee plantations were introduced in Travancore. By plantations, we mean capitalist units, employing hired labour to produce a single crop (coffee) for the market. This definition is useful

[2] Ferguson, 1878, pp. 20, 175: Pp. 159–62 list 101 coffee estates but for three of them, situated near Tencasy, no acreage is given and, most probably, they were not yet opened then. Figures for Ceylon may include a small number of acres under tea or cinchona.

N.B.: south Travancore includes Tencasy, but not Courtallum.

[3] Rajaratnam, p. 2.

[4] In 1896 4,643 acres in south Travancore were still planted with coffee as against 6,685 acres with tea, see The Planting Directory, 1896, p. VII.

[5] Varghese, p. 121.

to distinguish the plantation from the so-called native coffee gardens, working mainly with family labour on plots not exceeding 10 acres. Attention will be given to Government policies meant to stimulate the commercialization of agriculture and to the pioneering role of foreign entrepreneurs. In the previous chapter we have seen that people from south Travancore played an important part in the labour migration to the coffee estates in Ceylon. Now, our main question will be how the same people, and especially the low caste Christians among them, reacted to the emergence of coffee plantations in their own state.

After 1860, the commercial-capitalist development of agriculture came to receive strong encouragement from the Travancore government. The start of this period of active government intervention coincided with the appointment of a new *dewan*, T. Madhava Rao, a student of Madras High School, and the accession of a new *Raja*, Rama Varma, who had received his education from Madhava Rao. Before 1857, Travancore, accused of maladministration, had been on the verge of annexation by the East India Company. Therefore, the new leadership realized that only a vigorous policy of modernization could guarantee independent survival of the state.

Forced by pressure from European capitalist interests, the new government started abolishing a number of state monopolies. In 1860, the monopoly of pepper was abolished, followed in 1863 by that of tobacco. The removal of all inland transit duties in 1836 was now extended to a wider field: in 1865 Travancore joined the British Indian system of free trade, adopting British Indian tariffs and removing most of the duties on trade between Travancore and other parts of British India. Exports, especially from Alleppey, rose dramatically.[6] In 1861 postal services were opened to the public and together with the introduction of the telegraph, these innovations facilitated international communications.

Another important measure was taken in 1865, when a royal proclamation conferred full ownership rights on cultivators of *sirkar* lands (the majority of all the tenants), subject only to due payment of land revenue. The same law also allowed unrestricted transfer of landed property. A few years later further land reforms ensured protection and permanent occupancy rights

[6] Jeffrey, 1976, p. 97; Tharakan, p. 71.

to tenants of private landlords.[7] Those *uliyams* or *corvées* that were still enforced were finally abolished in 1865. In the same year a law was introduced, similar to the one in force in British India, making any breach of contract by workmen or labourers a criminal offence.[8] These measures created conditions necessary for the commercialization of agriculture and the emergence of plantations.

In 1861 the government had opened an experimental garden in Pirmed, north Travancore, where cinchona and tea were tested for their suitability to local circumstances. Coffee had then already passed the experimental stage. The government, however, did not choose a new state monopoly of coffee, but decided to encourage the initiative of private planters. To serve that purpose, it had to offer land on favourable terms, to alleviate economic burden and to improve internal communications.

As far as land was concerned, Varghese has already pointed out that planters in Travancore were in a fairly advantageous position. They could obtain lands directly from a sympathetic government, whereas in Malabar it was more expensive and rather insecure to lease land from private landlords.[9] To facilitate the sale of land, the government of Travancore had established a survey department in 1865. Before a piece of forest land suited for coffee cultivation was put up for auction, this department mapped out its area and roughly sketched its boundaries. As soon as the land was sold, a surveyor went up to the hills a second time to make up the final accurate survey and only after that title deeds were issued to the proprietor.[10]

At first the price of land amounted to Re. 1 per acre only. When in 1871–72 and 1872–73 bumper harvests were gathered and enormous profits made, many people who had some capital to spend were infected by a "coffee fever" and wanted to invest in land. The following year the price of land rose to Rs. 10 per acre and in 1874–75 competition made land prices soar to the unprecedented height of Rs. 76 or even 82 per acre. In these years, the government realized Rs. 85,254 and Rs. 214,761 respectively from the sale of land[11] (Appendix V).

[7] Varghese, pp. 64–7.

[8] Report on the Administration of Travancore 1865–66, p. 30; Nagam Aiya, vol. I, p. 545.

[9] Varghese, p. 116.

[10] Report on the Administration of Travancore 1870–71, p. 31 ff.

[11] See the Reports on the Administration of Travancore for these years; also Mateer, 1883, pp. 230–31.

As the survey of the blocks sold in previous years could not keep pace with the new sales, many disputes over boundaries cropped up between old and new purchasers. In these circumstances, the government decided to suspend the sale of land, primarily with a view to completing the surveys of land already sold.[12] At that time, November 1874, 40,000 acres had been sold, some parts yet unfelled or in the first stage of cultivation. Approximately 23,000 acres were planted, of which 14,000 acres were bearing.[13]

In 1878 the British Resident suggested resumption of the sale of forest land. The Travancore government, however, seriously doubted the wisdom of such a policy. In a memorandum, the *dewan* argued that denudation of forests not only tended to affect the fall of rain, but also threatened to destroy fuel reserves, grazing grounds and the general quality of the soil. For that reason, he preferred to reserve all forests above an elevation of 500 feet and to prevent the unrestrained clearance of lower hills by the demarcation of reserved tracts. The Resident was not impressed. He apprehended that the real aim of the Travancore government was to impede European enterprise, more so as an acre planted with coconut paid the government much more in tax and duty than an acre of coffee. He expressed the opinion that, if the felling was judiciously done, the dangers of diminished rainfall and destructive floods could be averted. The Madras government fully supported the Resident, but in the meantime the depression had set in and the coffee fever was replaced by a feeling of disillusionment.[14]

Sales of land for the cultivation of coffee had been made on the stipulation that it remained open to the Travancore government either to increase the land tax or to levy export duty on coffee. The land tax was modest and amounted to no more than 12 *annas* per acre in 1870.[15] To woo the planters, it was also ruled that land taken up for coffee was tax-free for the first five years. The exact yield of tax on coffee land is difficult to determine. For a long time these taxes remained included in the general collection of garden land assessments and only in 1878–79 they appeared under a

[12] Memorandum of *dewan* in Crown Representative's Records, R/2 (879/18).

[13] Report on the Administration of Travancore 1875–76, p. 26.

[14] Memorandum of *dewan* and connected correspondence in Crown Representative's Records, R/2 (879/18).

[15] In Wynad, Malabar, the land tax on coffee plantations was Rs. 2 on all land in bearing. Markham, p. 18.

separate heading. In that year the total tax demand under this head was Rs. 17,105 (Appendix V).

The export duty on coffee was 5 per cent ad valorem and yielded the government Rs. 26,224 only in 1875. This duty was remitted for the first five years on the condition that one quarter of the land should be cleared and planted within the first three years.[16] Nevertheless, the planters earnestly requested the government to abolish the export duty. They argued that the government received sufficient benefit from the plantations by the growth of employment enabling the population to buy taxable commodities and to pay revenue to warrant remittance of the export duty. The government agreed in 1875, but announced that henceforward the land tax was liable to increase. In view of developments in the coffee business after 1875, the planters, on second thought, preferred to leave the land tax unchanged and the government fully obliged. Thus, in 1877 an export duty on coffee was reinstituted but now at the reduced rate of 2.5 per cent ad valorem.[17] As the depression in the cultivation of coffee continued, the government complied again with the planters' wishes and suspended for the time being the collection of the land tax. The export duty, however, was restored to 5 per cent.

Another important government measure, finally, was the improvement of the internal system of transport and communication, which may also be seen as a crucial factor in the emergence of a commercialized agriculture. A prominent part in this was played by the Public Works Department (PWD). This department was started during the great 1860 famine as a "food for work program" and was led by British civil engineers.[18]

At the beginning of the 1870s, the Department numbered a permanent executive staff of 39 members, apart from Division or Range Offices. Instituted for the construction of roads, canals and bridges, the PWD soon became one of the major items of the Travancore annual budget (Table V).

Among the first major works by the Department of Public Works, was the Martanda Varma or Southern Canal from Cape Comorin to the immediate neighbourhood of Trivandrum. Also, a

[16] Mateer, 1883, p. 229.

[17] Report on the Administration of Travancore 1876–77, p. 24.

[18] For a short history of the PWD, see Report on the Administration of Travancore 1873–74, pp. 107 ff. See also Maltby.

TABLE V: TRAVANCORE GOVERNMENT EXPENDITURE (RS.)[19]

Year	Total Expenditure	Expenditure on PWD (plus percentage of total)
1865/66	43,07,644	3,75,735 (8.7%)
1870/71	53,10,187	9,67,664 (18.2%)
1871/72	54,93,682	11,93,189 (21.7%)
1875/76	55,94,814	8,94,065 (16%)
1877/78	56,15,211	11,83,887 (21%)
1879/80	60,27,802	12,23,075 (20.3%)

cartable road was built from Nagercoil to the Ashambu hills, completed in 1865, and a similar road from Kottayam to the hill area around Pirmed. Branch roads were constructed and many rivers bridged. It proved very difficult to keep large bodies of workmen together and to feed them in deserted and unhealthy localities. Yet, the PWD made steady progress and in 1872 1,000 miles of road were completed or nearly completed. In 1859, Duthie had a difficult journey to Nagercoil by *palanqin* along a hardly passable road, whereas in 1902 Dr. Bentall of the LMS and his wife went for a pleasant bicycle-ride from Neyoor to Nagercoil in the cool of the evening.[20]

However, transport was not improved to make missionary life more easy. The construction of central roads to Ashambu in the south and Pirmed in the north, the most prominent coffee centres, indicates that the new network of communication was primarily meant to serve the plantation interest. Bullock carts with food, clothing, tobacco and arrack went up to the foot of the hills and returned laden with coffee to the coastal ports of Colachel, Quilon and Alleppey; from where the coffee was shipped. In his report of 1876 Barton, chief of the PWD, admitted that many roads, and

[19] Figures are taken from the Reports on the Administration of Travancore for these years. The building and repair of public offices, palaces and temples was the responsibility of a separate *Marhamut* Department and expenditure for that purpose has not been included under the head PWD. As explained in chapter II, the Travancore Government had also to pay an annual subsidy of Rs. 8,00,000 to the British-Indian Government.

The Government of the much larger Madras Presidency paid in 1870/71 Rs. 35,42,790 only for internal communications, see Memorandum by Sir Alexander Arbuthnot, 12.10.1874, in Crown Representative's Records, R/2 (879/3).

[20] Duthie, 1906, p. 11; LMS Chronicle 1902, p. 165.

indeed all the roads which skirted the foot of the hills, were designed to give ready access to the coffee plantations. But he rejected planters' demands to construct road approaches to the separate estates, as—unlike the situation in Ceylon—the estates in Travancore lay isolated along a narrow ridge varying in elevation from 2,000 to 3,000 feet which would make road construction very expensive.[21] Instead it was decided to give grants-in-aid to planters who wanted to build their own roads, but out of the allotment of Rs. 34,150 in 1879–80 only Rs. 8,400 were used for that purpose.[22]

Mateer was of the opinion that the government had heavily handicapped the coffee enterprise by its unwillingness to remit duties or to provide sufficient roads.[23] In view of the policies discussed above, there seems to be no ground for such a statement. After 1860, the commercialization of agriculture, which had alreadv started much earlier with the cultivation of paddy and pepper, was further stimulated by official legislation. Thus, the government had created conditions favourable to private enterprise. Let us now turn to the question, who made use of these conditions.

VI.2 Foreign Planters

According to Nagam Aiya, the coffee plant was introduced into Travancore by *dewan* Reddy Rao (1817–21). In 1843 Travancore was said to have exported 910 cwts, produced by local peasants and plantations of Messrs. Binny & Co. The plantations turned out to be a failure and were abandoned.[24]

An important contribution to the later emergence of coffee plantations was rendered by General Cullen, British Resident in Travancore (1840–60). Cullen had his own bungalow in the Ashambu hills with a garden at a height of about 3,000 feet, where he experimented with European fruits and Oriental spices. About the year 1854, he started planting some coffee shrubs and this experimental garden later grew into a flourishing coffee estate.[25]

[21] Report by Barton in Report on the Administration of Travancore 1876–77, pp. 35–7.

[22] Report on the Administration of Travancore 1879–80, p. 42.

[23] Mateer, 1883, p. 233.

[24] Nagam Aiya, vol. I, p. 472; Mateer, 1883, p. 225; according to Varghese, p. 69 Europeans had started plantations in the Travancore hills in 1834, but he gives no further particulars and mentions no source.

[25] Smith, p. 116; Mateer, 1883, pp. 225–226. At his death Cullen left three other gardens apart from the one in Ashambu, see Correspondence relating to Estate of General Cullen in Crown Representative's Records R/2 (879/6).

European planters were the most prominent group among those who invested money in the coffee enterprise. As might be expected there was a close connection between the cultivation of coffee in Travancore and that in neighbouring Ceylon. The pioneer of large-scale coffee planting in the Travancore hills was John Grant, who had gained rich experience in Ceylon and came over to Travancore with his two brothers in 1862. To encourage him the government allowed him a free grant of 500 acres of forest land in Mahindragerry near Ashambu, where planting began in 1864.[26] He was soon followed by others. In Pirmed, east of Kottayam, the first plantations opened at the same time. Planters here received also free grants of land from the government for the experiment. The first Travancorean planters, that will be discussed in the next section, had also gained experience on plantations in Ceylon.[27]

In 1868, Travancore numbered 50 coffee estates owned by European planters; in 1878 the number had risen to 128, apart from estates and gardens owned by local people. One big company, the Scottish Indian Coffee Company Ltd., with offices, stores and a bank at Colachel, were agents of no less than 52 plantations in south Travancore alone, owning 12 of them. Nevertheless, the number of European planters in Travancore remained small, at least according to official information.[28]

Among the names of the early coffee planters, we find those of the *dewan* Madhava Rao and the crown prince, Vishakham Tirunal. After the death of General Cullen (1862) they had taken over his plantation, which enabled them to combine their commercial and botanic interests. John Cox, the former LMS missionary, was asked to serve as Manager of their property[29] and here, we come across another small but interesting group of estate holders.

In the 1870s, LMS missionaries started coffee planting, first a

[26] Ferguson, 1878, p. 40; Mateer, 1883, p. 228; Saradamoni, pp. 114–5.

[27] Mateer, 1883, p. 228; Jeffrey, 1976, p. 99.

[28] The Census of Travancore 1875, p. 261, counted 34 "European cultivators", most probably meaning planters, but the actual number must have been higher. Many Europeans entered Travancore in search of land or work on the coffee estates, but since passports were no longer required from people travelling from British India, the government in Trivandrum had lost control, see Confidential Letter Nanoo Pillay, *dewan*, 3.12.1877, in Crown Representative's Records R/2 (879/13).

[29] For Cox's personal background and forced retirement from the LMS see chapter III, p. 49 ff.

few acres to support their hot-weather bungalow in the Ashambu hills; then, they launched their own Glenroy Estate with 50 acres under cultivation to finance an additional European teacher for the Nagercoil Seminary.[30] Of course, the management of this and other ventures, being inconsistent with the missionaries' proper duties, had to be left to local converts, but the missionaries played an important part by taking shares, rendering advice and establishing links with British exporters like the Scottish India Coffee Company. The LMS missionaries were no exception. Caldwell, working for the SPG in Tinnevelly, had his own coffee estate in Ashambu in the 1860s and the family of H. Baker, CMS missionary in north Travancore, was also in planting.[31] Coffee seemed a safe investment, but leaf disease destroyed all hopes and much money was lost. Duthie had engaged an additional teacher on the basis of prospective returns and when the Seminary plantation turned out a failure, a somewhat irritated correspondence with headquarters in London followed about the question who had to be charged for the additional teacher's travelling-expenses.[32]

Altogether, there were eight plantations in south Travancore in 1877 owned by (ex-)missionaries. Their average number of acres under cultivation was 107, and with their total acreage of 863 they covered 4.1 per cent of all the land planted with coffee (see Table VI, p. 132). The largest estate was Balmoral, situated near Tencasy and owned by Jones,[33] Cox and others, having 273 acres planted. John Cox owned two estates, Olivers[34] and Blackrock, and Duthie had

[30] Jeffrey, 1976, p. 132 assumes that the Glenallyn Coffee Company, formed by the missionaries and owning the Glenallyn Estate, served that purpose, but most probably it was the Glenroy Estate, owned by the Mission Seminary and listed by Ferguson 1878, p. 159.

[31] Nyanacan, letter from Nagercoil, 21.6.1865, in LMS Archives, Odds, Box 16/mf. 1120; for a list of early coffee planters see Report on the Administration of Travancore 1865–66, pp. 29–30.

[32] The teacher was Norbert Caldwell of the Free Church Training College Glasgow; enganged in 1877, he left in June 1878; see Whitehouse, acting Foreign Secretary LMS, letter 31.10.1879 from London to Duthie in LMS Archives, Outgoing Letters, Box 21/mf. 458 and Duthie, letter from Nagercoil, 2.12.1879, in LMS Archives, in idem., Odds, Box 17/mf. 1126.

[33] The personal papers left by Samuel Jones clearly testify to his large investments in coffee estates, garden lands etc. and his extensive dealings with the Scottish India Coffee Company which served as the agency for Balmoral, see LMS Archives, Personal Papers, Box 3/mf. 904.

[34] Title deeds for Olivers, named after Cox's parental home in Gloucestershire, were issued in 1869, see Report on the Administration of Travancore 1870–71, pp. 28–9.

the smaller Crownhill North Estate registered in his name with 25 acres under cultivation. Apart from the Glenallyn and Glenroy Estates, mentioned earlier, there was a Mission Land Estate, owned by the LMS and managed by P.D. Devasagayam, numbering only 10 acres and Caldwell's Woodlands Estate.[35]

The commercial interest of people who had been sent to sow the Gospel and not to harvest coffee is not so strange as it may seem. As we have seen in the third chapter, the missionary movement in nineteenth century Britain was also a social emancipation movement of an emerging lower middle class. As representatives of that class, the missionaries combined a predilection for a sober and industrious life with a keen eye for the economic opportunities that their situation offered. They always strongly emphasized the importance of improvements in agriculture and cottage industries and, depending on their own occupational background, pleaded for the introduction of ploughs, weaving machines or trading facilities. The department for lace and embroidery, where hundreds of poor women were enabled to earn some money, and the Nagercoil School of Industry were the institutional expressions of this developmental interest. When in the 1820s the cultivation and manufacture of indigo experienced a short period of prosperity in south Travancore, Mead contacted the owners and ensured that his converts became actively involved in this business.[36] So, when the cultivation of coffee seemed to offer bright prospects, the missionaries were ready to respond, and encouraged their converts to undertake coffee cultivation.

VI.3 Indian Participation

Varghese regards the influx of foreign capital into Travancore as an opportunity for indigenous groups, especially Christians, to benefit from the economic trend by starting their own plantations. He is speaking primarily of the first part of the twentieth century.

[35] Ferguson, 1878, pp. 159–62. Total acreage usually was much larger than the area actually planted.

[36] Jacob, Manuscript History, pp. 98–9, 185; Mateer, 1871, pp. 105–6. idem., 1883, p. 2; Cox, pp. xxiv–xxv, B 18; Agur, p. 720; Mead, letter, 26.9.1820, in LMS Archives, Incoming Letters, Box 1, and letter, 7.2.1849, ibidem., Odds, Box 16/mf. 1108. The pressure by Mead and Mault for the introduction of European trades and implements was accompanied by the dubious argument that "it raises the English character greatly to see the superiority of our own workmanship", extract of letter, 1819 or 1820, ibidem., Odds, Box 15/mf. 1101.

Jeffrey, dealing with the nineteenth century, states that several Syrian Christians took service with coffee plantations in north Travancore and, in some cases, opened sizable plantations around Pirmed, north Travancore, on their own account.[37]

In contrast to their opinion, Mateer remarked, that "few, if any ... Syrian Christians availed themselves of the opening which the coffee enterprise afforded".[38] He is supported in this by the *Planting Directory* of 1878, which listed 30 coffee estates in Pirmed, a Syrian Christian area, but all the names of owners, agents or managers are English or at least non-Indian.[39] For south Travancore, the case was different. There, the coming of the coffee plantations did indeed offer new opportunities which local initiative could profitably make use of.

As was mentioned erlier, the first Travancorean planters had been introduced to the skills and opportunities of large-scale coffee planting when working as migrant labourers in Ceylon. Back in Travancore, some of them took up land and started coffee planting on their own. A few life histories of those who made a successful career may help to explain the interrelation between labour migration, coffee planting and Christian mission.

One of the first to migrate from Travancore to Ceylon was Daniel Motchakan, a *Shanar* from Jamestown. He was born a Christian and attended the Nagercoil Seminary at the time of Charles Miller, where he was a class-mate of the two later *dewans*. Because of his excellent command over English, he became the personal assistant of Pattison, the missionary of Quilon, whom he accompanied on all his travels. In Quilon he heard of the coffee estates in Ceylon and, when in 1844 Pattison was recalled, Motchakan decided to cross over to the coffee island to seek his fortune there. He collected a few friends and in the port-town of Tuticorin he met Mr. Lambert, a coffee planter from Kandy, who had come to south India in search of labour. That was the beginning

[37] Varghese, pp. 116–7; Jeffrey, 1976, pp. 126–7; Tharakan, p. 57 is basing himself completely on Varghese and Jeffrey when writing, that Syrian Christians took up commercial agriculture earlier than other communities. But he does not claim a pioneering role for Syrian Christians with regard to coffee planting in particular; in fact, the Syrian Christian presence in the planting arena was a phenomenon largely associated with rubber (personal communication by Tharakan).

[38] Mateer, 1883, p. 236.

[39] Ferguson, 1878, p. 156; the same is true for the Planting Directory of 1896, pp. 31–3. There were only very few Syrian Christians in south Travancore.

of a long lasting relationship between Motchakan and Lambert. Motchakan worked for several years as *kangany* and did pioneering work in starting coffee plantations. He retired in 1859 and became deacon of the Jamestown church, his eldest son serving the LMS as assistant missionary in Tittuvilei.[40]

Among the first so-called coffee coolies, recruited by Motchakan, was P.D. Devasagayam (1822–1884).[41] This Devasagayam came from a poor *Shanar* family, converted by Mault. After receiving his education at the Nagercoil Seminary he worked for the LMS as a catechist and a teacher. In 1844, or shortly after that, he emigrated to Ceylon, where he served several planters as *kangany* and was eventually employed in a large estate, drawing a salary of Rs. 100 per month. In view of this salary, Mateer may be right in suggesting that Devasagayam had risen to the post of manager. In 1859, he returned to Travancore to invest his savings in land. He asked the *dewan* for permission to buy 60 acres of forest land in the Ashambu hills, which was granted in 1861, and started his own Victoria Estate, later followed by Joaja Estate with 40 acres under cultivation and Lower Victoria (10 acres).

Devasagayam invested his earnings also in paddy lands and in a magnificent house in his native place Nagercoil. This two-storeyed building proudly challenged the old restrictions imposed on *Shanars* and similar castes,[42] and after completing the house Devasagayam had to set an armed guard round the premises for about six months, as the high castes had threatened to set it on fire. Apart from that, he became a deacon and generously supported missionary education and church building, giving regularly a tenth of his income to the LMS and, till coffee failed about 1880, donating Rs. 200 to every Christian widow who remarried. In 1874

[40] Jacob, Manuscript History, pp. 161–2.

[41] This life history has been reconstructed from bits of information in Jacob, Manuscript History, pp. 66, 160–1; Mateer, 1883, pp. 226–8; Duthie, 1906, pp. 45–46; Jeffrey, 1976, pp. 131–2, 336; Nyanacan, letter from Tittuvilei, 21.2.1867, in LMS Archives, Odds, Box 17/mf. 1122; Duthie, Seminary report, 1878, in idem., Reports, Box 2/mf. 3312; Crown Representative's Records R/2 (879/25). Jacob and Jeffrey are rather inconsistent as far as dates are concerned.

[42] In 1833 a district court had ruled that Christians, when building houses had to conform to the fashion of the caste to which they belonged before conversion; for Christians from untouchable castes, this meant that no improvements like the construction of a second storey were permitted, Report of Nagercoil, 1833, in LMS Archives, Odds, Box 16.

he assisted his wife's nephew, P.C. Joseph, in launching the *Travancore Times*, a trimonthly Christian journal with a circulation (in 1895) of about 420 copies.

It might very well be, that Devasagayam was also inspired by the nearby experimental coffee garden of Resident Cullen, which grew into a large coffee estate, managed by Cox and later by Devasagayam himself. In view of the early start of his Victoria Estate (1861), however, Devasagayam certainly deserves the distinction of having been the first to enter upon the professional production of coffee in Travancore. His enterprising spirit was publicly praised by Vishakham Tirunal, first prince and later *Maharaja*, who in an address on Travancore's industrial status called the Victoria Estate one of the best managed and best paying coffee plantations he had ever seen. The prince exhorted his people to follow Devasagayam's example and presented him, among other things, with a *palanqin* and a four wheeled chariot.

The life of P. Paul, a born Christian from Mayiladi, bears a close resemblance to that of Devasagayam. After receiving his education in Nagercoil Seminary, Paul went to Ceylon and was employed for several years as *kangany* in the coffee estates. After his return, he took up land in the hills close to Nagercoil and started coffee planting in his Love Hill Estate (20 acres planted), surrounding himself with Christian labourers and friends. He was a great help to the pastor of the Mayiladi congregation and from his newly acquired wealth, he gave liberally to the poor, paid half of the building costs of a school in Mayiladi and footed a Rs. 600 bill to roof the Nagercoil chapel with iron.[43] M. Paul, a convert from the *Maravan* caste in Tinnevelly, was in charge of the LMS press after he had completed his Seminary education. He gave up mission work and joined P.P. Joseph in running a coffee estate, paying generously for the improvement of chapels in Jamestown and Zionpuram.[44]

The way shown by Motchakan, Devasagayam and Paul was followed by many others. The missionary reports abound with references to successful Christian *kanganies* and in the 1870s Agasteesvaram, to give one example, numbered four conductors

[43] Mateer, 1886, pp. 151–2.

[44] Lee, 1882, in LMS Archives, Odds, Box 17, also in LMS Chronicle, November 1894; Report of Nagercoil, 1880; in LMS Archives, Reports, Box 2/mf. 3316.

and six *kanganies* among its 251 LMS adherents.[45] A number of these people used their earnings to open their own coffee plantations in Travancore and friends placed additional capital at their disposal. When more plantations had been laid out in south Travancore, Ceylon experience became less important, and migrant labourers and prospective planters went straight to the hills in their own country. The profits that could be made by people from humble origin would have been impossible in pre-plantation days and, as Jeffrey has pointed out, Devasagayam's imposing two-storeyed house symbolized a changing order in which caste alone would not determine rank or status.[46] Most missionaries tried their utmost to keep their precious seminarists from entering on more mundane professions. But at the same time, they were perfectly aware that the income from the coffee plantations could only save their budget from an always threatening deficit. Therefore, they brought their converts' skills to the attention of virtually every planter and assisted the people in their own ventures by lending advice, useful introductions and even shares of capital. The Christian involvement in the coffee business can clearly be seen from the level of local LMS contributions. Till the 1860s these contributions amounted to Rs. 4,000 annually, but from 1866 onwards they averaged Rs. 10,000 per annum, showing a sharp fall in 1879 (Rs. 6,000).[47] In 1883 the missionaries noted that

> the failure of the Coffee Enterprise ... has caused the withdrawal from the country of much money which circulated largely amongst our people and by which the funds of Congregations in various places have been benefited....[48]

[45] Duthie, report of Nagercoil, 1877, in LMS Archives, Reports, Box 2/mf. 3311; conductors, if used as a separate category, should be seen as head-*kanganies*; among the prominent conductors and church benefactors mention may be made of Vethanayagam of Nagercoil, Peter of Neravilley and M. Daniel of Agasteesvaram.

[46] Jeffrey, 1976, p. 134; Duthie, 1906, p. 48.

[47] Yesudian, report of Tittuvilei, 1878, in LMS Archives, Reports, Box 2/mf. 3312. After 1879 the local contributions soon recovered and continued at the old level, suggesting that the income from coffee was replaced by other sources, see Reports on the Administration of Travancore and Annual Reports of the LMS for these years. The local contributions mentioned by the Annual Reports of the Travancore District Committee, used by Jeffrey 1976, p. 133, are slightly different and reflect more clearly the fluctuating value of coffee exports from Travancore in the corresponding years.

[48] Travancore District Committee Minute Book, 1883, Annual Meeting Neyoor.

Maybe, it was no coincidence that the main centres of coffee planting, Ashambu in the south and Pirmed in the north, were situated close to the headquarters of the LMS in Nagercoil and the CMS in Kottayam. The coffee planting industry had made several Christians very wealthy. Many inhabitants of Nagercoil had followed Devasagayam's example by building two-storeyed houses with large rooms and a reception hall, and in 1861, the local congregation had become entirely self-supporting, paying its own pastor, Bible women, teachers etc.[49]

TABLE VI: (INDIAN) CHRISTIANS IN COFFEE ESTATES
SOUTH TRAVANCORE 1877[50]

	Number of Estates (opened)	Total Acreage under Cultivation
Indian Christian Estate owners	22 (22.4%)	811 (3.9%)
(Ex-) Missionaries as Estate owners	8 (8.1%)	863 (4.1%)
South Travancore (total)	98 (100%)	20,884 (100%)

In 1877 south Travancore numbered at least 22 plantations owned by Indian Christians and having Nagercoil as their post station. That was almost one quarter of the total number of plantations in south Travancore. Their total acreage under cultivation, however, was only 811 acres, averaging a planted area of 37 acres per estate against a total average of 213 acres.

Usually, coffee plantations were much larger than the area actually planted. The plantations owned by local Christians,

[49] The Neyoor home church became self-supporting about the same time, LMS Chronicle 1869, p. 14, 1882, p. 10; at the turn of the century about one hundred congregations had become self-supporting, Duthie, 1906, p. 42.

[50] This table has been computed from Ferguson, 1878, pp. 159–62. My own count of the list given by Ferguson brings the total number of acres under cultivation up to 15,884 acres instead of 20,884 (Ferguson, 1878, p. 175), which means that Indian Christians and (Ex-)missionaries in fact had planted 5.1 per cent resp. 5.4 per cent of the total area under cultivation.

The Love Grove and Rosehill Estates are included among the plantations owned by Indian Christians, as the name of their owner, Paramanandam, is frequently mentioned in missionary reports and a gentleman of that name was deacon of the Nagercoil church. The Thylemalley Estate of P.D Packianathen and others has not been included, although Packianathen's name appeared occasionally on LMS donation lists.

however, used to have their total acreage under cultivation. Because of their smaller size, many owners were at the same time managers of their property. They gave their estates beautiful names, like Eden, Providence and Honey Rock, sometimes naming them after their missionaries like Dennis and Newport Estates. Among the owners we find the names of A.R. Benjamin, S. Daniel, A. Devasagayam, P.D. Devasagayam, C. Isaac, J.G. Jacob, A.M. Joseph, P.P. Joseph, M. Luke, A. Moses, A.R. Nathaniel, P. Paul, N. Peter, Sebagnanam and A. Welcome; there may have been more, before or after 1877.[51]

As said before, the size of these estates was small, especially if compared with the European enterprises. But this share in the coffee business was extremely important for the local Christian community which derived much prestige and self-confidence from it. Even more important was the fact that, as far as there was Indian ownership in the south Travancore plantation industry, it came almost exclusively from the local Christian community, the only exception being the Ashambu Estate of the Crown Prince and the *dewan*.

Another important fact is that already in 1852/53 1,033 cwts. of coffee were exported from Travancore (Appendix V). This is a clear indication that, just as in Ceylon and elsewhere,[52] the small holder coffee production, i.e. production by local peasants on plots smaller than 10 acres, preceded the plantations. Therefore, Mateer is absolutely mistaken and inconsistent with his own praise of Devasagayam and other Christian pioneers, when he states that "European push and activity have moved and guided the inert natives".[53] It is much more likely, that people like Devasagayam, strengthened by their earnings saved from Ceylon, merely transferred an already existing small holders production to a larger and more capital-intensive scale. After the emergence of plantations the peasant production on smaller coffee gardens, both on the hills and in the

[51] A LMS donation list of 1879 mentions a Penshurst Estate of V. Joseph, Seminary Report, 1879, in LMS Archives, Odds, Box 17/mf. 1126.

[52] In 1836 there were only a handful of European planters and the bulk of Ceylon coffee was still being grown by Kandyans on small plantations, see *Ceylon Journal of Historical and Social Studies*, VII, 1 (1964), p. 44; Bandarage, p. 70; for south India, see Planting Directory 1896, pp. vii, ix, and the diary of a European planter in the India Office Library, Eur. Mss. A 123.

[53] Mateer, 1883, p. 237.

plains, remained important as government reports and missionary sources amply testify.[54] Unfortunately, the proportional share of this production in the Travancorean export is unknown. Also, the social groups who engaged in this kind of production are never mentioned by name. But we may assume that *Shanars*, and especially the Christians among them, played a significant part. As was to be expected, the majority of these plantations and coffee gardens were too small and financially too weak to survive the depression of the 1880s.

Nevertheless, the 1860s and 1870s were rather prosperous for those Christians who had been able to enter the coffee business, either as *kangany* or planter, or as clerk, cook and, maybe even, coolie. The missionaries, grappling with their old dilemma, welcomed this commercial involvement of their people, but at the same time expressed grave concern. Duthie informed the Directors, that thoughts about property, money and coffee estates bulked much more largely in the minds of evangelists, catechists and even some pastors than he feared to be good. The eagerness to make money and—later—the necessity to pay off debts led many of these agents to neglect their congregations. Therefore, the European missionaries, who in some cases had large interests in coffee themselves, reminded the Indian pastors that the LMS required all its personnel to abstain from secular work of any kind.[55] For that reason, the end of the coffee boom must have been a blessing in disguise to some missionaries. In 1878 Duthie reported with relief that he had less difficulty than before in keeping his students in the

[54] Report on the Administration of Travancore, 1868–69, p. 31; Baylis in his report of Neyoor, 1875, stated that one of his evangelists had visited 16 native coffee gardens on the hills near Neyoor, LMS Archives, Odds, Box 17/mf. 1125.

In Ceylon, where the coffee industry had assumed much larger proportions, peasant production was also more extensive. Hobbs, in a letter of 24.11.1859, CMS Archives, referred to 46 little coffee gardens in the neighbourhood of Kandy, and Ferguson, 1878, pp. 87 and 103 mentioned 82 Sinhalese, 33 Chettiars, 20 Tamils and several others as owners of regular plantations, apart from hundreds of native coffee gardens. According to Bandarage, p. 186, new cash needs like taxes encouraged the Kandyan peasants to take up small holder cash cropping rather than hiring themselves out as wage labour on the European coffee estates.

[55] Duthie, letter from Nagercoil, 20.2.1872, and Meeting Travancore District Committee, Neyoor 8.2.1872, in LMS Archives, Odds, Box 17/mf. 1123. The missionaries seem to have delegated much of their financial responsibilities to the Scottish Indian Coffee Company Ltd., see Travancore District Committee Correspondence 1875–76.

Seminary, and Yesudian wrote that those who had left the service of God for the search of material profit had now experienced the treacherous nature of their new sphere of labour.[56]

VI.4 Labour Questions and Cooly Mission

A very important condition for the development of plantations, which has not yet been discussed, is the availability of sufficient and cheap labour. In view of this need of free labour, it might be presumed that the abolition of slavery was induced by the interests of the emerging plantation economy. In this connection the time sequence is very suggestive: in British India, slavery was abolished in 1843 and the first plantations were opened in the 1840s and 1850s. In Travancore, abolition came in 1855 and plantations started shortly after 1860. Was the emancipation of slaves, which had ruined so many plantations in the West Indies, a condition for their emergence in south Asia?

Benedict Hjelje has pointed out that in south Asia the abolition of slavery coincided with a growing availability of alternative employment opportunities, like the opening of plantations. She does not mean to say that abolition was enforced with the express purpose to further the plantation economy, but rather that the newly acquired freedom of the slaves could only make sense, when alternative means of support became available. Srinivas makes the same point in his well-known study of the Coorgs: the end of slavery had but little effect, till the opening of coffee plantations in Coorg district with their cash wages cut the bonds binding the slaves to their traditional masters.[57]

Both may be true. Even if it was not the express purpose, slavery abolition did create an agrarian proletariat which could be tapped by an emerging plantation economy. On the other hand, the formal abolition of slavery could receive real substance only by the presence of alternative employment opportunities, or at least assume a different shape under the new system of plantation labour. Let us now turn to Travancore.

The population of Travancore contained large numbers of slaves

[56] Duthie, Seminary report, 1878, in LMS Archives, Odds, Box 17/mf. 1126; Yesudian, report of Tittuvilei, 1878, in idem., Reports, Box 2/mf. 3312.

[57] Hjelje, pp. 102, 106; Srinivas, 1965, p. 19; see also Logan, vol. I, pp. 148, 151, 178; Hardgrave, p. 10.

or soil-serfs, especially *Pulayas* and *Pariahs*, who were owned by the government or private landlords. Kusuman and Saradamoni have argued, that their liberation was hardly motivated by economic considerations, but rather by political pressure from the British Indian government and moral arguments from local missionaries. Other historians, like Kurup, however, emphasize that the Christian and humanitarian efforts in favour of abolition were in fact primarily meant to create the free labour market that was needed by local capitalist planters.[58] Now the problem is, that the LMS sources themselves do not explicitly link a ban on slavery with plantation labour, whereas the economic disadvantages of abolition like reduced tax income and possible labour scarcity are freely discussed.[59] I personally tend to think, however, that in spite of the absence of straight evidence, the mentality and economic outlook of the London missionaries were certainly conducive to the creation of a free labour market, even though there were as yet no plantations on the spot.

These ex-slaves do not seem to have crowded the gates of the emerging coffee plantations. Saradamoni states that the plantations could not recruit a large number of ex-slaves, as "by habit and tradition they were unused to leaving their huts and hamlets".[60] She gives no source, but might be basing herself on the Travancore Administration, which also reported that people, as a rule, preferred agricultural work in the well watered plains to shifting their habitations to inhospitable mountainous districts.[61] No reference is made to any groups in particular, but at least this information does not suggest that many ex-slaves availed themselves of the plantations as an economic alternative.

Where, then, did the plantation workers come from? Current opinion has it, that the neighbouring districts in Madras Presidency were the main suppliers of cheap labour, more so, as the mountain-ridge which separated Travancore from Madras could

[58] K.K.N. Kurup, pp. 194, 196–7.

[59] The same applies to the government documents published by Kusuman. An exception is the 1847 memorial of all British missionaries in Travancore, where it is stated that "slavery ... is the most costly labour" and "its extinction greatly conduces to the wealth ... of man", text in Kusuman, p. 80.

[60] Saradamoni, p. 114–5.

[61] Report on the Administration of Travancore 1865–1866, pp. 28–29, idem., 1868–1869, p. 33.

easily be reached from the east.[62] Nevertheless, this opinion is not completely satisfactory.

Local missionaries reported that labour in Travancore was cheap, even cheaper than in Madras. And the higher wages in Ceylon induced many workers from Travancore to cross over to that island. Apparently, they were not so tied by "habit and tradition" as government reports will make us believe. But most important is that missionary correspondence suggests that many workers from Travancore did go to the plantations in the neighbouring hills. Most probably, that was especially the case in south Travancore and it concerned *Shanars* as well as ex-slaves.

The Government Administration Report of 1869/70 stated that coffee plantations and Public Works Department had ameliorated the condition of the ex-slaves, in as much as the demand for labour thus created enabled them to procure better terms from their old masters. Especially in the south, this amelioration could be observed, as in the more northern *taluks* the ex-slaves were said to be as yet too dependent on the landowners and too wanting in self-reliance to migrate to the distance of even a few days journey in search of other means of livelihood.[63] A report by the *dewan peishkar* of Padmanabhapuram confirms the impression that in the south the situation was different. In 1873 this official informed the government that many ex-slaves in his division were no longer in the service of their old masters, and went about for work just as other labourers, acquiring property in the shape of land, cattle and houses. Especially in the *taluks* of Tovala, Agasteesvaram and

[62] Saradamoni, p. 114; Jeffrey, p. 100. Jeffrey refers to a note by coffee planters in Travancore, informing the Government of Madras, that much, and on some estates all their labour came from the Tamil districts in British India (1879). In a note to the Government of Travancore, however, the same planters reminded the authorities that by their investments profitable labour, which had been diverted to other countries, was recalled to Travancore (1872), see Mateer, 1883, p. 238. Apparently, the information from the planters was to a large extent determined by their addressees.

A comparative table of labour recruitment of 1896, given in K.K.N. Kurup, p. 197, reveals that 60 per cent of the estate labour was imported from British India, 20 per cent from Mysore and 20 per cent from Travancore itself. But this table refers to Travancore as a whole and does not allow for regional disparities.

[63] Report on the Administration of Travancore 1869–70, p. 39; the *dewan peishkar* of Kottayam reported on 27.3.1873 that in his division the ex-slaves "appear to continue still in the same condition with little or no change ...", Kusuman, p. 144.

Eranial, many ex-slaves had found employment in the Public Works Department and coffee estates, although the *dewan peishkar* unfortunately was unable to state their exact number.[64]

As we have seen above, almost all the coffee plantations in south Travancore held by Indians were owned by LMS converts. In their estates as well as in many others the leading positions of conductor or *kangany*, writer, and sometimes even manager were occupied largely by those who had received their education from the LMS.[65] In 1874, Duthie could write that nearly all the conductors and many of the smaller proprietors in the Ashambu hills were associated with the Christian church.[66] There may be some exaggeration in Duthie's words, as they were partly written to counter CMS claims on the Ashambu mission field. But donation lists for these years also show that the LMS received a large amount of financial support from the leading cadre of both Indian and European plantations.[67]

In view of the fact that a large number of conductors or *kanganies* were Christian and that they usually recruited the necessary labour from among their own family and friends, we may assume that many Christians from south Travancore were working as coolies in the plantations in the Ashambu hills. This assumption is confirmed by missionary sources, and a LMS report of 1867 observed that a majority of the workers in the Ashambu coffee estates were Christian, coming from different missionary districts.[68] That claim sounds a bit exaggerated, even if we take into account that some of these missionary districts may have lain in Madras Presidency. But it surely indicates, that south Travancore did supply plantation labour and that a substantial part of them was Christian.[69]

[64] Letter and Memo from the *Dewan Peishkar* of Padmanabhapuram to the *Dewan* of Travancore, 1.4.1873, in Kusuman, pp. 145–7.

[65] Mateer, 1883, p. 236; Jeffrey. 1976, p. 100.

[66] Duthie, letter from Nagercoil, 27.6.1874, in Travancore District Committee Correspondence File 1874.

[67] See, for instance, Thomson, report of the Medical Mission, 1875, in LMS Archives, Reports, Box 2/mf. 3307 and 3308, and Hacker, report of Neyoor, 1880, ibidem., mf. 3315.

[68] Annual Report Travancore District Committee, Tittuvilei 1867, p. 2; see also Report of Neyoor, 1876, in LMS Archives, Reports, Box 2/mf. 3309.

[69] S. Zechariah reported from Neyoor village, one of the old LMS headquarters, that several male members of the congregation used to be absent because of work as *kanganies* or coolies on the coffee estates in the adjacent hills; reports of the Neyoor Home Church, 1876 and 1879, in LMS Archives, Reports, Box 2/mf. 3309 and 3313.

As we have seen, the migration to Ceylon was mainly a movement of *Shanars*. Returning to the question, which social groups the south Travancore plantation workers came from, we may conclude from the scarce information available that the same *Shanars* were working in the south Travancore hills. There, they worked together with other groups, such as the ex-slaves. Confirming the report by the *dewan peishkar* of Padmanabhapuram, quoted above, Mateer wrote in 1883, that the labour of *Pariahs* and *Pulayas* had gained a market-value and that many of these people with their women and children had obtained employment and good pay on the estates.[70]

The south Travancore hills were the dwelling-place of hill tribes, called *Kanikars* or *Mala Arayars*. These *Kanikars* were organized in patriarchal clans, pursued shifting cultivation, and sometimes lived in trees to be out of harm's way of elephants or tigers. They never left their hills for the plains, and because of their ignorance they fell prey easily to itinerant traders.

Missionaries like Emlyn and Mateer were convinced that the opening of coffee plantations had greatly benefited the *Kanikars*. They were drawn within the orbit of civilization and received large pay for clearing and weeding. Most *Kanikars*, however, were not to be lured by high wages. They regarded themselves as the hereditary proprietors of the land and refused to herd with common coolies. When planters came to claim the land they had purchased, the hill tribes withdrew, if they were not driven away. They worshipped the gods of the jungle, and their priests pronounced the most awful curses on the invaders who dared to fell trees in defiance of the spirits of the forest. But they could not resist the advance of the plantation economy. For centuries they had been able to live with the wild animals of the mountains; but the planters were different.[71]

In view of the large number of people working on the south Travancore coffee estates, the District Committee of the LMS decided in 1875, that each missionary should undertake mission

[70] Mateer, 1883, pp. 235–6; we may assume that women were recruited as part of the family labour, but on the estates there were sometimes separate conductors of cooly women, like for instance Elizabeth Motchakan from Jamestown, mentioned in a donation list in Lee, Report of Nagercoil, 1881, in LMS Archives, Reports, Box 2/mf. 3319.

[71] Travancore District Committee Minute Book, 1886, Annual Meeting Pareychaley; Mateer, 1883, pp. 63–71.

work in those hill areas that geographically belonged to his district. The many Christians on the estates were seen as sheep without shepherd who away from home might degenerate in character. For non-Christians the unfamiliar surroundings in the hills were expected to have the opposite effect: uprooted and not hindered by the restrictions of village society, they were thought to be more receptive to the teaching of the Gospel.[72]

From the beginning, the so-called Coffee Cooly Mission had to cope with serious difficulties. The first problem was to find suitable agents. People working in the hills were exposed to many dangers, such as change of climate, diseases like jungle fever, and roaming tigers or rogue elephants.[73] The missionaries enlarged on these dangers to explain their own personnel problem. But we may infer from this that working conditions must also have been far from favourable to plantation labour in general, a fact that has remained rather neglected in missionary correspondence.

The planters did not have the same difficulty in finding qualified assistants, and here we come across a second problem of the Cooly Mission. The planters could offer attractive wages, whereas the missionaries were always short of money. No wonder that several missionaries had vested all their hopes on the planters and their leading cadre as possible suppliers of the necessary funds. The same had happened in Ceylon, where Hobbs' CMS Cooly Mission was financially supported by European estate-owners.[74] In south Travancore, planters in general were favourably disposed to the mission and proved willing to render valuable assistance. Unfortunately, however, shortly after 1875, leaf disease manifested itself and the financial position of the coffee planters was severely affected.

Nevertheless, some work among the plantation workers was done. Mateer reported for Quilon, that a few catechists had been sent to the estates in Colatoorpoley, a hill territory that seemed naturally connected with the Quilon mission district. They were

[72] On the establishment of the Cooly Mission, Baylis, report of Neyoor, 1875, in LMS Archives, Odds, Box 17/mf. 1125.

[73] Hacker, report of Neyoor, 1880, in LMS Archives, Reports, Box 2/mf. 3314.

[74] Hobbs was paid by the CMS and his catechists by the planters. This local support made Hobbs' mission dependent on the export prices of coffee and restricted his freedom to criticize the planters' management of labour, see Hobbs, Journal 13.7.1859 and Letter 24.11.1859, in CMS Archives, Tamil Cooly Mission.

cordially received by the planters, and the contributions received from some of them enabled Mateer to appoint a special catechist for the Cooly Mission. That catechist itinerated three weeks every month, visiting the sick in the lines and holding prayer meetings with groups of workers. In his monthly reports, he wrote that he had met several conductors and writers who had been educated at the Nagercoil Seminary. From Trivandrum district also catechists were sent to the hills. They were kindly received by the European planters, but on these estates some Roman Catholic but no Protestant Christian workers were found.[75]

Emlyn visited all the coffee estates of his Pareychaley district himself in 1875, primarily to establish a good relationship with the estate managements. Since then, one catechist was employed on the two principal estates of the district, "Bridge" and "Auld Bar", owned and managed by the Young family, and another catechist visited once a fortnight the remaining plantations, numbering about twelve, most of them small and superintended by local Christians.[76] Baylis had an evangelist who went every month to the hills for 22 days, holding services also on weekdays with 100 or 200 men mustered in the morning before proceeding to their daily work. Sometimes, Christian conductors themselves took the lead in holding services with their workers, as catechists from Nagercoil reported.[77]

It is not always clear, whether the catechists were paid by the LMS or by the planters. In most cases the catechists visiting the estates seem to have been employed by the LMS. The planters, however, contributed to the cause of the mission in several other ways. First of all, they offered substantial contributions to the LMS in general and its Cooly Mission in particular. The LMS donation lists of these years contain the names of many prominent European planters, apart from their conductors, *kanganies*, waiters, writers, cooks and even coolies. Generous subscriptions were also received, amongst others from the Scottish India Coffee Company, for the LMS Medical Mission, which had opened one or two

[75] Mateer, report of Quilon, 1877, in LMS Archives, Reports, Box 2/mf. 3309 and report of Trivandrum, 1883, ibidem., Box 3/mf. 3324.

[76] Emlyn, report of Pareychaley, 1875, in LMS Archives, Odds, Box 17/mf. 1125 and Lee, report of Pareychaley, 1878, ibidem., Reports, Box 2/mf. 3311.

[77] Baylis, report of Neyoor, 1875, in LMS Archives, Odds, Box 17/mf. 1125 and Duthie, report of Nagercoil, 1877, ibidem., Reports, Box 2/mf. 3311.

branch dispensaries at the foot of the hills. For a new chapel in Attur financial assistance was received from "European gentlemen in this province", most probably planters, and when Lee fell ill, he was offered hospitality in the house of a planter on Mahindragherry.[78]

It is abundantly clear that in the relation between planters and missionaries, the planting community had much to offer, their most precious attribute being financial means. But the missionaries stood not altogether empty-handed. As we have seen, the mission provided a kind of personal training, imparting a modern education to many youngsters who later came to serve the estates as assistant managers, conductors and clerks. Next, the LMS Medical Mission was requested by the planters to open hill dispensaries for their own benefit and that of their workers. The planters offered personal and estate subscriptions to support it, and in one case the *Maharaja's* government granted the LMS an unused salt store in Colasagaram that was converted into a dispensary.[79] From the reports of this Medical Mission, we can see that the dispensaries at the foot of the hills were a great service to the plantations, treating fever afflicted workers, accidents from the estates, and cases of dysentery, for instance when people had eaten the stinking fish used as manure.[80]

Finally, the mission served the estates in instilling into the workers a new labour ethos that could not but satisfy the planting interests. Again, it is useful to refer to Ceylon for comparison. Hobbs, the CMS missionary on the Ceylon coffee estates, had noticed that most planters used to have a high opinion of Christian labourers. The reasons for this are not far to seek. Hobbs and his catechists did their utmost to fight the most current transgressions on the estates, like theft, drunkenness, quarrelsome behaviour and disobedience, and even if they may have been less successful than their reports suggest, they certainly contributed to the establishment

[78] Aruminayagam, report of Attur, 1869, in LMS Archives, Reports, Box 1/mf. 3292 and Lee, report of Nagercoil, 1881, ibidem., Box 2/mf. 3319.

[79] LMS Chronicle, 1873, p. 257 and 1881, p. 232.

[80] Thomson, reports of the Medical Mission, 1875, 1877 and 1880, in LMS Archives, Reports, Box 2/mf. 3307, 3310, 3315.

In 1880 the LMS Medical Mission with headquarters in Neyoor had branch dispensaries, superintended by Indian dressers, in Tittuvilei, Santhapuram, Nagercoil, Agasteespuram, Attur, Colasagaram and Neyoor.

of more orderly working conditions.[81] The same was true for south Travancore, where the missionaries were instrumental in creating a docile work force, preaching sobriety and subordination, and making some planters urgently ask the LMS catechists to come back every month.[82] As Wilson has already observed, the untouchables' consciousness for obedience to law and order got only further strengthened by conversion, and this perfectly suited the interests of the capitalist, European, and often Christian, planters.[83]

[81] Hobbs, Annual Letter 1857, and Arumaniagam's catechist journal, April–May 1857, in CMS Archives, Tamil Cooly Mission; Ferguson, 1868, p. 125.

[82] Mateer, report of Quilon, 1877, in LMS Archives, Reports, Box 2/mf. 3309.

[83] Wilson, pp. vii, 22.

VII. The Fight against Civil Disabilities

VII.1 The Threat of Annexation

"The [Travancore] Court combines the Oriental vices with English energy, ...". This spicy comment was approvingly quoted in the book by John Cox, entitled *Travancore: its present ruin shown and the remedy sought*. The ruin in this state, according to the author, manifested itself in an intolerable measure of misgovernment, and the remedy sought was British intervention and annexation. A piquant *detail* was that at the very time of the book's publication (1857), northern India was in the grip of the Mutiny, a resistance movement that was provoked by the same British policies of intervention and annexation. Apart from that, the missionary author had received royal permission to settle in the capital of Trivandrum only after much political hesitation and deliberation. To make things still worse, the book, which had a clear political tendency, was printed by the LMS Press in Nagercoil, although this society's stated aim was to abstain from all political interference. The following year, Travancore itself was the scene of a major conflict and many LMS converts were to a large extent involved.

The strains and tensions that surfaced in the 1858/59 conflicts were of a dual nature. Internally, the untouchables, mainly the *Shanars*, had to face fierce opposition in their attempts to shake off some of the most humiliating civil disabilities that had been imposed on them by the dominant castes. Dress restrictions were the most conspicuous of these disabilities, but by far not the only ones. Externally, the Travancore government had to resist mounting pressure from the British paramount power, which grew impatient with the heavy deficit accumulation, and with what it saw as mismanagement and official abuse. Both conflicts got intertwined, as the LMS missionaries tried to use the internal conflict as an argument for British intervention.

Because of these tensions and the resulting conflicts, the last years of the 1850s were rather turbulent in Travancore. The question may be raised, to what extent the missionary activities in Travancore caused the internal unrest. Another question is, whether the conflict was deliberately sought by the missionaries or whether it merely resulted from the specific way in which receiving groups in Travancore tried to harness the missionary effort for their own private purposes.

As we have seen in the third chapter, the East India Company observed a cautious neutrality in religious matters after the 1813 Charter had permitted Christian missionaries to enter the Company's territory. In spite of this official neutrality, individual Company servants could further the work of the mission in several ways, if they felt personally committed to the cause. The British Residents Macaulay and Munro, who enabled the LMS to start its operations in Travancore even before the Charter was renewed, are clear cases in point.

Munro's departure, however, ushered in a new era for the LMS. The Government of Madras, under whose competence Travancore came, refused to patronize the Indian Christians in any way. And the Travancore Government began to curtail several of the privileges that the Christians had acquired in course of time. In 1829 a proclamation was issued, forbidding the Christians to erect churches, chapels and schools without regular permission from the *Sirkar*'s officers.[1] Although the same rule applied to the building of pagodas and mosques, the LMS felt this measure to be especially meant to delay or frustrate building activities by Christians.[2]

The same proclamation reminded the people that there were no other tribunals in Travancore than those appointed by the *Sirkar*. Many *Shanars* and others who had embraced Christianity used to lodge their complaints with the LMS and, when the influence of the missionaries proved to be insufficient to settle these grievances, the LMS passed them on to the British Resident. In that way, a rather effective complaint-office was opened for those communities which otherwise would have found it next to impossible to get redress from the official courts of justice. To the government, however, the emergence of an alternative juridical machinery was unacceptable and they wanted to put an end to this practice.

[1] Text of Proclamation (3.2.1829) in LMS Archives, Odds, Box 4/mf. 961; also in Yesudas, 1980, pp. 259–61, and in Regional Records Survey Committee, vol. I, p. 64 ff.

[2] Mead, letter from Neyoor, 12.1.1833, in LMS Archives, Odds, Box 16; LMS memorial to Governor of Madras (18.7.1859) in Yesudas, 1980, p. 297.

Earlier, Munro had tried to legalize this informal machinery by appointing missionaries as judges at district courts. The opposition of the Government in Madras and the LMS Directors in London had forced him to abandon that policy.[3]

After 1829, it became much more difficult for the LMS to render assistance and protection to its adherents. The freedom of the missionaries themselves was also further restricted. In 1837, the British Government ordered that all Europeans residing in Travancore, who were not servants of the East India Company, must be held to be in all respects subject to the laws of that country. The London missionaries, to their great dismay, felt that they were left to their fate, and sent vigorous protests to Madras against the new regulation. They understood very well that the loss of their superior position as British subjects would further reduce their ability to intervene on behalf of their adherents. Mead added that henceforth he and his brethren were at the mercy of barbarism and could be sentenced to death for what he saw as a mere trifle, the desecration of an idol.[4] But the protests were in vain and the LMS had to accept the restrictions imposed by the government.

Finally, the LMS also lost the support of the Resident. Munro's successors had generally been rather favourably disposed to the mission. General Fraser's prolonged but gentle pressure, for instance, had finally resulted in permission for John Cox to settle in Trivandrum. However, after the appointment of General Cullen as Resident (1840) and the promotion of his protégé Krishna Rao as *dewan*, times had definitely changed for the LMS. Cullen, a Scotchman from Edinburgh, did not regard the spread of Christianity as a self-evident part of his commission, and he remained always suspicious that the missionary activities might unsettle, if not altogether subvert, the existing political arrangements in the state. The missionaries, referring to Cullen's personal way of life, criticized him as a "bad ... specimen of that religion which the missionaries laboured to teach the natives" and accused him to be

[3] Nevertheless, the British Resident still complained in 1854 that the missionaries "persist[ed] in referring to the Resident complaints which should always be brought previously to the notice of the local authorities", see British Government, "Copies of the Official Papers ...", p. 24.

[4] Nagam Aiya, vol. I, p. 500; Gladstone, 1984, pp. 172–3; letter from Mead to the LMS Directors, quoted in Agur, pp. 897–8; Memorial of the LMS to Sir C.E. Trevelyan, Governor of Madras, 18.7.1859, in Yesudas, 1980, p. 296.

even more opposed to the missionary effort than the "bigoted Brahmins".[5]

Right from the beginning, the missionaries had eagerly looked forward to British annexation of Travancore. After 1840, they started to press more openly for British intervention. They were convinced that the situation in Travancore needed radical change which, without the influence of the paramount power, would remain impossible. In petitions to the Government of Madras as well as in their own publications, the missionaries dwelled extensively upon the existing abuses, like the corruption in the administration, the extreme caste distinctions, the continuance of slavery, the malpractices around the monopolies of pepper and tobacco, and the disastrous neglect of economic opportunities. It will not take long, Leitch wrote in 1853, before we will be nicknamed political missionaries, as "we give no rest either to the Rajah or the Resident" on all these matters.[6]

From the repeated complaints forwarded by missionaries and other parties, the Government of Madras was forced to conclude that intolerable abuses did prevail in the *Raja*'s administration. Alarmed especially by the declining state of revenue, which might affect the annual payment of subsidy by Travancore, the Madras Government warned the *Raja* that prompt and effective measures for improvement were needed to save Travancore from being placed under the direct management of the East India Company.[7] Nevertheless, the *Raja*'s government proved slow in introducing the necessary reforms, and Cox, who had grown impatient, decided to submit the critical petitions of the LMS to a larger public by having them printed in his book (1857). His undisguised plea for annexation, however, was drowned in the uproar of the Great Mutiny that broke out in north India at the same time. Moreover, shortly after that, the LMS became completely occupied by violent conflicts emanating from the social aspirations of its most numerous group of adherents, the *Shanars*.

[5] Abbs, 1870, pp. 81–3; a more sympathizing comment on Cullen can be found in Nagam Aiya, vol. I, p. 532.

[6] Leitch, letter of 23.9.1853, in Smith, p. 166; the LMS petitions can be found in Cox; abstracts in British Government, Copies of the Official Papers, pp. 12 ff.

[7] See letter of Lord Harris, 21.11.1855, in Regional Records Survey Committee, vol. I, pp. 117–9.

VII.2 The Dress Controversies

In Travancore, lower castes like the *Shanars* were subjected to many civil disabilities. On account of their untouchability, they were refused entrance to temples and courts, they were not allowed to use public roads and wells, to wear sandals, jewels, golden ornaments or fine cloth, to build larger and more convenient houses, to carry water-jugs on the hip, to sit on cots or to have gongs in their places of worship. No infringements of these rules were permitted and Mault wrote home that

> ... here the people must not deviate from ancient usage in the construction of their houses—in the shape of their umbrella—in the quality of their iron pen and in a hundred similar matters—indeed it seems to be taken for granted that everything has arrived at perfection for by the laws of the land no further improvement among the lower classes can be attempted.[8]

The style of dress was one of the many ways to express distinctions in social status, and the peculiar styles of all castes and groups were meticulously observed. Brahmin women wore a blouse with a short body and short sleeves, made out of fine, often coloured cloth, and tied in front with a knot (*muditchi ravakkay*); also, a length of the lower garment was brought up across the breasts and over the shoulder, the so-called upper cloth. The women of the *Nayar* caste, which immediately followed the Brahmins in the hierarchy of status, contented themselves with wearing this upper cloth which was usually made of cotton. There were not many Syrian Christians and Muslims in south Travancore, as we have seen in the second chapter. But generally, women of these communities wore a long-sleeved blouse of white or coloured cotton, tied in front with a string or tape (*kuppayam*). The women of the fisher castes wore a coarse cloth tied around the body, covering the breasts but leaving the shoulders bare.[9]

One of the most glaring forms of discrimination that people from the lower castes had to endure was the rule which forbade them to cover the upper part of their body. In the symbolism of

[8] Mault, report of Nagercoil Station, January–June 1829, 24.7.1829, in LMS Archives, Incoming Letters, Box 1; see also Mateer 1871, p. 41 and Yesudas, 1975, p. 32.

[9] Lewis, letter from Santhapuram, 21.1.1859, in Yesudas, 1975, pp. 191–4; Mateer, 1871, pp. 61–2; Hospital, p. 148.

clothing as prevalent in Travancore, a bare breast was seen as a sign of respect to those considered to be of higher status. *Nayars* bared their breasts in the presence of *Nambudiris*, but Brahmins did so only for the deity.[10] For the *Shanars* and similar communities, this symbolism implied that they were not allowed to wear anything above the waist or below the knees. Their dress consisted of a single cloth of coarse texture, tied around the middle.[11] This dress restriction was the most conspicuous issue in the fight against civil disabilities, and the missionaries could not fail to get involved. But dress distinctions symbolized not only status but also power. Therefore, when the *Shanars* started attempts to appropriate high caste attributes like the upper cloth, violent clashes with the dominant castes were the inevitable result.

As early as 1812, Munro had issued a proclamation permitting women who had converted to Christianity to cover their bosoms as obtained among Christians in other countries. Two years later, this permission was further specified: Christian *Shanar* women were allowed to wear a *kuppayam* like the Syrian Christians and the Muslims, but not the upper cloth as was usual among the *Nayars*.[12]

In the 1820s, the missionary ladies Mead and Mault devised a jacket for Christian women, with a long body and short sleeves, fastened in front with a string or tape (*ravakkay*). But, as Hardgrave has pointedly observed, this jacket may have satisfied the modesty of the European ladies, but it did not meet the social aspirations of the Christian *Shanars*.[13] They preferred the upper cloth in addition to or instead of the *kuppayam* or *ravakkay*, and this pretension provoked a first wave of violence, especially in the Eranial and Kalkulam *taluks*, more or less coinciding with Mead's Neyoor district. Mead managed to get a decision from the Padmanabhapuram court permitting his people to wear the upper cloth.[14] But although he reports to have pressed his followers for moderation, fresh riots broke out at the end of 1828, this time caused by the refusal of Christian converts to render the traditional labour

[10] Mateer, 1883, p. 230; Hardgrave, p. 59.

[11] Mateer, although shocked by this custom, made the dubious comment that "the dark complexion of the natives ... makes this custom seem less unnatural than it would be amongst Europeans", Mateer, 1871, p. 61.

[12] Agur, p. 935, Appendix XVIII; Yesudas, 1977, pp. 53–4.

[13] Hardgrave, p. 60.

[14] Agur, pp. 780–2; Appendix XVIII.

services (*uliyam*) on Sundays. *Nayars* and local *sirkar* officials retaliated by seizing more *Shanar* men for labour service and beating their women in public for wearing the upper cloth. Chapels and schools were set on fire, making it unmistakably clear that missionary activities were seen as the root cause of *Shanar* pretensions. When the riots spread, armed forces were called in to quell the disturbances.[15]

In February 1829, the *Rani* issued a new proclamation. It reminded *Shanars* who had embraced Christianity of their remaining obligation to perform *uliyam*, but exempted them again from labour duties on Sundays and from services meant for Hindu temples and religious festivals. As far as the dress controversy was concerned, the *Shanars* could hardly feel satisfied by the new royal order. Overruling the Padmanabhapuram court decree, the proclamation confirmed the decision of 1814, allowing Christian *Shanar* women to cover their bosoms, but not in the same way as the higher castes. The proclamation added, that whatever Christian denomination people belonged to, they were not permitted "to act towards persons of higher castes contrary to the usages of their own castes before they [became] Christians".[16]

In the 1850s social tension between *Shanars* and *Nayars* further increased, partly in consequence of the growing adoption of the upper cloth by *Shanar* women. To avert a threatening outburst of violent clashes, the *dewan* issued a public warning, which was read out in streets and *bazars* with drum-beating, urging that existing rules and usages should be respected. If the *Shanars* desired modifications, they should represent them to the *Sirkar* and await its decision. On the other hand, the *Nayars* were ordered not to take matters into their own hands and to cause no breach of peace.[17] Nevertheless, in many cases the *Nayars* took violent action against what they saw as the *Shanar* pretensions which had become so clearly manifest in their change of dress, and the *Shanars* fought back. Attempts by some state officials and

[15] Mead, report of Neyoor, July 1829, in LMS Archives, Incoming Letters, Box 1; Mead, letter from Neyoor, 22.6.1830, and report January 1830, in idem., Odds, Box 16; Agur, p. 835; Hardgrave, pp. 60–1.

[16] Text of the *Rani*'s Proclamation (1829) in LMS Archives, Odds, Box 4/mf. 961 and Incoming Letters, Box 3; also in Yesudas, 1980, pp. 259–61.

[17] Text of Proclamation by the *dewan* (27.12.1858) in Yesudas, 1975, p. 170, and in Nagam Aiya, vol. I, p. 527.

missionaries to put the blame for the outrages exclusively either on the *Shanars* or on the *Nayars* should be seen as merely motivated by partiality.

The main difference between the 1858/59 conflict and earlier outbursts was the geographical spread. The violence now affected a wider area and Nagercoil was in the thick of the trouble. Again, *Shanar* women were publicly stripped of their breast cloth, without distinction always being made between the disputed upper cloth and the legally permitted Christian jacket. *Shanar* men, especially Christians among them, were beaten, imprisoned or forced to take refuge in neighbouring Tinnevelly, their houses were plundered and destroyed, churches and schools burnt, and books torn to pieces. In a few cases, there was even forced reconversion to Hinduism. Remarkably, the south Travancore Muslims also turned against the *Shanars*.[18]

The *Shanars* did not leave these attacks unanswered. They retaliated by molesting *Nayar* women and looting a village inhabitated by caste Hindus. In the beginning of January 1859, a group of about 350 *Shanars* attacked the *bazar* in Kottar, pulled down some shops, and took away money and merchandise. The market was instantly closed and the *Nayars* tried to prevent the *chunam* burners from selling that article which the *Shanars* needed to prepare the jaggery.[19] Rumours that *Shanars* in Tinnevelly assembled with the intention to come to the rescue of their caste brethren, were most probably a ruse of the Travancore authorities who hoped to induce the district collector of Tinnevelly to arrest the *Shanar* refugees.[20]

Taking a larger view of the 1858/9 conflict, we find a rather close cooperation between *Nayars* and state officials to be one of its main characteristics. *Nayars* were well represented in vital government services like the administration of justice and police, and could wield state power as one of their most important weapons

[18] For a more detailed description of these conflicts, see Yesudas, 1975, pp. 132–50 and Hardgrave, pp. 63–9.

[19] Reports by the *dewan peishkar* (4.1.1859) and the *dewan* (12.2.1859) in Yesudas, 1975, pp. 176–7 and pp. 209–12; British Government, "Copies of the Official Papers ...", pp. 8–10; Nagam Aiya, vol. I, pp. 528–30; Russell, report of Nagercoil, 1859, in LMS Archives, Odds, Box 16/mf. 1112.

[20] Caldwell, letter from Edeyengoody, 5.2.1859, to Whitehouse, in LMS Archives, Odds, Box 16/mf. 1114.

against the *Shanars*. "All the officials are banded together against the unfortunate applicant for justice", Baylis complained.[21] Since an appeal to the government held out little prospect of success, the LMS saw no alternative way but to address the Resident or Madras Government directly. Resident Cullen, however, was hardly interested in the problem "that certain people wanted to wear more clothes than the climate demanded or their neighbours thought lawful".[22] Apart from that, the social composition of local officialdom prevented it from acting as a very effective instrument. The new *dewan*, Madhava Rao, had to cope with the same problem. But he had the best of intentions and tried to instill a more professional attitude into his officers by having them punished or discharged for every proven breach of rules.[23]

Next, the violence seems to have been directed especially against the poorer *Shanars* whose women had only recently appropriated the upper cloth. In the extreme south, the more wealthy *Shanars*, called *Nadans*, wore the upper cloth much longer, in some cases even before the work of the mission had begun.[24] These people remained largely unmolested. Russell, the missionary of Jamestown, attributed this to the better economic position of these *Nadans*, their self-confidence which was further strengthened by their early association with the mission, and the small sprinkling of high caste people to be found in this area. Baylis reported, that also in Neyoor the more respectable and better educated Christian women, who already wore the upper cloth, with or without a jacket, had nothing to do with the disturbances.[25] Apparently, the violence of 1858/59 was primarily meant to stem fresh transgressions of social boundaries. Only Lewis' correspondence does not confirm this conclusion. He wrote from Santhapuram, that just the most wealthy and influential *Shanars*, both Protestant, Roman Catholic and Hindu, had to suffer most from the oppression by the high castes.[26]

[21] Baylis, letter from Neyoor, 1.1.1859, to the Resident, in Yesudas, 1975, pp. 171–3.

[22] Quoted in Hacker, 1908, p. 48.

[23] Cox, report of Trivandrum, 1859, in LMS Archives, Odds, Box 16/mf. 1114.

[24] G.T. Mackenzie, quoted in Thurston, vol. VI, p. 365; Gladstone, 1984, p. 82.

[25] Russell, report of Jamestown 1859, in LMS Archives, Odds, Box 16/mf. 1113; Baylis, letter from Neyoor, 19.8.1859, ibidem, mf. 1114.

[26] Lewis, letter from Santhapuram, 21.1.1859, in Yesudas, 1975, pp. 191–4.

The missionary letters and reports for these years further show that the *Shanars'* wish to shake off their disabilities did not remain confined to dress restrictions alone. Already in the 1830s, caste Hindus in Mayiladi complained that local Christians presumed the right to walk on public roads, to put on clean clothes, and to build houses in a style superior to what they were entitled to by caste.[27] That must have been the reason why during the 1858/59 riots, so many houses were destroyed. Violent action against the wearing of finer cloth or jewels (in one case a Christian *Shanar* woman was robbed of Rs. 20 worth of jewelry), a change in hair dress, the use of gongs in churches and the carrying of water-jugs on the hip clearly indicate that the *Shanars* were striving for a much more comprehensive change and that the fight for the upper cloth did not stand alone.[28]

As a last characteristic, it may be mentioned that representatives and institutions of the LMS were among the most prominent victims of the disturbances of these years. All missionaries except Russell, who continued to tour through his district in the extreme south, remained confined to their headquarters for three months. Lewis described his bungalow as a beleaguered fortress which was guarded every night by 12 to 15 men of his congregation, while the clergyman himself kept fire arms within reach.[29] We will come back to the role of the LMS later.

In February 1859 the worst was over. In spite of the many reports about "gross outrages", the overall damage proved to be limited. There were people wounded and, according to unofficial information, even two men killed, but the official report of the *dewan* stated that there was "no loss of limb or life". The *dewan* estimated the damage to schools and churches at Rs. 128, but according to Cox, twelve churches had been laid in ashes, costing Rs. 1105, quite apart from the destruction of houses and property.[30] Without further discussion, the Travancore *Raja* granted Rs. 1000 to rebuild the churches.

[27] Mault, typed extract of note about social limitations of outcastes, 1830, in LMS Archives, Odds, Box 15/mf. 1103; Chamberlain, reader at Mayiladi, 1843, ibidem., mf. 1105.

[28] LMS, Brief Statement of the Gross Outrages, pp. 10–11.

[29] Lewis, letter from Santhapuram, 18.1.1859, in LMS Archives, Odds, Box 16/mf. 1114.

[30] Report of the *Dewan* to the Resident, 12.2.1859, in British Government, Copies of the Official Papers, pp. 8–10, with hand-written comment by Cox in the margin.

Not only the damage, the social gain was also limited. In August 1859, a proclamation of the *Raja* was read on all public places, permitting all *Shanar* women to put on a jacket like the Christian women, or to dress in coarse cloth like the fisher-folk, or to cover their bosoms in any other way, but—and that was the most important thing—"not like the women of high caste".[31]

VII.3 Socio-Economic Backgrounds of the Conflicts

The dress disturbances were mainly caused by the *Nayar's* concern about the changes that took place among the *Shanars*; these changes were seen as infringements of rules that had been in force "from time immemorial". Also, the *Nayars* contended that changes of dress threatened to obscure all caste distinctions, and that the *Shanars* with the help of the London mission wanted to shirk their traditional obligations. Resident Cullen definitely concurred in the latter opinion. He was annoyed that the partial exemption from *uliyam* services did not only apply to Christians who had received baptism, but to all people whose names had been entered on a LMS congregational list—by far the largest category! For the rest, Cullen's chief and only concern was that the missionaries, whom he thought to be misled by the exaggerated reports of their own followers, might upset the existing social relations in Travancore and thus endanger the continuation of British rule. Obviously, he regarded the reforming zeal of these missionary busybodies as extremely irksome.[32] The Mutiny had no influence on the disturbances, although Queen Victoria's proclamation afterwards was seen by many caste Hindus as a denunciation of all outside interference in Hindu caste and religion.

In her reports, the LMS mentioned the same facts, but—as could be expected—offered a completely different interpretation. The missionaries argued that the Christian *Shanars* were depicted as sedition-mongers, merely because they refused to be exploited any longer. As slavery had been abolished in 1855, partly through the untiring efforts of the LMS, the land-owning castes were alleged to

[31] Text of the Proclamation of the *Raja* of Travancore, 26.7.1859, in Yesudas, 1980, p. 311; Nagam Aiya, vol. I, p. 531.

[32] Cullen's correspondence with Chief Secretary to Government of Madras in British Government, Copies of the Official Papers, pp. 7–8, 14–5, 24 etc.; Cox, p. xxix.

have sought compensation in a new demonstration of their superiority. But the main reason for the 1858/59 conflicts, according to the LMS, was the socio-economic progress, which the *Shanars*, and especially the Christians among them, had made and which had aroused the envy and violent opposition of the high castes.[33] Let us look at that argument a little more closely.

As we have seen, education had been one of the main concerns of the LMS right from the beginning. Its village schools were visited by many Christian children and in the schools for girls the number of Christian pupils was much larger than that of all other creeds. In the 1850s, no less than 15.5 per cent of the south Travancore Christians (school-going children not included), were able to read, and congregational literacy rates of 30 per cent were no exception.[34] This achievement stood in marked contrast to a general literacy rate of 5.7 per cent recorded by the 1875 Census.[35] Even if this could not directly be turned into remunerative employment, it did give the Christians a lead over other communities and heightened their self-esteem.

The LMS itself had not much to offer in terms of paid work. The mission owned some land and printing presses, and employed a number of teachers and catechists. These means were important but limited. Another development however, which owed nothing to the LMS, considerably increased the employment opportunities of *Shanars* and similar groups. That development was the opening of plantations, especially coffee, in Ceylon and Malaya from the 1830s onwards. As a major part of the necessary labour was recruited from Tinnevelly, this region soon experienced a lack of palmyra tree climbers. To fill up the vacant places *Shanars* were brought in from south Travancore. The tapping seasons in Tinnevelly (March–August) and south Travancore (September–February)

[33] Mault, notes from a written report, July to December 1829, in LMS Archives, Odds, Box 16; Petition of the LMS to the *Raja* of Travancore (7.2.1859), in LMS, Brief Statement of the Gross Outrages, pp. 12–15, and in British Government, Copies of the Official Papers, pp. 39–41; Lewis, letter from Santhapuram, 19.8.1858, in LMS Archives, Odds, Box 16/mf. 1114.

[34] Statistics for the South Travancore Missions, 1858 and 1859 (figures of Pareychaley district missing), in LMS Archives, Odds, Box 16/mf. 1112–1113; see also chapter V, p. 89.

[35] Census of Travancore 1875, pp. 232–3; the most southern *taluks*, coinciding with the LMS area, had slightly higher rates, varying from 5 per cent to 10 per cent, ibidem., pp. 236–7. Census and LMS both defined literacy as the ability to read and write the mother-tongue.

perfectly alternated,[36] and so, a regular labour migration came into being which substantially contributed to the material improvement of the migrants' families who were enabled to earn an additional income in what usually was a slack season. This migration was also of social importance: the *Shanars* of Travancore started to adopt the ways of their caste-fellows in Tinnevelly who under British administration were freely allowed to wear the upper cloth. Therefore, the LMS emphasized the social effects of this labour migration as a major cause of the dress controversy, and the period of violence (October 1858-February 1859) indeed exactly coincided with the tapping season in Travancore.[37]

The Ceylon plantations also contributed in a more direct way to an amelioration of economic prospects. Many Christian *Shanar* students of the Nagercoil Seminary, the pride of the LMS, preferred migration to missionary employment and went to Ceylon. As English-speaking intermediaries, they were perfectly suited for the role of labour recruiters and, as we have discussed earlier, they gave the south Travancore Christians a considerable stake in the Ceylon plantation economy.

Finally, the *Shanars*, and many Christians among them, increasingly turned to trade with jaggery, tamarind and cotton as their main articles. The profits were used for the purchase of land and especially in the extreme south many Christian *Shanars* were in easy circumstances. Russell reported in 1856 that about half of the *Shanars* in his congregation possessed land planted with palmyra or cocoa trees, and not unfrequently they even owned small paddy fields. But the poorer *Shanars* did not completely lag behind. By a more careful outlay of their means, some of them managed, with or without missionary assistance, to save money and build more comfortable houses.[38]

Therefore, the conclusion seems justified, that in several ways the *Shanar* community experienced an improvement of their

[36] Russell, description of *Shanars* and *Pariahs*, 24.1.1856, in LMS Archives, Odds, Box 18/mf. 1147; Mateer, 1871, p. 123.

[37] Lewis, letter from Santhapuram, 19.8.1859, in LMS Archives, Odds, Box 16/mf. 1114; LMS Petition to the *Raja* of Travancore (7.2.1859), in LMS, Brief Statement of the Gross Outrages, pp. 14–5.

[38] Russell, report from Jamestown, 24.1.1856, in LMS Archives, Odds, Box 18/mf. 1147; Duthie, letter from Nagercoil, 7.12.1859, ibidem., Box 16/mf. 1113; Baylis, letter from Neyoor, 17.1.1859, in Yesudas, 1975, pp. 187–8.

economic position. Their attempts to appropriate the attributes of high castes were undoubtedly founded on this strengthening of their material position. In that sense, their social aspirations were not dissimilar to those of other groups which tried to adjust their ritual status to their improved economic conditions.

One may feel tempted to regard the joint fight for a breast-cloth by *Shanars* and missionaries as a unique fusion of two distinct processes, i.e. Sanskritization and Christianization. Following that line of reasoning, the LMS, whose primary aim was to free its adherents from all heathen superstitions, would in fact have contributed to give the *Shanars* a more solid footing in the Hindu caste system. Jeffrey, though clearly distinguishing status from decency, seems inclined to such an interpretation, when he observes that "the low castes were able to harness missionary zeal for decency to their own ideas of prestige".[39] Yet, that view is valid only to a very limited extent.

The proclamations of 1829 and 1859 far from satisfied the *Shanars*' aspirations for prestige. They wanted to emulate the higher Hindu castes and for their women that meant wearing the upper cloth; some Christian women even assumed coloured jackets as worn by Brahmin women.[40] The permission to dress like the Syrian Christians could not reconcile them to the ban on wearing the upper cloth. South of Trivandrum, there were too few Syrians to make "Syrianization" attractive as an alternative frame of reference.[41]

For the LMS, on the other hand, the dress controversy was entirely a question of decency. The exposure of uncovered limbs in general and of bare bosoms in particular was in the missionaries' view "incompatible with the modesty and decorum which the Christian religion inculcates and promotes",[42] and Abbs had found a suitable Bible passage in 1 Timoth. 2: 9, where the women were admonished "to dress modestly and quietly in seemly garb".[43]

[39] Jeffrey, 1976, p. 58.

[40] Shungoony Menon, deputy *peishkar*, letter to *dewan*, 3.1.1859, in Yesudas, 1975, pp. 173–5.

[41] Forrester, 1980, p. 114.

[42] LMS Petition to the *Raja* of Travancore, 7.2.1859, in LMS, Brief Statement of the Gross Outrages, p. 14; Horne, p. 296–7, 299.

[43] Lectures by Abbs in Pareychaley 1858 in LMS Archives, Odds, Box 16/mf. 1112

Mateer, who prior to his missionary employment had worked in a linen and cotton manufacturing firm in Belfast, added as a practical consideration that even commercial improvements were retarded by these restraints in dress. The manufacturer, he observed, might find a ready market for his commodities in Travancore, if only civilization and comfort were allowed to spread.[44]

For that reason, the wives of the missionaries had designed a special blouse or jacket, which was made in large numbers by the girls of the LMS boarding schools. From Neyoor, Baylis reported that in the 1850s, 500 to 600 jackets were produced annually, which were sold at the cost of the material or distributed free of charge to those unable to pay.[45] This jacket completely satisfied the missionary zeal for decency, whereas the loosely folded upper cloth provided far from sufficient cover. But with their preference for the upper cloth, the Christian *Shanars* clearly indicated that they were led by other considerations than the missionaries. Already in the 1820s, the missionaries urgently recommended the jacket as devised by their wives, but they had to acknowledge, in the words of Mault, that

> this is looked on as an invidious badge of distinction from which the people turn away with as much abhorrence as respectable farmers in England would from a badge worn in a parish workhouse.[46]

Therefore, the missionaries often had to apply strong pressure when introducing the jacket. That pressure was not only necessary to counter an explicit preference for the upper cloth. From their reports we can also infer that many people were afraid to put on the jacket, because they were under the impression that it meant an infringement of the existing laws of the country. Apart from

[44] Mateer, letter from Pareychaley, 22.8.1859, in LMS Archives, Odds, Box 16/mf. 1114; idem., 1883, p. 2; personal information on Mateer in LMS Candidate Papers, Box 11/mf. 456.

[45] Baylis, report of Neyoor, March 1856, in LMS Archives, Odds, Box 16/mf. 1111, report of Neyoor, 1860, ibidem., Incoming Letters, Box 5/mf. 2667, and letter from Moottam, 10.1.1859, to the Resident, in Yesudas, 1975, pp. 181–3.

[46] Mault, report of Nagercoil station, January–June 1829, in LMS Archives, Incoming Letters, Box 1.

that, many elderly women showed great aversion to "these new-fangled customs".[47]

The question remains to what extent the LMS realized that for all those involved, the upper cloth also implied notions of social status and prestige. From the correspondence it appears that the missionaries were chiefly occupied by the legal aspects of the matter. They emphatically explained the wearing of the upper cloth by Christian women

> not from any opposition to the Government, but simply from the love of appearing decent in public.[48]

Maybe, Baylis came closest to the heart of the matter when he surmised that the upper cloth was preferred for much the same reason as English ladies wore crinoline, "to appear more respectable". And when the 1859 proclamation was issued, the missionaries did not fail to protest against the clause referring to the coarse cloth of the fisherwomen, as they could not but regard this as a gratuitous insult to the *Shanar* community.[49]

However much the missionaries considered greater respectability to be an acceptable aim, they declared never to have encouraged their adherents to wear the upper cloth. Cox wrote that he had always exhorted his people to adopt the dress which the law permitted and decorum required.[50] On this point the ways of the LMS and the *Shanars* clearly diverged. Only in those places where the wearing of the upper cloth by Christian *Shanars* had found general acceptance, the LMS had more or less acquiesced in it. When in 1859 the disturbances broke out, Baylis had advised his people to abandon the upper cloth, as far as it was actually worn. Strangely enough, however, he ends his letter with the concluding

[47] Baylis, report of Neyoor, March 1856, in LMS Archives, Odds, Box 16/mf. 1111, and letter from Neyoor, 19.8.1859, mf. 1114; Lewis, letter from Santhapuram, 18.1.1859, ibidem., Box 16/mf. 1114.

[48] LMS Petition to the *Raja* of Travancore, 7.2.1859, in LMS. Brief Statement of the Gross Outrages, p. 14; see also Hospital on the symbolic meaning of cloth.

[49] Baylis, letter from Neyoor, 19.8.1859, in LMS Archives, Odds, Box 16/mf. 1114; LMS Petition to Sir Charles Wood, 1859, ibidem., mf. 1115.

[50] LMS Petition to the *Raja* of Travancore, 7.2.1859; Cox, letter not dated, in LMS Archives, Odds, Box 16/mf. 1114 and Cox Annual Report Travancore District Committee, Trivandrum, 1858. p. 7.

observation that "some of the other missionaries agreed with me in this, but not all".[51] Apparently, the *Shanars'* aspirations were not entirely rejected after all.

VII.4 Interpretations

The 1829 proclamation had declared that all the inhabitants of Travancore were permitted without opposition to embrace whatever religion they might be inclined to adopt. It continued, however, by stating that Christians of whatever denomination were not permitted to act towards persons of higher castes contrary to the usage of their own castes before they became Christians. In other words, when a *Shanar* became a Christian (or a Muslim), he must never cease to be a *Shanar*. This official view was reconfirmed by the Edict of 1851.[52]

In this connection, it may be useful to refer to the distinction between "orthodoxis" and "orthopraxis". The caste Hindus in general did not show much interest in what the missionaries had to say and remained indifferent to the doctrinal contents of the *Shanars'* newly-adopted Christian faith. This indifference greatly disappointed the LMS people, who eagerly sought a debate and sometimes complained in their letters, that there was nobody who cared to contradict them.[53] But the same caste Hindus immediately rose in protest against any violation of the established orthopraxis and resisted with all their might the adoption by others of attributes, which they considered to be the exclusive privilege of their own caste. *Shanars* who during the disturbances of 1858/59 threatened to become Muslims were told that they were perfectly free to do so but, whatever religion they might like to join, they would never be allowed to wear the upper cloth.[54]

Many *Shanars* were also more interested in the practical aspects of their new faith than in its doctrinal contents. With their generous

[51] Baylis, letter from Neyoor, 18.8.1859, in LMS Archives, Odds, Box 16/mf. 1114.

[52] Text of Edict of 1851 in Yesudas, 1975, pp. 163–4.

[53] Aruminayagam, report of the Attur Division, 1869, in LMS Archives, Reports, Box 1/mf. 3292; Newport even suggested to give up street preaching altogether in view of the utter indifference of the people, Newport, Seminary report, 1875, idem., Odds, Box 17/mf. 1125.

[54] Lewis, letter to the Resident, 21.1.1859, in Yesudas, 1975, p. 192.

contributions in money and personnel, the more well-to-do *Shanars* of southern Jamestown, were the backbone of the mission. Nevertheless, Russell, who worked here for many years, was often at a loss to tell what bound these people to Christianity in view of their religious apathy and lack of a real change of mind.[55] The women of these *Shanars*, however, proudly wore the uppercloth and it was that privilege which other *Shanars* wanted to share. In 1859, Baylis informed the Resident that lately many *Shanars* would have been willing to join the LMS, if he had only held out some hope of assistance being given to obtain the upper cloth. But in spite of his sympathy with their endeavours, the missionary had refrained from giving any promise to these *Shanars*, as he did not want to propagate Christianity by such means.[56]

Another reason, why the social mobility of the *Shanars* was not coterminous with missionary intentions, was a fundamental difference in their views on caste. The *Shanars*, who had to submit to Brahmins and *Nayars*, demanded in their turn due deference from castes below them like the *Pulayas* and *Pariahs*. An official document suggested that the *Shanars* were passing down the humiliations received from above, and Cox wrote in the margin as his personal comment: "Too true".[57] Their own experience forced the missionaries to acknowledge that considerations of caste continued to play an important part among their converts. We will return to that in the next chapter. Suffice here to say that, what the *Shanars* in general were after was not so much social equality as well as an improvement of their own position within the existing social hierarchy.

The LMS on the other hand was fundamentally opposed to the caste system as such. From his Lutheran background Ringeltaube had tended to adopt a tolerant attitude towards the institution of caste. But the Anglo-Saxon missionaries that came after him, soon agreed that caste and Hinduism were indissolubly interrelated and, therefore, should be fought as part and parcel of the same "debased superstition".

[55] Russell, letter from Jamestown, 24.1.1856, in LMS Archives, Odds, Box 18/mf. 1147.

[56] Baylis, letter from Muttam, 10.1.1859, to the Resident, in Yesudas, 1975, pp. 181–3.

[57] Minute by Walter Elliot, Government of Madras, 3.3.1859, in British Government, Copies of the Official Papers, p. 11. The copy preserved in the LMS Archives, Personal Papers, Box 2/mf. 20A/898 contains Cox' handwritten comments.

The class background of the missionaries may also have played a part in their attitude towards caste. In contrast to most British civil servants in India, the missionaries, as we have seen above, came from the less privileged sections of British society like artisans, small traders and skilled labourers. That could not have made them too favourably disposed to social institutions blocking individual progress or emancipation. Mead, to quote one example, was a fierce adversary of the caste system, which he accused of restricting occupational mobility and economic innovation, and of hindering the full development of one's natural gifts.[58] His views can be seen as representative of a more general feeling in missionary circles.

Yet, the LMS zeal for social equality was not without bounds. Those missionaries who wanted to marry an Indian wife were forced to resign, evoking the bitter comment from their converts that the missionaries wanted them to be only their brothers but not their brothers-in-law. At the same time, the missionary organization strongly reflected colonial attitudes, and the confession of equality in Christ was constantly exposed to the infection of paternalism or more pronounced forms of racial discrimination.[59]

In sum, *Shanars* and LMS missionaries showed considerable differences in aims and motivations. Even during the height of the 1858/59 conflict, these differences could not be bridged entirely. The *Shanars* wanted freedom for their women to dress according to their own taste and preference, whereas the LMS championed the abolition of all dress restrictions for all castes. For the *Shanars*, the 1859 proclamation was greatly disappointing, as the freedom of dress granted by the *Sirkar* did not include the much desired uppercloth, whereas the reference to coarse cloth as worn by the fishing women could only be seen as adding insult to injury.[60] The LMS shared the opinion that the 1859 proclamation was insufficient but for different reasons: it protested against the fact that women from other low castes like *Ezhavas, Pulayas* and *Pariahs* remained

[58] Mead, letter 26.9.1820, in LMS Archives, Incoming Letters, Box 1. For a broader discussion of the missionaries' interest to exploit local economic opportunities, see Chapter VI, p. 127.

[59] Wilson, p. 18; Alter, pp. 24, 28.

[60] According to a LMS Petition to Sir Charles Wood, no date, in LMS Archives. Odds, Box 16/mf. 1115 the reference to "coarse cloth" did not form part of the draft proclamation that had been submitted to the LMS; Mateer, 1871, p. 306.

subjected to the barbarous law which forbade them to cover their bodies in any way whatever above the waist.[61] Therefore, the LMS continued its fight against the remaining dress restrictions and in 1865 the Travancore government extended the 1859 proclamation to all lower castes. Interestingly, some missionaries reported in the following years that *Pulaya* women, who had never dared to wear the upper cloth, took more easily to the jacket than many *Shanars*.[62]

Much ink has been spoiled on the question who has to be held responsible for provoking the 1858/59 disturbances. Some missionaries and Madras officials were of the opinion that Hindu *Shanars* were the first to wear the upper cloth, inspired by their caste-fellows in Tinnevelly or otherwise, and that Christians only followed suit.[63] The government of Travancore and General Cullen, however, asserted that the Christian *Shanars*, with the active support of the mission, had started to infringe the caste rules and that they had encouraged their Hindu caste-fellows to do the same. In the same vein, the *dewan peishkar* of the Southern Division advised the *dewan*, that

> when the disloyal conduct of the Christian *Shanars* is properly dealt with, the Hindoo *Shanars* would behave themselves as they ought to do.[64]

According to Jeffrey, the Christian *Shanars* were the main cause of the trouble, but Hardgrave seems more inclined to share the missionary point of view.[65]

I think this question to be rather irrelevant and to suggest too great a difference between Hindu and Christian *Shanars*. The

[61] Memorial of the LMS to Sir C.E. Trevelyan, Governor of Madras, 18.7.1859, in Yesudas, 1980, pp. 303–4.

[62] Newport, report from Pareychaley, 1866, in LMS Archives, Odds, Box 17/mf. 1121.

[63] Baylis, letter from Neyoor, 19.8.1859, in LMS Archives, Odds, Box 16/mf. 1114; T. Pycroft, Chief Secretary to the Government of Madras, note of 27.1.1859, in British Government, Copies of the Official Papers, pp. 6–7.

[64] Letter from Shungoony Menon, *Dewan Peishkar* of Southern Division, 3.1.1859, in Yesudas, 1975, p. 174; also, *tahsildar* of Eranial in Madras Political Proceedings, 24.8.1858, quoted by Gladstone, 1984, p. 81 and report by Madhava Rao, *dewan*, 12.2.1859, in British Government, Copies of the Official Papers, p. 8 ff.

[65] Jeffrey, 1976, p. 59; Hardgrave, pp. 57, 60, 63.

Shanar community was trying to improve its social and economic position and those *Shanars* that were most successful in this endeavour had to endure the most vehement opposition from the higher castes. Hindu and Christian *Shanars* both suffered from *Nayar* retaliation and on several occasions they stood shoulder to shoulder to protect their life and property. The 1859 proclamation did not make any distinction between Hindus and Christians, and declared the regulation of 1829 to be valid for all *Shanar* women. The use of violence against Christian women wearing their legal *ravakkay* was not a specifically anti-Christian act, but above all an indication that the *Nayars* wanted to push the *Shanars* back into their old position of submissiveness, irrespective of their religion. Therefore, the title of the LMS publication *Gross outrages ... committed ... by the heathen natives on their Christian countrymen* (1859) is misleading. Even some missionaries regarded the conflict primarily in terms of *Nayar* versus *Shanar* and not as Hindu/heathen versus Christian,[66] although the violence against their converts was, as a matter of course, more fully documented in their letters and reports.

A large part of the violence had been directed against the LMS and its institutions, most probably because the mission had proved to be highly instrumental in the social mobility of the *Shanars*. In exculpating itself from any part in the outbreak of the conflict, the LMS was, whether consciously or not, underrating its own influence. The lower castes in south Travancore drew their own conclusion: at the end of 1859, the LMS registered an increase in number of more than 1500 people, most of them *Shanars*. "The late disturbances", Duthie wrote home, "have done these Missions much good."[67]

The LMS' insistence on British intervention in Travancore drew renewed strength from these dress disturbances. After the 1859 proclamation, the missionaries, in their letters to the LMS Directors kept harping on the theme of annexation as the only remedy for

[66] For instance Lewis, letter from Santhapuram, 21.1.1859, in Yesudas, 1975, p. 192.

[67] Duthie, letter from Nagercoil, 7.12.1859, in LMS Archives, Odds, Box 16/mf. 1113. Agur, p. 940 and Gladstone, 1976, pp. 64–5, basing himself on Jacob, Manuscript History, p. 126, claim an increase of 3000 and 4500 adherents respectively which is not borne out by the statistics in the LMS Annual Reports.

the ruin existing in Travancore. In their memorial to Sir C.E. Trevelyan, Governor of Madras, the same message was formulated more cautiously: in order to carry out the needed reforms, the Governor was asked to institute a strict inquiry.[68]

After 1857, however, the colonial authorities had lost interest in further political interference in the Indian native states. When at the end of 1857, the last remaining princess of Travancore died, the royal family was threatened with extinction, as succession was only in the female line. Baylis, the missionary of Neyoor, welcomed this want of heirs as an excellent opportunity for annexation, but the British government preferred adoption by the *Raja* of two young princesses to secure new successors to the *musnud*.[69] During the conflict, Resident Cullen was instructed to take a clear stand against all forms of caste discrimination and to convince the *Raja* that the existing dress restrictions were unworthy of an enlightened monarch. But in the end, the British authorities acquiesced in a compromise, permitting of all the lower castes only the *Shanar* women to cover their bosoms. The intention to start an official inquiry into Travancore's internal affairs—temporarily pushed to the background by the Mutiny—was taken up again in 1859. But for the time being, the governments of British India and Madras were at variance on the question whether the discharge of General Cullen should be a precondition or possible outcome of the same inquiry. The LMS kept arguing for intervention, but after the Mutiny, the political climate was no longer favourable to radical solutions.

The fight of the LMS against dress restrictions was only one aspect of its more general fight against caste and Hinduism. There were several other civil disabilities, not less degrading and humiliating, which the missionaries in joint cooperation with some sections of the untouchable communities tried to do away with.

In 1861, the LMS sent a petition to the *Raja* of Travancore asking him to change the laws of inheritance.[70] Apart from that they requested him to grant the lower castes free usage of

[68] Memorial of the LMS, 18.7.1859, in Yesudas, 1980, pp. 294–309.

[69] Baylis, letter from Neyoor, 18.11.1857, in LMS Archives, Odds, Box 16/mf. 1112; Nagam Aiya, vol. I, p. 520.

[70] The discussion on inheritance rights has been shortly referred to in Chapter IV, p. 84.

public roads, unrestricted approach to places of justice and permission to carry umbrellas etc. The petition also reminded the head of the state that untouchables in dealing with other groups were still obliged to use "such terms of address and speech as are objectionable and degrading".[71]

At first there was no response. But at the end of the 1860s Resident Ballard asked the LMS for more detailed information, as he had been ordered to make a report about the remaining disabilities of the lower castes. Baylis had the impression that it was the Resident himself who had brought this subject before Lord Napier, the Governor of Madras. He wrote home to have heard that on their latest visit to Madras, the *Maharaja* and the *dewan* had been given to understand very plainly by Lord Napier what ought to be done in this matter. Official pressure from Madras resulted in a new proclamation from the government of Travancore (1870), granting all castes free access to public roads, market places, courts and *cutcherries* and releasing the untouchables from the obligation to use degrading terms when speaking about themselves, their families etc. Baylis also managed to get two *sirkar* English schools in his neighbourhood thrown open to Christian, i.e. untouchable boys, and he observed with full satisfaction that the missionary efforts for the general good of the country had not been in vain.[72]

The 1870 proclamation was not very effective. Access to courts and public offices gave the people something definite to appeal to, but few officials cared to take the trouble of enforcing the rule. On the suggestion of the Resident a new circular was issued in 1884, reminding the people of the rules laid down in 1870. Again, the available evidence from the following years does not suggest a dramatic change of situation. A missionary reported, that he constantly saw poor people proceeding to their daily work driven or ordered out of the way outside the mission house in Trivandrum, and much more so in his travels throughout the country, where it would seem as if such rules as proclaimed in 1870 and 1884 had

[71] Text of Petition by the LMS on Disabilities of Christians (1861) in LMS Archives, Odds, Box 17/mf. 1117.

[72] Baylis, letter from Nevoor, 19.5.1870, in LMS Archives, Odds, Box 17/mf. 1123; Regional Records Survey Committee, vol. I, p. 66; Gladstone, 1984, pp. 161–5.

never been heard of.[73] Sometimes, the efforts of a catechist or missionary led to the punishment of offenders who had beaten Christian converts for daring to walk on a public road; but it also happened that untouchables who refused to leave a public thoroughfare were not only caned but also had their goods damaged by police officers themselves.[74] The same ambivalence prevailed with regard to female dress. Even at the end of the century, the fight against civil disabilities still had a long way to go.

[73] Report from Trivandrum, 1885, in LMS Archives, Odds, Box 17.

[74] Mateer, report of Trivandrum, 1889, in LMS Archives, Reports, Box 4, and Edmonds, report of Quilon, 1899, ibidem., Odds, Box 17.

VIII. Conversion and Cultural Change

VIII.1 Perceptions of Change

The LMS missionaries in south Travancore were undoutedly the most staunch and convinced believers in the possibility of radical social change. Their written reports abound with references to the rapid progress made from absolute barbarism to civilized and refined society. Russell, the missionary of Jamestown, described part of the local population as "brutally ignorant, superstitious, drunkards, liars, pilferers, and quarrelsome", of whom not a few, by the benign influence of the Gospel, have become eminent in knowledge, faith, sobriety, and honesty.[1] In support of this pleasant conviction, the missionaries could refer to no less a person than the *Maharaja* Rama Varma who, on his accession to the *musnud* (1880), prized their efforts as "the links of civilization, enlightened progress, and moral regeneration between the West and the East".[2]

In this last chapter, we face the intriguing question, to what extent conversion to Christianity really effected a perceptible change in the daily life, the customs and culture of the Indian adherents. The missionaries themselves, perfectly in line with the vision of Charles Grant, perceived their work as the spreading of light that was gradually but irresistibly making its way amidst utter darkness. As a matter of course, there was a strong bias in this perception. By painting a dark picture of Travancore as a superstitious and immoral society, they justified their fiery determination to reform it in accordance with their own principles, whereas their optimistic progress reports clearly indicate an overestimation of the practical results of these efforts.

In fact, the missionaries did realize very well that much change was only skin-deep, and they often felt discouraged when seeing the tenacity with which the native Christians clung to their old

[1] Russell, report from Jamestown, 24.1.1856, in LMS Archives, Odds, Box 18/mf. 1147.

[2] Quoted in Hacker, report of Neyoor, 1880, in LMS Archives, Reports, Box 2/mf. 3314.

ways and habits. In more private utterances, they admitted that Christianity in south Travancore was large in body, but little in heart, and that in many cases, the adoption of a Christian family name was the only mark to distinguish the converts from their neighbours. William Miller, on his death-bed, sighed that he had seen so much duplicity among the local people, that he had become suspicious of the LMS' successes, while Ringeltaube—who was never noted for cautious phraseology—thought that in some cases people had even grown worse after conversion.[3] More official reports indirectly confirm this lack of thorough change by listing numerous dismissals from the congregations, principally on account of caste feeling, non-Christian marriages, demon worship and sometimes drunkenness.

Most missionaries were inclined to ascribe this lack of more substantial change in their converts' lives to the lasting hold of native religious ideas, which prompted them to fight "heathen superstitions" with still more vigour. Yet, from their long acquaintance with the people of south Travancore, the missionaries also knew that wretched economic conditions seriously hampered all spiritual and intellectual life. Speaking of the *Shanars*, most of whom were sent to do the laborious work of drawing palmyra juice when mere boys, Mateer concluded that "their minds are so dull that they cannot take in much".[4] Their wives, whose daily routine was to collect firewood in the jungle, boil the juice and make the jaggery, sell it in the nearest market in exchange for food and then return home to prepare the evening meal, had scarcely any time left "to attend to their soul's wants", as an Indian female teacher observed.[5] The consciousness of sin, so crucial to the Christianity as propagated by the LMS, merely took the form of regret (if at all) for some specific act, like killing a squirrel and eating its flesh, cutting green and immature leaves from the palmyra tree, or

[3] Miller has been quoted by Abbs, 1870, p. 239, whose book for the rest was primarily meant to convince his English critics of the Christian character of the Indian converts. Ringeltaube's answer to a question by Resident Munro has been quoted in Agur, p. 598. Leitch, to give yet another example, discovered on his arrival in Neyoor (1853), that many catechists and teachers had not been baptized themselves and that there existed "a church only in name", see his letter in Smith, p. 89.

[4] Mateer (1886), p. 31.

[5] See her vivid description in Annual Report Travancore District Committee, Pareychaley, 1865, p. 26.

seeing one's betrothed before the day of marriage. Professing Christians generally had the same ideas. Mault complained that the ignorance of many was so great that "they scarcely possessed of two connected ideas on any subject" and were "incapable of comprehending the simplest truth ...". An 1880 report noted with hardly concealed irritation: "they nod assent to all we say but do not understand a bit".[6]

In contrast to this ignorance and often total indifference as to Christian doctrine, high caste people sometimes showed a refreshing interest in religious discussion and reflection. In Trivandrum, caste Hindus were regular visitors of Mateer's lectures—adorned with magic lantern and transportable harmonium—on various Christian and scientific subjects. Elsewhere, Brahmins might stand by the doors and windows of a chapel and after service with the confidence of rank and birth enter into long conversation with the European missionary and the principal readers on the merits of the sermon. Some of them were even able to repeat Scripture passages and catechisms much better than many Christians could ever hope for.[7] But, to the utter dismay of the missionaries, they never seriously thought of entering the Christian fold. For its support, the LMS remained primarily dependent upon people from low and untouchable groups who confronted the mission with a completely different and much more mundane set of questions. Samuel Mateer, who spent the better part of his life among the *Pulayas* of Trivandrum district, summarized their frank inquiries about the temporal benefits of Christianity in the following way:

> What is the profit of learning your religion? Will you feed us? Shall we be freed from dying? Shall we be allowed to steal when we are hungry and have nothing to eat? May we take as many wives as we please? Must we not give contributions to the Mission? We are in these respects freer than the Christians themselves are. And when we die, we are quite willing to inherit whatever place our high-caste and respectable neighbours enjoy.[8]

[6] Mault, Letters from Nagercoil, 6.1.1829 and 12.1.1830. in LMS Archives, Incoming Letters, Box 1; Report of the Travancore Medical Mission for 1880, ibidem., Reports, Box 2/mf. 3315.

[7] Annual Report Travancore District Committee, Trivandrum 1884, p. 9; Abbs, 1870, p. 154; Lewis, letter from Santhapuram, 28.1.1851, in LMS Archives, Odds, Box 16/mf. 1108.

[8] Mateer, report of Trivandrum, 1880, in LMS Archives, Odds, Box 17/mf. 1126.

The problem that will be discussed here is, whether a change of religious belief as apparent from the profession of Christianity by many people in south Travancore has also led to a change of their customs and general culture. The formulation of this question has been derived from a study by Srinivas.[9] But we should issue a note of warning, as we are on slippery ground here. First of all, the formulation of this question suggests too much that the adoption of a new set of beliefs implies the complete eradication of all previously existing religious sentiments. It is much more likely to assume an evolutionary displacement of one religious belief system by another, or—as Kuper has done for Africa—to interpret conversion as a continuing process of mutual accommodation between the two.[10] The question then should be to what extent the customs of the south Travancore Christians were determined by their old or by their new faith.

Next, I would like to emphasize, that it is not my intention to give an evaluation of south Travancore Christians by the application of a definition of Christianity of cross-cultural validity. Such a definition may or may not exist. The point is that the LMS missionaries did have their own particular definition in mind and from that perspective they kept exhorting their people "to come out, and be different from the heathen". In order to ascertain the practical effect of that call, I will concentrate on four issues that may serve as possible indicators of cultural change, i.e. caste relations, marriage customs, folk religion and the use of the sabbath day. An analysis of these issues eminently suits our problem: they played not only a vital role in local society but the nineteenth century British missionaries were also absolutely convinced that their converts' attitude towards these issues determined the quality of their Christian faith.

Finally, it should be understood that a discussion of this problem is not meant to slight the first generations of Christians in south Travancore, nor to doubt the sincerity and devotion of the missionaries. I sympathize with both. The only intention is to elucidate a neglected part of the history of south Travancore's untouchables by focusing on the socio-cultural limitations of a conversion movement.

[9] Srinivas, 1969, p. 60.
[10] Kuper, pp. 83–90.

VIII.2 Remaining Caste Feeling

Ringeltaube, the first LMS missionary in south Travancore, had assumed a tolerant attitude towards caste. In his opinion, it was impossible to make converts, if the mission were to insist on the losing of caste. He was also frank enough to ascribe the results of his work to a certain adjustment to the prevailing social system. In one of his letters to the LMS Directors, he informed them, that he knew many pious caste Christians, and that it was sufficient to protest against all vestiges of caste pride.[11] His immediate successor, Charles Mead, held the same view and wrote that "the renunciation of caste [was] injudiciously and unreasonably demanded of everyone wishing to become a Christian".[12]

Very soon, Mead's attitude and that of the LMS began to change. For the greater part of the nineteenth century, as Forrester has shown, the Anglo-Saxon Protestant missions in India were engaged in a fierce fight against the caste system which they regarded as part and parcel of Hindu religion and, therefore, incompatible with Christian life and doctrine. The question whether caste, even if part of Hinduism, might be reconciled to Christian faith, was not raised. This rigid stand led to the rejection of many innocent customs as processions, the use of flowers and bells, the beating of the tom-tom etc., and seriously discouraged more indigenous expressions of Christianity. The opposite extreme, however, also occurred. In a letter by Mault we read that some converts condemned themselves and others for practising things that were indifferent in their own nature, only because they happened to be customs common among their non-Christian friends and neighbours.[13]

Even among the poorer sections of society, there was a strong sense of caste. Often, *Shanars* proved to be as disposed to oppress, or at least to despise, *Pulayas* and *Pariahs*, as the *Nayars* were to oppress them. One missionary suggested that the dissatisfaction of the *Shanars* with their present low and degraded position might

[11] Ringeltaube, letter from Colombo, 9.4.1816, in LMS Archives, Odds, Box 15/mf. 1091.

[12] Mead, letter from Nagercoil, 10.8.1819, in LMS Archives, Incoming Letters, Box 1.

[13] Forrester, 1980; Mault, report of Nagercoil, 12.1.1830, in LMS Archives, Incoming Letters, Box 1.

have been the main factor in inducing them to come over to Christianity in large numbers.[14] *Pariahs*, with their claims of a former free and elevated position, did not mix easily with groups of similar standing and even practised caste distinctions among themselves.

The remaining caste consciousness among Travancore Christians can be gleaned from their avowed preference to form caste congregations and to build places of worship exclusively meant for their own community. The missionaries were determined not to accept this, but in many cases, their stubborn resistance to these practices was self-defeating. In 1867 Mateer, almost laconically, reported

> I scattered a congregation of about 30 ... by merely permitting two Pulian [Pulaya] Christians to enter the chapel and attend the service along with other Christians, instead of compelling them to go to a distance to a Pulian congregation.[15]

In Veeranakavu, the same missionary discovered that a separate prayerhouse had been erected within the mission compound for the use of *Pariah* converts who were refused admission into the chapel by *Shanar* and *Ezhava* Christians. When he called the former into the original church which had been built some years before, the *Shanar* Christians jumped up and went out. Caste did not create any fellow-feeling, neither did Christianity. Thus, the missionaries were constantly worried by the misgiving that many of their adherents would renounce the profession of Christianity altogether, if promiscuous communion were introduced into their locality.[16]

This attitude was by no means confined to members of the *Shanar* or *Ezhava* community. *Kuravars* regarded themselves as superior to *Pulayas* and were not always prepared to share with them the same place of worship. Many *Pariahs* in their turn clung to their own prayer-sheds instead of going to a larger chapel in the immediate neighbourhood. Wherever Christians from different

[14] Abbs, p. 151.

[15] Mateer, letter 20.8.1867, in LMS Archives, Incoming Letters, Box 7.

[16] Mateer, report of Trivandrum, 1872, in LMS Archives, Odds, Box 17/mf. 1123; Annual Report Travancore District Committee, Trivandrum 1884, p. 4; Abbs, letter from Neyoor, 29.3.1841, Incoming Letters, Box 3.

castes happened to join in worship, it was expressly and approvingly mentioned in the local annual report.

As has frequently been pointed out before, the transfer of caste linkages to church organization could attract as well as deter new entrants. For people of the same caste or social status, conversion to Christianity was made much easier. For the higher castes, however, Christianity became closely associated with low status and they carefully kept their distance. Less known is that in several cases converts from higher castes were far from cordially received in the church fold, at least in Travancore. Mateer, confining his remarks to "former times", wrote that *Shanar* converts did not wish the *Nayars* to become Christians, because they regarded the *Nayars* as their hereditary enemies and oppressors. Abbs made a similar observation. He wrote that converts who were far above the *Shanars* in social rank had told him that the chief temptation to return to Hinduism had arisen from "the jealousy, insolence, and unlovely conduct of some of the *Shanar* Christians".[17]

What could the missionaries do to weed out these evils from their congregations and to create a real Christian fellowship in its stead? One of the main weapons resorted to, especially in times of crisis, was the giving of a love feast. At such a feast, usually held before or after a Sunday service, people from different castes joined together in eating the same rice and curry, paid for by the mission or by a more well-to-do member of the congregation. In Nagercoil, in 1861 no less than 250 Christian converts shared the same meal. Some years later, the missionary in Pareychaley invited one or two couples from every caste represented in his church to a similar celebration at his bungalow. Some of them did not turn up (the number is not mentioned), but 29 people accepted the invitation, among them *Shanars* of two subdivisions, *Pariahs* of three subdivisions, *Pulayas* of two subdivisions, *Nayars, Ezhavas, Chettis*, barbers, washermen and hunters.[18] Also, special meetings were held with the Indian agents, to instruct them on the unchristian nature of the caste system.

Another weapon in this fight was to make the complete renun-

[17] Mateer, extract from letter. 20.8.1867, in LMS Archives, Odds, Box 17/mf. 1122; Abbs, 1870, p. 156.

[18] Annual Report Travancore District Committee, Nagercoil 1861, p. 7; Emlyn Jones, report of Pareychaley, 1872 & 1873, in LMS Archives, Odds, Box 17/mf. 1124.

ciation of caste an absolute condition to church membership. As church membership was the highest position attainable for Christian laity, it was at the same time indicative of the emergence of a new ranking system alongside the old one. It became the usual procedure, that only after about six months of regular attendance and probation, aspiring Christians could reach the first level of this hierarchy by having their names entered on the list of a local congregation. After a certain period of instruction, persons thus listed could receive baptism and become candidates, but only after several examinations and sufficient proof of good Christian conduct were they admitted to full church membership and Holy Communion. At first, this privilege was carefully guarded by the missionaries who tried by all means to keep this inner circle of the Christian community select and pure. Subsequently, the church members themselves became also very strict in admitting new entrants to their circle.[19] Any trace of caste observance effectively sealed the way to that lofty position and on an average only 4 to 8 per cent of all Christians achieved this highest rank of the hierarchy. Yet, in spite of all the care, even from this select number, dismissals took place.

There was also the question of the *kudumi*, the tuft of hair left over after shaving the head that men of the more respectable castes were accustomed to do at regular intervals for coolness and cleanliness. This *kudumi* was associated with *Parasurama* who was said to have drawn the *Nambudiris* by their *kudumi* from over the mountains into Kerala. Maybe, that is the reason why the Malayalis wore it at the front of the head, whereas Tamilians wore it at the back. The missionaries regarded it as a decided mark of caste and Hinduism, and required their adherents to remove it. According to Mateer, *Shanars* and others had made marvellous progress under the influence of Christianity

> but many are, I fear, grasping at more, claiming an absurd and untenable position in the scale of Hindu caste. With this is connected, I believe, the more general wearing of the *kudumi* or topknot, which I made many others regard as a decided mark of Hinduism ....[20]

[19] Jones, report of Nagercoil, 1875, in LMS Archives, Reports, Box 1/mf. 3305; Mateer (1886), pp. 26, 28 and 34; Abbs, 1870, pp. 160–1.

[20] Mateer, report of Trivandrum, 1872, in LMS Archives, Odds, Box 17/mf. 1123.

Some acquiesced and gave up this long-cherished custom, but other Christians kept their *kudumi* and ridiculed those that had it cut off.[21]

Their fight agianst caste made the LMS also protest against the separate columns for caste and religion in the enumeration papers of the first systematic census (1875). Two missionaries saw the British Resident and requested that the original caste of Indian Christians might not be entered. Caste was said to conflict with their converts' new identity as Protestant Christians and—a consideration not made explicit—might arouse caste-feeling within their congregations. The request was accepted, also for later years.[22]

Nevertheless, even the most uncompromising missionary had a soft corner in his heart for a Brahmin, provided he appeared in the shape of a Christian convert. The exceptional conversion of a Brahmin was always celebrated as a main event and the new convert could count upon a most respectful treatment. John Abbs, missionary in Pareychaley, admitted that he could not bring himself to ask a Brahmin convert to associate with his low and ignorant fellow Christians whose habits were not so refined as his. Instead of that, Abbs invited him to be his companion in evening walks, promised to introduce him to his friends and visitors, offered him the membership of committees and employment in the highest services, and assured him that he might live in decency and comfort. "I cannot promise this to all our converts, but I may and can promise it to you." Similarly, an influential *Nayar* convert in the same district was soon promoted as evangelist and his three sons were enabled to join the ministry.[23] This preferential treatment of

[21] Mateer, 1871, p. 56; Annual Report Travancore District Committee, Neyoor 1858, p. 10. Caldwell, missionary in Tinnevelly district, wrote in 1875 that a large majority of the Christian *Shanars* in his region had adopted the *kudumi* together with Christianity, quoted in Thurston, vol. VI, p. 372; see also on *kudumi* the Indian Evangelical Review, III: 12 and IV: 13 (1877).

[22] Baylis, report of Neyoor, 1875, in LMS Archives, Odds, Box 17/mf. 1125; Travancore District Committee Correspondence, File 1875; Census of Travancore, 1875, p. 62.

In 1931 Protestant Christians feared that their political interests might suffer from their inclusion with the more advanced sections of the (Syrian) Christian community and wanted to have their numbers shown under their castes of origin. Again, the request was accepted. Census of Travancore, 1931, Part I, p. 329.

[23] Abbs, 1870. p. 158; Jacob, Manuscript History, p. 190. In its eagerness to gain

a few high-caste Christians, undoubtedly served to maintain caste distinctions within the south Indian church. High-caste converts were viewed as a quality, untouchable converts as a quantity, a *Dalit* Christian recently remarked bitterly.[24]

The main victims of a surviving caste feeling within the local church seem to have been the *Pariahs*. They were the people who had invited Ringeltaube to come over to south Travancore and had formed the first congregations in Mayiladi and its immediate neighbourhood. But after the arrival of Mead and Mault these congregations were subsequently dissolved; some members were admitted into the new organization, the rest on account of their general attitude and conduct were deemed unsuitable for membership. When the LMS headquarters were shifted to Nagercoil, local Christian authors like Jacob and Yesudas both agree that a *Shanar* predominance began gradually to emerge. In many places the *Shanars* established their supremacy in the church, thereby making a subtle return to casteism and forcing other groups to form their own congregations, if they wanted to maintain some independence.[25]

This decline of *Pariah* influence can be illustrated when we look at the career of Masillamani, the grandson of Vedamanickam, often called the first Protestant Christian of south Travancore. Masillamani, ordained in 1866, was intended to be appointed as pastor of the Nagercoil church. It was, however, clearly intimated to him by members of the local congregation that in spite of his abilities, he would not be welcomed as a pastor by people from a caste higher than his own. Therefore, he was placed in charge of the Dennispuram pastorate which consisted chiefly of people of his own *Pariah* community. Since then, Masillamani kept not only himself but also the congregations of his pastorate away from others, making some missionaries suspicious that he wanted to separate his pastorate from the LMS.[26] Because of this personal

---

a footing among the higher castes, the LMS organized magic lantern lectures in the villages, where LMS adherents were not always admitted, partly because "some classes of our people would entirely prevent caste hindus attending", Mateer, report from Trivandrum, in LMS Archives, Odds, Box 17.

[24] Wilson, p. 18.

[25] Jacob, Manuscript History, p. 64; Yesudas, 1980, p. 94.

[26] See Travancore District Committee Correspondence re Masillamani, in LMS Archives, Incoming Letters, Box 11/mf. 2836.

background, people like Masillamani were the most thorough opponents of caste, but at the same time they were easily inclined to take offence on that account. In 1886, Masillamani went over to Madras for employment with another missionary association. With him, the last prominent agent from the *Pariah* community left the LMS.

During the last decade of the century, *Pariah* Christians in south Travancore openly started to express the feeling that they were neglected by the LMS and that the European missionaries were prejudiced in favour of the *Shanars*. They complained that all the higher posts in the mission were given only to *Shanars*; in substantiation of that complaint, they brought forward that among the 18 ordained ministers and 24 evangelists, there was not a single member from the *Pariah* caste. A few years earlier, Mateer had indeed acknowledged in a letter to the Directors that since Masillamani had left all LMS pastors and ministers without exception were *Shanars*.[27] But nothing was done to eradicate caste dominance from that "sacred enclosure", the Christian church. This feeling of being subjected to a new variety of the old caste hierarchy led many *Pariahs* and *Pulayas* to leave the LMS and join other missions, especially the Salvation Army, that had established its headquarters in Nagercoil in 1889. Their changeover most probably accounts for the loss of about 5,500 LMS adherents in 1894 and 1901. At the 1931 census Christian *Pariahs* and *Pulayas* in this southern region exceeded their Hindu caste fellows in number. But the former caste unity, weak as it was, had been replaced by mutual rivalry and division among LMS, Salvation Army, American Lutherans, Roman Catholics and other missionary societies.

VIII.3 Problems about Marriages

The missionary reports contain a wealth of information on marriage customs and family life. They note with approval that the *Shanars* showed great respect for the marriage bond and usually were

[27] Mateer does not mention the few Christian agents from the Brahmin or *Nayar* caste. Mateer, letter 23.11.1889, in LMS Archives, Odds, Box 17; P.N. Peter, letters to Travancore District Committee on behalf of the *Pariah* Christians, October 1893, ibidem, Incoming Letters, Box 13, also quoted in Gladstone, 1984, p. 137.

faithful in its observance. Economic considerations played an obvious part in this, as a *Shanar* toddy-tapper would climb the tree in vain, if he had no wife to boil the *pataneer* and make the jaggery.

The *Ezhavas* of the northern districts were considered much inferior to the *Shanars*, as far as marriage was concerned. The *Ezhavas*, Mateer observed in 1865, had similar customs as the *Nayars*, having no regular marriage apart from "the trivial form of giving a cloth", and leaving their inheritances to nephews instead of sons. This matrilineal system, which virtually denied the father's parental rights, was abhorred by the missionaries as a gross immorality, both causing and proving the depth of *Nayar* depravity.[28] Therefore, *Ezhavas* and other groups following matrilineal customs, like some *Kuravars* and *Pulayas*, and willing to join a congregation were required to marry in Christian form the women or men with whom they were living. And whenever professing Christians were found to live in a state of temporary or loose marriage, they had to undertake the obligations of matrimony or their names were struck from the congregational list. In 1872, 13 of the 33 marriages celebrated by Mateer in Trivandrum district were of that character.[29]

Another cause for numerous dismissals, as well as defections, was marriage with non-Christian partners, the so-called unequal yokings. Wealth and rank, Newport wrote from Nagercoil, were the main thing considered in marriage apart from caste. On account of that, families preferred to give their children in marriage to Hindu partners, when suitable candidates of comparable standing were hard to find within the Christian community. Even where property was not an issue, as in most cases, Christians were often more inclined to conform to traditional marriage networks than to restrict their options to the smaller circle of church people. Although the marriage situation must have improved with the increasing number of converts, in 1875, 210 of the 476 dismissals in Nagercoil district were still on account of connection with "heathen

[28] Mead, letter from Neyoor, 1833, in LMS Archives, Odds, Box 16; Mateer, report of Trivandrum and Quilon, 1865, ibidem., Box 17/mf. 1120; Annual Report Travancore District Committee, Trivandrum and Quilon 1858, p. 4; Mateer, 1871, pp. 40–2.

[29] Mateer, report of Trivandrum, 1872, in LMS Archives, Odds, Box 17/mf. 1123.

marriages". Adherents, who joined in countenancing such a marriage, were placed under discipline, as happened to 22 Christians in the village of Zionpuram in 1877.[30]

From these data it may be concluded, that in the nineteenth century the boundaries between the Christian community and caste society were as yet far from closed. At the same time, within that Christian community old distinctions persisted, as can be seen from the marriage pattern. In Mayanadu, for instance, a village in Quilon district, all Christians belonged to the same caste. But within the congregation, there was no intermarriage among the different subdivisions of that particular caste. Even a missionary agent in that district would not invite to his marriage any Christian except of his own particular subcaste.[31] Therefore, in spite of all missionary encouragement, intercaste-marriage among Christians remained a rare phenomenon. A well-known exception was Devadasan, a Brahmin convert and one of the first ordained Indian ministers (1866), who married a *Pariah* girl from the LMS boarding school in Nagercoil. The exceptional character of this kind of marriages was made perfectly clear by Lewis, who in 1851 united the *Shanar* Paul and the *Pariah* Eusebial in marriage. As they were the first in Nagercoil district to break through caste by intermarriage, the missionary cherished them as a romantic idyl, and built them a neat little cottage at his own expense to show publicly his approval of their "Christian fortitude and consistency".[32]

The form of marriage could raise additional problems for the new Christians. One of the local customs of the *Shanars*—to cite just one example—was to beat drums at marriages and to go in procession to the bride's place, where the bridegroom's party was received in a seven pillared porch or *pandal*. After the missionaries had discovered, that this was meant as representation of the manner in which *Shiva* was received when he went to marry *Parvati*, they immediately demanded a break with these "heathen

[30] Information has been gathered from Newport, reports of Nagercoil, 1869 and 1875, in LMS Archives, Odds, Box 17/mf. 1122 and mf. 1125; Jones and Duthie, reports of Nagercoil, 1875 and 1877, ibidem., Reports, Box 2/mf. 3305 and mf. 3311; Zachariah, report of Neyoor, 1879, ibidem., Reports, Box 2/mf. 3313.

[31] Mateer, report of Quilon district, 1879, in LMS Archives, Odds, Box 17/mf. 1126.

[32] Lewis, letter from Santhapuram, 28.1.1851, in LMS Archives, Odds, Box 16/mf. 1108, also quoted in Annual Report LMS 1851, p. 74.

relics". But these relics were very popular and several Christians, who wanted to keep up these customs and found that they were forbidden them, became disappointed and left.[33]

The general custom of tying a *tali* round the bride's neck, as the badge of matrimony, however, was allowed in Christian marriage and was even incorporated into the church ceremony. Most Christians seem to have adhered to this tradition, though a few preferred to use the European marriage ring.

In a study on social reform, Heimsath has expressed the opinion, that in the nineteenth century women in Kerala—except in *Nambudiri* and some Muslim households—enjoyed already a fair amount of liberty and independence. Social evils like *sati* and female infanticide were never mentioned in foreign and local accounts of this region. Widow remarriage, a highly charged issue throughout India, caused no ripples either, because most low caste and *Nayar* widows freely remarried. And infant marriages among all communities were rare, even among *Nambudiri* Brahmins. Heimsath assumes that these social disabilities of women failed to emerge in Kerala, because of the wide prevalence of mother-right cultural norms and matrilineal traditions.[34]

As far as *sati* and female infanticide are concerned, the LMS sources seem to confirm Heimsath's statements. In 1848, the British missionaries in Travancore submitted a joint memorial to the *Raja*, asking him to abolish *sati*, infanticide and slavery. But the main issue in those years was slavery, and *sati* and infanticide were never mentioned again in missionary correspondence with the state authorities. Occasional debates about *sati* with local Brahmins seem to have been of a theoretical nature.[35].

The case of widow remarriage, however, was different. The remarriage of widows was forbidden among the higher castes in India as well as in Travancore, and introduction of this ban was usually indicative of social mobility. Among the matrilineal castes, the problem did not arise, as their women were permitted to have more partners than one and used to remain in their own *taravad*. *Pariahs* and *Pulayas* freely allowed widows to remarry, subject

[33] Abbs, 1870, pp. 171–3; Baylis, letter from Neyoor, 18.8.1859, in LMS Archives, Odds, Box 16/mf. 1114.

[34] Heimsath, pp. 24–6.

[35] Cox, 1857, p. xiv; Yesudian, report of Tittuvilei, 1878, in LMS Archives, Reports, Box 2/mf. 3312.

only to marginal restrictions.[36] There is, however, some dispute whether there was a ban on remarriage among the *Shanars* and if so, whether the ban was introduced in the nineteenth century as part of a process of Sanskritization.[37]

The missionary reports contain some early references to a ban on widow remarriage in Neyoor and Agasteesvaram, known centres of the *Shanar* community. Mead believed, that the laws of Travancore state prevented *Shanar* widows from remarrying and Abbs, who never was a keen observer, thought that the prohibition applied to widowers as well. In spite of their imperfections, these reports clearly indicate that remarriage was not allowed to *Snanar* widows when British imperialism entered Travancore.[38]

Occasionally, the missionaries made mention of the presence of many widows in their congregations. These women were described as much despised, neglected and often ill-treated, which may explain why many of them looked for protection from the mission. Often they were quite young. But it turned out to be very difficult to convince these widows and their relatives that it was no disgrace to marry a second time. Missionary agents in Neyoor reported that instead of remarriage a widow used to live with any man, widower or single, who happened to like her, and that she was treated as his regular wife with the only exception that she did not wear the matrimonial badge or *tali*. It is not clear, whether children born in that state, had a claim to the property of the father. But in any case, these unions were generally considered respectable and disgrace would come not from their living together, but from a second marriage.

Missionaries insisted on regular remarriages, for widows living on their own as well as for couples living together. As far as Christians yielded to this persuasion, they had to face strong opposition from their non-Christian relatives, who in some cases managed to stop remarriages on the very day fixed for the celebration. But the main problem, according to Baylis, was attachment

[36] Krishna Iyer, vol. II, pp. 91, 177.

[37] Hardgrave, p. 107, (note).

[38] Mead, letter from Neyoor, 1833, in LMS Archives, Odds, Box 16; Abbs, letter from Neyoor, 1.11.1841, ibidem., Incoming Letters, Box 3; Annual Report LMS 1827, p. 76; Caldwell, in his 1857 lectures on Tinnevelly, also stated that *Shanars* allowed no widow remarriage, quoted in Hardgrave, p. 22.

to their long-cherished customs by the Christians themselves.[39] In 1826, Mault married a widow in Agasteesvaram, and three years later, Mead, working among *Shanars*, wrote home that progress was made in the marrying of widows.[40] But progress was very slow, if there was any at all. Widow remarriages were often reported with sufficient emphasis to betray their exceptional character, and in the nineteenth century the number of these remarriages remained low.

In Trivandrum district, to cite another problem, some *Ezhavas* and *Shanars* had adopted the marriage customs of the *Nayars* before their conversion to Christianity. Pleading inability to meet the marriage expenses or anticipating problems in the settlement of property, many of them had delayed the celebration of Christian marriage. Mateer, however, was not the kind of person to show much patience. In 1867, he visited these congregations, called up all those who had delayed the celebration of their marriage, and married those who consented on the spot. Marriages of this kind amounted to no less than 68 out of the 88 marriages celebrated in that year. The names of those who declined to be married in Christian form were struck off the congregational list, and Mateer felt pleased "that this question is now satisfactorily settled".[41] But similar problems were to crop up the following years.

On one occasion, the LMS became involved in the remarriage of a Brahmin widow. In 1872, a young Brahmin student of the Nagercoil Seminary died. The father of his betrothed, the *vakil* Iyengar, wanted to save his 13-year old daughter from impending misery and addressed a circular to members of his caste, printed at the LMS press, in which he set forth his daughter's case and invited young suitors to come forward, backing his offer with quotations from the *Shastras* and a very handsome dowry.[42] Several applicants turned up and Duthie was not a little amused to find that he was expected to express an opinion on the merits of the

[39] Baylis, statistics of Neyoor, 1869, and letter from Neyoor, 25.6.1869, in LMS Archives, Odds, Box 17/mf. 1122; Aruminayagam, report of Attur, 1869, ibidem, Reports, Box 1/mf. 3292; Abbs, 1870, pp. 205–6.

[40] Annual Report LMS 1826, p. 76; Mead, letter from Nagercoil, 6.1.1829, in LMS Archives, Incoming Letters, Box 1.

[41] Annual Report Travancore District Committee, Trivandrum 1867, pp. 6–7.

[42] Complete text of this "Appeal to the Enlightened and Philanthropic Members of the Hindu Community of South India" (1872) in LMS Archives, Personal Papers, Box 3/mf. 904.

various candidates. Outraged Brahmins tried to disturb the procedure and the father of the bride was formally excommunicated, but a marriage was concluded and the newly-married young man entered the Seminary as a student.[43]

Infant marriage, finally, may not have been that rare as Heimsath suggests. Among *Nambudiris*, where only the eldest son or *karanavan* was allowed to marry, husbands were scarce and dowries high. Therefore, infant marriages were said to be unknown among them. Their daughters married well after twelve years of age, sometimes even at thirty, though instances of pre-puberty marriages occasionally did occur.[44] Among Tamil Brahmins, however, like the above mentioned Iyengar family, child marriage was universal and stringent. In the second part of the century, the LMS opened schools for high caste girls, and several Tamil Brahmin families made use of this facility. The girls that came were usually reported to be bright and intelligent. But to the dismay of the teaching staff, the Brahmin girls were promised in marriage when seven years of age or younger. In consequence of this, these girls were withdrawn from school and placed in seclusion until they joined their husbands.[45]

Matrilineal castes like *Nayars* and *Ezhavas* also married their girls at an early age. But these marriages were not binding, left the partners freedom of choice when grown-up, and cannot be regarded as infant marriages in the strict sense of the term.

[43] Duthie, Seminary report, 1872, in LMS Archives, Odds, Box 17/mf. 1123; Mateer, 1883, pp. 295–6.

In a discussion with local Brahmins missionary agents argued in favour of widow remarriage with profusive quotations from the *Vedas*. Their final argument for those still unconvinced was that widow remarriage not only was the source of much domestic comfort, but also the basis for England's superior position in the world; summary of these discussions in Yesudian, report of Tittuvilei district, 1878, in LMS Archives, Reports, Box 2/mf. 3312.

[44] Thurston, vol. V, p. 197; Meadows, "Child Marriage in South India", in the Indian Evangelical Review, IV: 15 (1877), p. 358 ff; Mateer, 1883, pp. 290 and 302 is not very consistent on this question. An official proclamation of 1823, noting that daughters from Malayalam Brahmin families were married off after 30 or 40 years of age with huge dowries, laid down that all girls should be married between the ages of ten and fourteen and that dowries should not be higher than Rs. 100; the effect of this proclamation is unknown, Regional Records Survey Committee, vol. I, p. 122.

[45] Mrs. Duthie, report of Nagercoil, 1878, in LMS Archives, Reports, Box 2/mf. 3312, and Hacker, report of Neyoor, ibidem., mf. 3314.

Pariahs married their girls after puberty, between twelve and fifteen. *Pulaya* girls in Quilon district married only after the age of sixteen, but in the most southern districts of Travancore, pre-puberty marriages among *Pulayas* did occur.[46]

An interesting question that remains is, to what extent the patrilineal *Shanars* practised infant marriage, and whether they changed their customs after conversion. According to Abbs, *Shanars* considered it a great misfortune if their daughters remained without a husband until maturity. Their girls were often married off when not more than nine years old. It was only with great difficulty that Christian *Shanars* could be persuaded to allow their daughters to remain free till their fourteenth year.[47] To raise the age of marriage the missionaries went so far as to excommunicate families from the church for giving their daughters in marriage before that age, as happened for instance in Santhapuram in 1880.[48] There were many more dismissals on account of "improper marriages", but unfortunately, it is seldom clear, whether "improper" referred to infant marriages, marriages with non-Christians or both. But at least, these few pieces of information indicate that infant marriage did occur among groups that associated with the mission, especially the *Shanars*, and that the missionaries fought that practice. In the 1880s, many *Shanars* made large profits out of the coffee cultivation in Ceylon and the Ashambu hills. This improved economic position may have induced also Christians among them to introduce infant marriage as part of an attempt to achieve a higher, more sanskritized, ritual status. For such a conclusion, however, more evidence will be needed than is as yet available.

VIII.4 The Influence of Folk-Religion

In the LMS sources the traditional religion of the groups from

[46] Krishna Iyer, vol. II, pp. 89, 176 and 186.

[47] Abbs, 1870, p. 169; Gladstone, 1975, p. 79, quoting from The Indian Evangelical Review, July 1876, p. 71.

[48] Pastor of Santhapuram, report of Nagercoil, 1880, in LMS Archives, Reports Box 2/mf. 3316; Gladstone, 1975, p. 79.

From Trivandrum it was reported that people—caste not mentioned—proved willing to learn the *Vedam* (Bible), but objected to the rule which forbade them to give their children in marriage at ten or eleven years old, Annual Report Travancore District Committee, Trivandrum, 1867, p. 5.

which most of the converts were drawn, is generally described as devil worship. Here, we prefer the term folk-religion. This term covers a bewildering variety of cults and practices that most of the lower castes and tribes held to a large extent in common, and in which even *Nayars* and sometimes Brahmins participated, the latter as officiating priests. In view of the great importance given in this worship to spirit-possession and blood-sacrifices—alongside many Brahmanical elements—, the question could justifiably be raised whether people taking part in it should be considered Hindus or not. Instead of entering into that problem, however, we will set ourselves to the task of giving a short description of this folk-religion.

There were believed to be hosts of deities, demons and evil spirits, flitting through the air, dancing on the surface of the water, dwelling in trees and groves, and haunting houses and burial grounds. Everything that struck the people as threatening or painfully sudden, like sickness, death or failing rains was attributed to these supernatural powers. One of the chief and most dreaded among them was *Madan*, who was said to afflict men and beasts with sudden illness. Then, there was *Mallan*, the giant, revered especially by hill tribes; *Kuttichattan*, who was willing to place his powers at the service of his devotees, and *Muppan*, who lurked at cross-roads, frightening and injuring the passers-by. The female elements among them in particular were supposed to be malicious and cruel. *Kali*, the wife of *Shiva*, was thought to delight in devouring children. As *Bhadrakali*, she was believed to spread the seeds of small-pox and cholera according to her whims, just like *Amman*, the mother goddess and village guardian. In the same vein *Bhagavati*, a principal goddess also of the *Nayars*, was associated with disease, death and destruction.[49] A distinction could be made between deities derived from the Hindu pantheon, primarily as manifestations of *Shiva*, and deities and demons of the local folk tradition, several of whom were originally human beings, supposed to have transformed into demons because of sudden or violent death. But the boundary lines are not always clear.

[49] This paragraph and the following ones have been pieced together from Mateer, 1871, Chapter XIV; idem., 1883, Chapter III; idem., (1886), pp. 20 ff. and idem., "The Pariah Caste ..." pp. 7, 11 ff; R. Caldwell, "Demonolatry", in the Indian Evangelical Review, vol. XIV (1887–88), pp. 192 ff; Gladstone, 1984, pp. 28 ff and Ayrookuzhiel, pp. 121 ff. For the religious practices of the *Ezhavas* see also Chandramohan, p. 58 ff.

The *Shanars* worshipped mainly in their own houses. In a few places, they had village temples for *Amman, Bhadrakali* and several other deities. The *Pariahs* performed their rituals in shrines which were nothing more than a small building with a few rough stones in the centre on which turmeric powder was rubbed. They worshipped *Madan, Mallan, Bhadrakali, Karumkali* and many others, offering coconuts, plantains, rice, fowl, goats and arrack; but according to Krishna Iyer no animal sacrifices were offered to *Amman* or *Mariamman*. The southern *Pulayas* largely shared the same worship and offered similar gifts to deities represented by rude stones.[50] The numerous "devil temples" mentioned in the missionary sources were usually simple buildings or mere sheds, only a few yards in length and containing the implements of worship like garments and bells, but mostly quite empty. Images were not an essential element in these cults and where they were found, they might have been adopted from the Brahmanical worship.

Almost all the lower castes in south Travancore worshipped the spirits of deceased ancestors. If not pacified, these spirits could strike their own children with misfortune and disease. Offerings of coconuts, parched rice, goats, cocks and fowl were needed to avert these impending dangers. Many poor people spent a large part of their meagre earnings in sacrifices to these spirits and in presents to their priests. *Shanars* sometimes had separate small buildings for the worship of the deceased, whereas the *Pariahs* and southern *Pulayas* used sheds tied at the bottom of a palmyra tree or squares in the midst of groves as places of worship.

Priests from these castes or so-called "devil dancers" played a prominent part in these cults. They were slightly acquainted with a few medicines, professed to cure snake bite, and could repeat some tales of the Hindu gods. Pretensions to witchcraft and divination also belonged to their usual stock-in-trade. Their office was not hereditary and anyone, women not excluded, could act as a priest or dancer, provided he or she was convincingly inspired or possessed by the demon invoked. *Pariah* dancers were frequently employed by all castes, even by *Nayars*, to drive out a demon or to counteract an enchantment. A spirit possession might be unexpected and involuntary. But most ceremonies were aimed at

[50] Krishna Iyer, vol. II, pp. 93 ff. and 180 ff.

bringing a demon into the soul of the dancer, who for such an occasion was adorned with a multi-coloured dress, a frightening painted mask, trident and jingling bells. Accompanied by the beating of the tom-tom and the music of various bells fastened to a gigantic bow, the dancer used to work himself up into a frenzy, using medical draughts and drinking the blood of decapitated fowls. After the deity had taken possession of the dancer, he was venerated by the assembled crowd, presented with gifts and consulted on matters like disease, crop failure or the welfare of distant family members.

Admonishing one of these local priests, a catechist was plainly told that he was considered to be of the same trade: "we are accustomed to cheat people ... so we get presents. You are also just preaching for a livelihood. Who has seen heaven or hell?".[51] Some demon dancers who later became Christians confessed to Mateer that their dancing was a mere trick to obtain money; but others asserted that "something came over them" which they could not explain.[52]

Ideas connected with these cults and practices had a strong hold upon the minds of those people from whose ranks the Christian converts were principally drawn. This influence could work in two ways. In 1860, continued drought destroyed the rice crop and led to a sharp decline in the yield of palmyra juice. Famine broke out, further aggravated by cholera, resulting in an appalling death-rate. Offerings were made to the demons, who were supposed to have been enraged, and dancers went round asking 50 *fanams* (about 15 sh.) to appease the demons and restore health. As even the most abundant and costly offerings brought no relief, many people started to doubt the power of the priests and the use of their old religion. They went over to Christianity in large numbers and many demon temples were destroyed. Individual cases of sudden deaths of misfortune could produce the same result and made the people more susceptible to Christian teaching.[53]

[51] Annual Report (printed) Trivandrum District, 1884, p. 7 in LMS Archives, Odds, Box 17.

[52] Mateer, 1871, p. 218. Missionary Caldwell in Tinnevelly district did not exclude the possibility of spirit possession, but his own experience made him observe that "the devil always fled before a turpentine enema", The Indian Evangelical Review, vol. XIV (1887–88), p. 198.

[53] Report of Santhapuram, and report of Neyoor, 1860, in LMS Archives, Incoming Letters, Box 5/mf. 2663–2664, 2666; see also Mead, letter from Neyoor, 22.7.1830, ibidem., Odds, Box 16.

However, among those people that had already embraced Christianity, the same process could also work the other way round. When in 1860 the awful ravages of famine and cholera terrified them, many Christian converts feared that they had provoked the evil spirits by leaving their traditional worship and went back, offering sacrifices to their demons as before.[54] The same happened in individual cases of emergency. Continually, defections took place on account of smallpox, cholera or some other personal misfortune. What happened to Abbs may serve as an illustration. Once he was confronted by an angry father who held a sick child and demanded of him to restore it to health immediately. As the child was caught at school, the father was convinced that the sickness of the child had been inflicted by a demon as a punishment for attending a place of Christian instruction. Allan reported a similar case from Nagercoil district. When his daughter was seriously ill, the head of a family who was born a Christian was led by his neighbours to attend the worship of *Muthukutty*, a demon said to be the incarnation of a Hindu god. The daughter improved and the whole family became devotees of *Muthukutty*.[55] The missionary reports contain many such cases.

Apart from this shifting of loyalties, people were used in case of trouble or illness, to visit both the Christian church and the demon shrine at the same time, keeping—as the missionaries wrote disparagingly—their feet in two boats. Also, in many congregations, the missionaries observed what they called "extravagances", like visions of evil spirits or pretensions to prophecy. In Pareychaley, a young female convert was possessed on her first visit to the chapel, and an agent described her as "wildly untying her knot of hair, shuddering and shaking her head while the expression of her countenance was terrible".[56]

[54] Annual Report Travancore District Committee, Trivandrum and Quilon 1860, p. 6.

[55] Annual Report LMS 1856, p. 92; Allan, report of Nagercoil, 1888, in LMS Archives, Odds, Box 17.

Elsewhere, crop failure or epidemics could produce the same results, causing people to forsake their old religion and making Christian converts to return to the faith of their fathers. For Africa, see Bucher's study of the Shona community, p. 134 ff. For Indonesia Dutch missionaries reported similar effects of epidemics in the Minahassa in their Mededeelingen vanwege het Nederlandsche Zendelinggenootschap, Vol. XXIX (1885), pp. 225–71, Vol. XXX (1886), pp. 307–58, Vol. XXXII (1888), pp. 24–86. I owe this last reference to Mieke Schouten. See also pp. 81 ff. of this book.

[56] Agent's report included in report of Pareychaley, 1880, in LMS Archives, Reports, Box 2/mf. 3314.

Another interesting case was related by Mateer. Yohanan, a Christian belonging to the small elite of church members, fell seriously ill. Immediately, he suspected that he was bewitched, and that his enemies had made a small image of him, had nails driven into it at those places where he was afflicted with disease, and had buried it secretly somewhere in his garden. The protestations of the catechists notwithstanding, Yohanan set for demon priests to dig up the ground in front of his house in search of the supposed hidden charm, and ordered the celebration of the usual ceremonies.[57]

Even missionary books and tracts were sometimes expected to operate as charms. Abbs was surprised to find that these publications were eagerly sought after by persons unable to read. On inquiry he learned, that they slept with them under their heads, "as proper instruments both for keeping away the devil and making their possessors good and happy".[58]

A most remarkable but much neglected aspect of the history of the south Travancore mission is the large number of local priests that sooner or later came over and joined the LMS. There is no question of exaggeration in the official LMS publications, as the incoming letters made it abundantly clear that many demon priests, devil dancers, sorcerers, native doctors, musicians etc. entered the Christian fold.[59] Several of them were men of property, held in high esteem in their society.

Kali, to cite one example, was a respected and wealthy demon dancer in Trivandrum district. He used to lead the singing and dancing at worship, played the musical bow hung with bells, and took a prominent part in the annual festival of a *Bhadrakali* temple. 'Attracted by the Christian lyrics and shaken by the death of three fellow-priests, old Kali came to the chapel on his bullock cart one fine Sunday morning, removed his *kudumi*, and asked for baptism. He died shortly after that and was buried a Christian.[60]

[57] Mateer, 1871, p. 212; for a similar case, see previous note.

[58] Abbs, 1870, p. 133.

[59] The same was reported from south Canara, where most converts were toddy drawers, but among them those "who were formerly devil priests, sorcerers, beggars, musicians etc., callings which are entirely incompatible with Christianity", see Muller, pp. 167 ff. The LMS Archives, Odds, Box 17, Nagercoil 1892, describe a "mass conversion" of six devil dancers.

[60] Wilkinson, report of Trivandrum, 1881, in LMS Archives, Reports, Box 2/mf. 3317; also in LMS Chronicle 1882, pp. 109–13.

As might be expected, there were many priests who fought the mission and tried to keep their people away from Christian instruction. Presumably, they feared a weakening of their own prominent and profitable position. However, it is less clear, why old Kali and so many other priests decided to join the mission. Generally, missionary accounts attribute these conversions to a deep dissatisfaction with heathenism and a growing awareness of the moral superiority of the Christian faith. Yet, a closer scrutiny of these sources may yield indications that there were also other factors at work.

In some cases, conversion to Christianity seems to have been nothing more than a flight or an attempt to save face. On one occasion, a dancer tried to convince a large gathering of people of his being possessed by supernatural powers. But he failed and hurt himself severely by beating his chest with a coconut and leaping into the fire. After that, he resolved to abandon his old profession and became a Christian.[61]

Other cases strongly suggest that priests might also have been motivated by a desire to retain or even reinforce their traditional influence under a new guise by entering the church and working in association with the British missionaries. Masillamani, pastor of Dennispuram, praised the valuable assistance received from Visuvasam, formerly a devil dancer and a serpent charmer, who "now cheerfully performs the work of a deacon, teaching and praying with the Christians, [and] giving bazaar medicines to the sick".[62] In Vellangode, Pareychaley district, a congregation could be formed only after the conversion of Peter and his brother, whose chief profession till then was the making of music in honour of the demon gods. On account of his leadership and liberal support, Peter became the mainstay of this congregation. Another priest, who was well versed in Tamil *Puranas*, became a deacon after his conversion and used the tom-tom to invite his people for prayers.[63] The continued influence of these priests, demon dancers, shrine owners etc. is obvious from the numerous instances, mentioned in the LMS documents, where the conversion of one of

[61] Mateer, "The Pariah Caste ..." pp. 9–10.

[62] Pastoral Report of Dennispuram, 1866, in LMS Archives, Reports, Box 1/mf. 3281.

[63] Emlyn, report of Pareychaley, 1880, in LMS Archives, Reports, Box 2/mf. 3314; Jacob, Manuscript History, p. 162.

these people led not only their own family, but whole clusters of families or even entire villages to come over to the mission.[64]

Another example of this continuity in change, is the case of a local doctor, who found his practice gone after the establishment of a LMS medical station in his neighbourhood. The man turned up at the station, professed himself to be a convert to the English medical system, and entreated the missionaries to employ him in the dispensary.[65] Probably, the explicit wish of this man to continue his old profession under new conditions was a motivating factor also for many other doctors, priests and musicians.

LMS reports from the latter part of the nineteenth century assert, that in the missionary districts the old folk-religion was definitely on the wane. Many temples, places of worship and stone images were destroyed, often with the help of former priests and dancers. Other temples and holy places—but not those supported by the *sirkar*—were in a deserted state. The people neglected their temples and idols, the pastor of Dennispuram wrote,

> partly because they are not able to celebrate idol worship without the assistance of the Christians who used when they were heathens to contribute much for it, and partly through the want of devil dancers or priests, many of whom have become Christians.[66]

It also happened that former temple sheds were changed into places of Christian worship. Among the new Christians in Attur—to cite just one example—was an old demon dancer, who gave up to the mission a new temple, made of good timber, which he had just built at considerable expense. Henceforth, it served as the chapel of the local congregation.[67]

Nevertheless, we may assume that the decline of this folk-religion was due to more factors than the missionary presence alone. Apart from that, the results of the missionaries' fight against "superstitious devil worship" should not be overestimated in view of the continued influence of this folk-religion within the Christian church, and the popularity of its cults in this region far into the twentieth century.

[64] Jacob, Manuscript History, p. 185; Lowe, pp. 97–99; Smith, p. 118.

[65] Abbs, 1870, p. 132.

[66] Pastoral report of Dennispuram, 1866, in LMS Archives, Reports, Box 1/mf. 3281; Aruminayagam, report of Attur Division, 1869, ibidem., mf. 3292.

[67] Annual Report Travancore District Committee, Neyoor 1867, p. 9.

In a discussion with missionary agents, a village headman declared: "The supreme God has created many demons also in the universe to be worshipped by men". Therefore, with due respect for that supreme creator, he preferred to continue the adoration of the same demons which his ancestors had adored. On the other hand, the *Kanikar* hill tribes, pushed back by the opening of coffee estates, believed that their demons had fled for fear of the mighty God of the white men.[68] These scraps of information seem to agree with Horton's assumption that the High God in one form or another was a universal feature of traditional religion.[69] Whether there was a need for a closer relationship with a High God because socio-economic change had widened the boundaries of social experience beyond the local sphere where demons and spirits operated, is a hypothesis that deserves further investigation.

VIII.5 The Observance of the Sabbath Day

Finally, the LMS missionaries had no doubt that a proper observance of the Sabbath day was a good standard by which to measure the quality of Christian life in their congregations. This proper observance required not only that one should refrain from pursuance of all usual occupations, but included also regular attendance at the church services held on that special day. Stringent rules were framed, and in some congregations fines were imposed on Sunday labour. Nevertheless, it proved to be very difficult to integrate some kind of observance into the life and work of the south Travancore Christians who in many cases were led by other priorities. Belonging to the poorest sections of society, they simply could not afford to abstain from one day's income.

Those Christians, who depended for their livelihood on the palmyra trees, as was the case with many *Shanars*, had to work everyday, at least during the tapping season. In the early years, Christian tappers interrupted their work on Sunday for a few hours, but immediately after church service they climbed back their trees. Most missionaries considered this arrangement to be far from satisfactory, but the situation was to grow worse in the

[68] Zachariah, report of Neyoor, 1879, in LMS Archives, Reports, Box 2/mf. 3313; Mateer 1883, p. 70.

[69] Horton; also M. Wilson, *Religion and Transformation of Society*, Cambridge University Press, 1971, quoted in Kuper, pp. 83 ff.

middle of the century. The opening of coffee estates in Ceylon had drawn away much *Shanar* labour from the neighbouring Tinnevelly district, increasing the local demand for tappers. As the tapping seasons in Tinnevelly and south Travancore perfectly alternated, the Tinnevelly trees yielding juice from March and the Travancore ones from September, many *Shanars* from Travancore migrated to Tinnevelly, part of the year.

Russell wrote from Jamestown, that consequently those Christian *Shanars* in his district who still lived from tapping—about half the number—spent all their time from early morning till late at night with the exception of an hour or two during the heat of the day in one continual round of climbing trees as high and as bare as the mast of a ship. The short afternoon nap had also to be used for bringing as much jaggery as possible to the nearest market to trade it for fish or other food. During their absence in Tinnevelly, these migrant labourers could receive no Christian instruction, but when at home there was not much time either, and if present at Sunday service at all, they usually fell asleep.[70] Russell showed at least some understanding of their working conditions, but not all missionaries were that kindly disposed.

In defence of their position, the tree climbers advanced not only loss of income; they also contended that if they did not tap on Sunday the productivity of the tree, "the *Shanar's* milch cow", would seriously be damaged. Mateer, who combined linguistic talent with a great botanic interest, showed his aptitude for scientific experiment and decided on a test. He ordered thirteen trees in the mission compound to be left wholly untouched on Sundays, and the daily produce of juice to be carefully measured. As this was found to be, on the average, about two pints from each tree daily, while other trees climbed every day, including Sundays, produced five to fifteen pints, Mateer felt obliged to conclude that the tapping should better not be interrupted.[71] Even then, missionaries like Emlyn, speaking of Pareychaley district, still held the opinion that palmyra climbing on Sundays had "much to do with the deadness and want of spirit observable in not a few

[70] Russell, letter from Jamestown, 24.1.1856, in LMS Archives, Odds, Box 18/mf. 1147 (also in Box 16/mf. 1111); the same labour migration is described by Allan, report from Nagercoil, 1888, ibidem, Box 17.

[71] Mateer (1886), pp. 126–7; idem, 1871, p. 125.

congregations".[72] In 1888, the Travancore District Committee expressed the hope, that Christians would at least feel constrained to devote the entire profits of their Sunday tree climbing to church purposes,[73] but there are no indications that this was more than a pious wish.

Field labourers had to cope with similar problems. A missionary report of 1830 noted that in some seasons of the year, "the temptations to work on the Sabbath are so powerful that the more worldly minded cannot resist them".[74] The same report, however, acknowledged that this "worldly mindedness" had much to do with a wish to avoid the wrath of the landlords who tried to prevent their slaves from associating with the mission. Yet, the most compelling reason was that the poor field labourers, being paid in rice, could not afford to refuse to work on Sunday and so lose one day's meal. Therefore, many Christians kept cultivating the fields on Sunday, even after relations between the landlords and the LMS began to improve in the second part of the century. If not required in the fields, the (ex-)slaves gathered firewood and sold it in the market on Sundays to supplement the little rice earned by their ordinary labour.[75]

There were many minor disappointments that the missionaries had to swallow. Mateer, to cite just one example, discovered one Sunday morning that a Muslim merchant was allowed to spread out his eatables for sale at the very door of a chapel. The catechist, Mateer observed disapprovingly, was "quite oblivious of the unseemliness of such a thing...."[76] This and other instances may serve to illustrate that the observance of the Sabbath day did not perfectly suit the needs of local society.

Our nineteenth century LMS sources turn out to be extremely

[72] Emlyn, meeting Travancore District Committee, Pareychaley 1886, in LMS Archives, Incoming Letters, Box 11; see also Emlyn's article in *Travancore Times*, 20.3.1885, cuttings in ibidem., Box 10.

[73] Travancore District Committee Minute Book, 1888, Annual Meeting Pareychaley.

[74] Extract of printed report, Nagercoil 1830, in LMS Archives, Odds, Box 16.

[75] Mead and Mault, letter from Nagercoil, 7.5.1820, in LMS Archives, Odds, Box 15/mf. 1101; Annual Report Trivandrum District 1884, printed report, ibidem. Box 17; Travancore District Committee Minute Book, 1883, Annual Meeting Neyoor.

[76] Travancore District Committee Minute Book, 1887, Annual Meeting Quilon.

useful in answering the question to what extent conversion really effected a cultural change among the people concerned. The missionaries themselves were scrupulously watching their converts' life in order to ascertain traces of veritable rebirth. Their letters and reports in spite of themselves strongly suggest that changes in the lives and thoughts of the LMS Christians were not substantial; at any rate, they fell far short of missionary pretensions and expectations. We will come back to that in the concluding chapter.

IX. Conclusion

In the nineteenth century, a large part of the population in the native state of Travancore may be said to belong to one of the numerous untouchable communities. Major groups were *Shanars, Ezhavas, Pariahs* and *Pulayas* who had their own status rivalries. On the periphery of local society, these groups eked out a miserable existence, rendering their valuable labour services but kept at a distance as polluted. Opportunities to improve their position were extremely scarce and the barrier towards caste society seemed insurmountable. Nevertheless, involvement in the exports of coconut products enabled the *Ezhavas*—who lived mainly to the north of the LMS mission area—to make enough social progress to lay a claim to a higher position in the ritual hierarchy of caste. *Shanars, Pariahs* and *Pulayas*, on the other hand, were less favourably situated in the local economy and many of them turned towards Christianity, as an alternative way to social mobility. Their adoption of Christianity, as a new religious identity, had much to do with the changes, that took place under colonialism.

In the wake of the Company's war with Mysore, Travancore state was forced to accept British sovereignty, and a Resident was installed in the capital, Trivandrum to keep a close watch on all political affairs. The nineteenth century saw a growing integration of Travancore, not only in the British empire, but also in an expanding world economy. Established institutions like slavery and state monopolies were abolished, a land market was created—accessible also to foreigners—and local agriculture became increasingly oriented towards the production of cash crops. Coconut products were the main export article compared to which coffee was only a minor item. From about the middle of the century this agrarian commercialization resulted in rice, the chief produce of the land, having to be imported to meet consumption demands at home. Internal communications were improved and a modern system of education was introduced. This was the situation in which the London missionaries operated and participated.

As we have seen, the LMS missionaries that came to south

Travancore in the nineteenth century, represented a very determined and fairly cohesive group. These "inner-directed" men and women shared a strong belief in being called by their Lord to go out and preach the Gospel to all mankind. For this purpose, they were ready to sacrifice personal comfort, material prospects and, if necessary, their lives. These lofty spiritual motives did not exclude the possibility of missionary employment bringing substantial improvement in social and economic position, as the careers of several missionaries indicate. Marriage ties further strengthened the personal cohesion among the small number of missionary families in south Travancore. These strong personal bonds did not prevent occasional conflicts from flaring up among these strong-minded and utterly convinced men and women, conflicts which shook the whole missionary community.

The kind assistance and protection received from the first British Residents enabled the LMS to start its operations in Travancore even before the 1813 Charter permitted Christian missionaries to enter and remain on Indian territory. Not all Residents had the same sympathy with the work of the mission. Yet generally, the local British officials responded favourably to missionary appeals and initiatives, giving the LMS a position of some influence and making the local people view the mission as an authority close to officialdom yet much more accessible. The successful interventions by the missionaries on behalf of their converts did not fail to make a deep impression on the low caste communities who had no friends in the state bureaucracy and now came to look upon the LMS as their trusted ally.

The London missionaries in Travancore retained their lower middle class background throughout the nineteenth century, and more so than their colleagues from other societies. Yet, this humble class background does not seem to have hindered their easy relationship with the colonial representatives in this native state, maybe also because of the small number of British officials and civilians on the spot. In its turn, the mission obliged the colonial government by the establishment of schools, printing presses and hospitals.

Its preaching of a foreign religion and association with the colonial power did not serve to make the London mission very popular among the dominant groups in Travancore society, who received the missionaries with distrust, if not with open hostility.

But after a last desperate revolt was violently suppressed, the traditional elite of landholders, bureaucrats and warriors had to swallow defeat and seek a modus vivendi with British colonialism and its local representatives. The painfulness of this accommodation process was mitigated by the fact that Travancore was allowed a continued existence as a semi-autonomous native state under its own royal family and bureaucracy. In that way, the internal social structure remained largely unchanged and the untouchable communities of agricultural labourers and slaves at the bottom of the social scale were suppressed and despised as before.

Very soon, it appeared that, as far as the Christian religion had any appeal among the local population, it was to the untouchables. For these exploited communities association with the mission offered the promise of an escape from social bondage and a possible way to a more respectable place in society. So, there developed a certain alliance between groups of untouchables who wanted to shake off their age-old oppression and the Christian mission eager to fight the dominant religion. As we have seen, that was one of the main reasons why the ruling classes in Travancore at first tended to resist conversion movements, as they could not fail to perceive it as a threat to their own position of power and authority. The fact that the British missionaries lent their wholehearted support to the first symptoms of a growing militancy among the untouchables only increased their hostility towards the Christian religion.

In their search for pure converts, i.e. people led exclusively by spiritual motives, the nineteenth century missionaries felt often disappointed, when they had to admit that social and economic considerations played a large part among their converts. Signs of genuine faith were not altogether wanting, but generally the groups that associated with the mission, tended to understand the message of the Gospel in terms of immediate interests and practical concerns. We should, however, not focus on motives in isolation—neither spiritual nor material—but rather view religious identity as encompassing all aspects of life. One might attempt to distinguish different kinds of motives and even evaluate their particular worth, as most nineteenth century missionaries had no hesitation in doing. But it ought to be emphasized, that the people themselves did not make these clear-cut distinctions, and expected the missionary to act as their leader both in spiritual and temporal affairs. And at the end of the century, the missionaries, taught by experience, came to show a growing awareness that concern for the material welfare of the people constituted a legitimate part of their calling and could only serve to make their preaching of the Gospel a more credible effort.

One of the main weapons that the mission could wield in its fight for social progress was education. From the beginning, education had been one of the main fields of missionary activity and especially the lower castes and classes, who were denied admission to government institutions, found their way to the mission schools. A system of education was introduced that strongly emphasized primary and vernacular instruction at the village level and found culmination in an English seminary at Nagercoil. Although this seminary was primarily meant to train Indian catechists and schoolmasters for missionary service, several students, to the great dismay of their teachers, preferred to turn to the market and use their education to gain more profitable employment in the emerging capitalist agriculture in the adjacent island of Ceylon.

Some of these Christian students managed to get *kangany* positions in the Ceylon coffee estates or served the planters in some other supervisory capacity. The savings brought back could be used for consumption purposes like the building of superior houses, but were also invested in paddy land or coffee cultivation. In the 1870s, almost one quarter of the coffee plantations in the south Travancore hills were owned by Indians, but all these Indian proprietors, with the exception of the crown prince, were Christian converts, associated with the London mission. Several missionaries expressed their conviction that the adoption of the Christian faith and its concomitant values had been the basis for a new, more enterprising economic attitude among their converts. Instead of referring to the Weber thesis as anticipated by the London missionaries, I want to emphasize the importance of education and personal contacts provided by the mission as factors to account for the remarkable economic progress enjoyed by a small but important section of the Christian community.

Shanars and similar communities seem to have been in a better position to profit from the socio-economic changes and missionary assistance than the slave castes. Involvement in the cultivation of coffee, from common labourer to independent planter, was largely a *Shanar* affair, at least in the beginning. The second half of the century, however, brought abolition of slavery and the promise of freedom also for *Pariahs, Pulayas* and other slave castes. The missionaries had actively championed the abolition of slavery which was finally proclaimed in 1855. Even though the missionaries themselves had no direct interest in plantations at that time, they had much in common with the colonial bureaucrats and European planters, at least in economic outlook.

The abolition of slavery loosened the old bonds between master and servant. But since it was not followed by any economic reform, the situation remained largely unchanged and the possible benefits of abolition did not become manifest to the newly liberated. In the following years, many ex-slaves went over to Christianity. But the always impecunious LMS commanded hardly any economic power and was not able to step in and to act as a new patron. For that reason, the missionaries welcomed the opening of plantations in the Travancore hills, since they offered alternative employment and cash wages that the ex-slaves needed to become more independent of their former masters. Many landlords had tried to prevent their (ex-)slaves from becoming Christians and therefore, abolition of slavery and work on the plantation also meant that the (ex-)slaves could gain more freedom to take their fate into their own hands.

This tendency of low caste Christians to turn to the cash economy was by no means an exclusive characteristic of south Travancore. In the first half of this century, many *Pariah* converts from Trichinopoly, often with the help of their missionaries, migrated to the Anamalai hills in Coimbatore and secured employment on coffee and tea plantations. Manickam informs us that most of the subordinate staff and many plantation workers in these hills were Christian.[1] A similar proportional concentration of Christian converts is noted by Shetty in the Kolar Gold Fields near Bangalore, where one-fifth of the mineworkers and their families belonged to the Christian community.[2]

The plantation owners in south Travancore had their own reasons for welcoming the flow of Christian converts to their estates. Though generally not moved by a great love for Christian

[1] Manickam, 1977, pp. 80, 87.
[2] Shetty, p. 116.

religion, the European planters were quick to discover that the missionaries' insistence on obedience and temperance helped in creating a docile labour force more easy to handle. And we may assume, that the LMS converts who owned the smaller estates were moved by the same considerations, apart from the fact that their recruiting ground largely coincided with existing social networks of family and friends. The planters showed their appreciation of the work of the mission by donation of generous subscriptions, at least as long as their trade could bear it.

Relations between the LMS and the *Nayar* landlords in the plains were much more strained, largely because the landholding castes accused the missionaries of undermining their traditional authority over the slave communities. But towards the end of the century there seems to have been a growing understanding between the two. The instilment of what the missionaries considered to be Christian virtues, like discipline and duty, strengthened a traditional submissiveness among the ex-slaves which even led some landlords to express their appreciation of missionary work. After starting as a promise of freedom and social improvement to the local labour force, Christianity in many cases turned out to be a new form of enslavement. At the same time, the ex-slave Christians were losing the little influence they had in the local church; they were neglected in the distribution of leading positions and faced increasing difficulties in gaining admission to the Nagercoil Seminary. The resulting frustration led many ex-slave Christians to leave the LMS for other missionary societies, which created further divisions in their own community.

Finally, let us turn to the question to what extent conversion really effected a cultural change among the people concerned. As we have seen, the lives and thoughts of the nineteenth century LMS Christians remained to a large extent determined by their traditional values. Now, one could argue that conversion should rather be seen as a gradual process allowing for various degrees of Christianization. These first generations of converts were as yet in an oscillation stage between old and new, and an active interaction between folk-religion and the Christian Great Tradition was to be expected among people who had only recently changed their religious identity. Following the same argument, the south Indian Christians of the twentieth century may have grown into a more clearly marked, internally homogeneous community, firmly shedding the more conspicuous vestiges of their former religion.

That hypothesis certainly deserves further investigation by empirical research. But the few studies that are available disclose a continuing influence of caste feeling, continuity of old marriage networks, and even incidental demon worship among Christians in the second part of the present century.[3] Therefore, we have to conclude that the Travancore converts have embraced Christianity in accordance with their own values and without completely rejecting their own cultural past. Whereas the missionaries attributed to the people only one religious identity at the same time, most converts were more inclusive and easily combined elements of Christianity with the traditions of their own culture. The interaction and accommodation between old and new is a structural quality rather than a transient process.

A more modest interpretation of the cultural change effected by conversion does not mean that all change is denied. First of all, the missionaries started a critical discussion of the cultural tradition in general which may be seen as an essential precondition to change and, with the help of the government, they made at least some progress in implementing social reform. But secondly, there was an indigenous process of cultural change that was in many ways similar to Christianization, i.e. Sanskritization as outlined in the first chapter. Both Christianization and Sanskritization are processes of adaptation to the customs and rituals of a prestigious Great Tradition and part of an attempt to achieve a higher status in society.

The (ex-)slave communities generally lacked the economic resources to lend force to their social ambition. But many of them attended the LMS village schools, which awakened their self-respect, and with the help of the missionaries they dared to fight some of the most glaring social disabilities. The *Shanars* benefited from the same missionary education and protection, but were more able to take advantage of the economic changes that took place in Travancore by their involvement in petty trade, labour migration and coffee cultivation. Therefore, some groups in these

[3] Alexander, 1972, pp. 156–8, idem., 1977, pp. 55–60; Wilson, p. 20, 24; see also the publications of the Caste-Class Study Program by the Christian Institute for the Study of Religion and Society, Bangalore.

communities, but more so among the *Shanars*, had attained that crucial level of economic independence and critical awareness through education which is necessary to make a convincing claim to a higher status in society.[4]

It may be true that Sanskritization aims at emulating the life style of the dominant Hindu castes—in this case the Travancore *Nayars*—who generally resisted these movements with all their might as an unwarranted infringement of their own caste privileges. Christianization, on the other hand, is actively encouraged by committed religious specialists, in our case the London missionaries, who tried to shape this movement of the lower castes in accordance with a Christian way of life as practiced in nineteenth century Victorian England. But in spite of all their efforts, the missionaries were often not able to prevent their converts from translating the social progress they made into an idiom derived from the local Hindu caste culture.

The basic convergence between Sanskritization and Christianization most clearly surfaced in the attitude towards caste. In theoretical terms, Sanskritization accepts and even confirms caste hierarchy, whereas Christianization is supposed to reject it altogether. But in practice, though often in a more subtle way, caste distinctions survived within the church, as can be seen from the forming of caste congregations and the continuation of the old caste-based marriage networks. The missionaries vehemently opposed all traces of casteism, but sometimes silently tolerated the same, especially in their treatment of that precious creature, the high caste convert. These continuing distinctions were not subtle enough to prevent a growing feeling of resentment, especially among the *Pariahs*.

The treatment of women is another case in point. The sanskritic Great Tradition and Christianity concur in emphasizing the reproductive role of women and both assign to women a central but subordinate place in family life. Since high caste Hindus used to restrict the freedom of their women, a ban on widow remarriage was a clear indication, that a group aspired to be respected in terms of the local caste hierarchy. This highly valued sanskritic custom was also found among the Christian *Shanars*, and

[4] The same conditions are mentioned in Matthews description of the mass conversion in Meenakshipuram 1981, Matthew, p. 1032.

missionary pressure could weaken but not break it. There are also a few references to pre-puberty marriages among the south Travancore Christians, though unfortunately, our evidence does not allow us to make a more general statement on that practice. But here, we should also note an important difference. Whereas Sanskritization tends to deny women all forms of creative self-expression, in the Christian congregations many women, at first reluctantly but later on more gladly, availed themselves of the education and employment opportunities offered by the mission.

The dress conflicts, that started in the 1820s and culminated in the 1858/59 riots, also showed a typical mixture of sanskritic and Christian elements. In the state of Travancore untouchable communities were not permitted to cover the upper part of their bodies. To end this humiliating practice, the lady missionaries devised a jacket for the Christian women, which was approved by the government and slowly found acceptance in the local congregations. The available evidence, however, makes it abundantly clear, that especially the better off sections of the Christian *Shanars* preferred the so-called uppercloth. That uppercloth may not have satisfied the missionary sense of decency, but had the important attraction of being a style of dress peculiar to the *Nayars*. Appropriation of that attribute provoked violent reprisals from the dominant castes. These reprisals may have been meant to insult not the women in particular but the caste community in general, yet the women were the main victims of the disturbances. It is worth mentioning that about fifty years later a similar social mobility took place among the *Pulayas*.[5]

By becoming Christians the untouchables acquired their own sacred scriptures. The reading or even the hearing of the *Vedas* was forbidden to the untouchables. But in the Bible they found their own *Veda* and Christianity was locally known as the religion of the *Vedam* or Book, parts of which the people carried with them written on palmyra leaf. Leaving their simple temple sheds they gained access to more imposing buildings, the most conspicuous being the large chapel in Nagercoil with its massive stone foundations that could contain thousands of people under its corrugated iron roof. There, the blood offerings to demons and evil spirits

[5] See for instance Edmonds, Quilon years report, 22.5.1916, in LMS Archives, Reports, Box 11/mf. 3428.

were replaced by the worship of one God, an element closely associated also with the Hindu Great Tradition. The destruction of many shrines and crude stone idols was unmistakably a significant change which the missionaries never tired of recording. But this change was as much a sign that people forsaked a religion that did not offer spiritual satisfaction, as it was an expression of their desire to be considered more respectable.

Another important element in the adaptation to both Great Traditions was the use of new, more prestigious names. Most untouchables used to have no family names and children were often named after the demons to whom they were dedicated. Hence the importance of new names after conversion. The adoption of the names of generous subscribers in England, as happened in the first part of the century, did not entail much prestige, as these names could not be written in the vernacular and were utterly unpronounceable by illiterate Hindus. Therefore, common Scriptural names were preferred like Daniel, Joseph etc., or high-sounding sanskrit names like Kamalan (lily) and Kesari (lion). This convergence is most clearly reflected in sanskrit names containing a Christian meaning like Yesudas (given to Jesus), Vedamanickam (gem of Scripture) or Masillamani (pearl without a flaw).[6]

Vegetarianism was an instance on which Sanskritization and Christianization clearly diverged. The touch of meat, especially beef, was strictly forbidden to a caste Hindu, whereas it did not mean anything sinful in the Christian tradition. However, the cheapest meat that came within reach of many untouchables was the flesh of cows and bullocks left dead by the roadside, sometimes in a putrid state. *Pariahs* especially were noted as carrion eaters, though not so in the extreme south. The mission strongly disapproved of it and all reports agree that in the course of the century the Christians among the *Pariahs* had broken with this custom.[7]

[6] Annual Report LMS 1823, p. 77; Mateer, report of Trivandrum and Quilon, 1865, in LMS Archives, Odds, Box 17/mf. 1120; Mateer, 1871, pp. 139, 195. To shake off the traditional inferiority traditionally associated with their name, *Pulayas* and *Pariahs* with the active support of the mission tried to change their names to *Cheramar* and *Sambavar*; these efforts received a distinct setback in the first part of this century. Census of Travancore 1941, Part I, p. 132.

[7] Mateer, "The Pariah Caste ..." p. 7; Annual Report Travancore District Committee, Nagercoil 1861, p. 4; idem., 1865, p. 3.

Although abstinence from alcohol was a value common to both Christianization and Sanskritization, on this point the agreement between both processes did not yield impressive results. Among the *Ezhavas*, the consumption of liquor was rampant and *Pulayas* could be found intoxicated even during church service. *Shanars* were generally said to abstain from the use of spirituous liquors, but quite a few of them became addicted while migrant workers on the coffee estates.[8] The LMS, having close connections with the temperance movement, fought excessive drinking by removing drunkards from the congregational lists, and making total abstinence conditional for church membership. Some progress was made and Abbs wrote that dealers in arrack had complained that the spread of Christianity was depriving them of their living.[9] But there were also many setbacks, and in 1883 a meeting of missionaries wondered whether intemperance was actually not on the increase.[10]

Of course, there remain some important difference between the two processes, especially when we look at the circumstances under which they were resorted to. In general, social groups that succeed in increasing their economic power or political influence will try to sanskritize their customs and beliefs in order to rise in the Hindu hierarchy of caste; but those lower castes whose social improvement is less impressive or even blocked and frustrated will be more inclined to turn to Christianity and associate with the mission as an alternative way to a higher and more dignified place in society.

In elucidation of this observation, an interesting comparison could be made with the *Ezhavas* in the latter part of the nineteenth century. Encouraged by economic developments that favoured them more than the *Shanars*, an emerging middle class, led by Shri Narayana Guru, started a movement to reform the *Ezhavas*' traditional customs and culture, as has already been hinted at in chapter IV. As part of that movement, the worship of one God and the equality of all people were emphasized, the offering to demons and evil spirits was forbidden, temples were built and consecrated where animal sacrifices and offerings of fermented drinks were

[8] Rajendran, p. 25: Hardgrave, pp. 22, 39–40; Zachariah, report of Neyoor, 1878, in LMS Archives, Reports, Box 2/inf. 3312.

[9] Abbs, 1870, p. 205.

[10] Travancore District Committee Minute Book, 1883, Annual Meeting Neyoor.

replaced by flowers and fruits, and *Ezhavas* were asked to outcaste the drunkards from their ranks.

Most scholars interpret this movement as an expression of Sanskritization, although some others prefer to stress its character of protest against the Hindu caste hierarchy.[11] The main point that I want to emphasize here, however, is the basic similarity between the movement led by Shri Narayana Guru and his close associates, and the efforts of LMS catechists and pastors to change the customs of the low caste Christians in the south of Travancore. Therefore, one of our main conclusions must be that Sanskritization and mass conversion towards Christianity are not as radically opposed as theoretical explanations may suggest. In many cases they are closely intertwined.

[11] Chandramohan, pp. 62 ff.

Population Distribution in LMS Area 1871[1]

Caste and Community	Padmanabhapuram Revenue Division					Trivandrum Revenue Division				Quilon Revenue Division	Total
	Tova:	Agas:	Eran:	Kalk:	Vila:	Neya:	Triv:	Nedu:	Sira:	Quil:[2]	
Malayali Brahmins	34	64	74	152	121	172	413	241	374	134	1779
Non-Malayali Brahmins	1146	3250	<500	1384	1109	634	6596	<500	1357	<500	
Nayars	603	935	3498	9939	12077	29568	29409	12851	22363	26252	147495
Shanars	3027	17164	33043	10865	16191	13388	<1000	<1000	<1000	<1000	
Pariahs	4048	8294	5797	5780	<2000	2292	<2000	<2000	<2000	<2000	
All Hindus	26062	61066	69494	43036	48372	84939	82698	43590	74506	81847	615610
Muslims	1245	3800	4491	2134	2367	5206	9144	2958	11695	10593	53633
Syrian Christians	none	none	<1000	<1000	none	<1000	<1000	nonc	<1000	3684	
Roman Cath. Christians	1017	6469	21121	4566	10039	3923	7532	<1000	1142	9181	
Protestant Christians	1288	10248	11579	12403	8773	12032	251	895	78	677	58224
Total Population	29635	81613	106732	62146	69553	106128	100413	47668	87992	106091	797971

[1] All information is obtained from the *Census of Travancore* 1875, pp. 152 ff.

Unfortunately, the Census gives no figures for *Ezhavas* and *Pulayas* in these *taluks*, but mentions that these groups were sparse.

A slave caste like the *Kuravars* was found in Sirayinkil *taluk* only (7996 persons); a farming caste like the *Vellalars* was numerous only in Tovala (6063 persons), Agasteesvaram (1865), Eranial (1706) and Trivandrum North (1966).

A small number of Europeans and Eurasians is included in the total population but not listed in a separate column.

[2] The Padmanabhapuram Revenue Division included the *taluks* Tovala, Agasteesvaram, Eranial, Kalkulam and Vilavankodu; the Trivandrum Division included Neyattankara, Trivandrum, Nedumangadu and Sirayinkil; from the Quilon Division only the Quilon *taluk* is listed here.

The *taluks* mentioned in this table are listed from south to north; they represent the closest approximate to the LMS area.

APPENDIX II

Population according to religion in LMS Area 1875–1901[1]

Religion	Padmanabhapuram Revenue Division				Trivandrum Revenue Division				Quilon Revenue Division		Total
	Tova:	Agas:	Eran:	Kalk:	Vila:	Neya:	Triv:	Nedu:	Sira:	Quil.	
				1875							
Hindus	26062	61066	69494	43036	48372	84939	82698	43590	74506	81847	615610
Muslims	1245	3800	4491	2134	2367	5206	9144	2958	11695	10593	53633
All Christians	2328	16747	32747	16976	18814	15983	8571	1120	1791	13651	128728
Protestant Christians	1288	10248	11579	12403	8773	12032	251	895	78	677	58224
Total Population	29635	81613	106732	62146	69553	106128	100413	47668	87992	106091	797971
				1891							
Hindus	26822	68634	74383	47117	56718	93618	93468	50766	83105	90737	685368
Muslims	1184	3387	4065	2420	2087	5143	9506	3308	13050	13650	57800
All Christians	1745	15220	26650	9937	9716	11994	8963	1423	1840	17538	105026
Protestant Christians	977	5737	5764	6461	5417	9046	899	1374	87	105	35867
Total Population	29751	87241	105098	59474	68521	110755	111938	55497	97995	121935	848205

				1901							
Hindus	26070	69095	75403	51059	58553	107248	106874	54895	93300	92070	734567
Muslims	1453	3371	3671	2839	2507	5908	12847	5811	15981	14462	68850
All Christians	4784	21047	31087	15332	17467	24778	14226	3328	2403	20553	155005
Protestant Christians	1493	6308	8232	5693	7393	14350	1593	1318	179	492	47051
Total Population	32410	93513	110161	70247	79584	139952	131196	67771	112823	129658	967315

[1] Source: *Census of Travancore* 1875, pp. 152 ff., 192 ff.; idem, 1891, Part I, pp. 378 ff., Part II, pp. 10 ff.; idem, 1901, Part III, pp. 14, ff., pp. 503 ff.

The sharp decline in the number of Christians in 1891 was merely due to the inclusion of many Syrian Christians into the column "caste" instead of "christian sect". In fact, the number of Syrian Christians showed a slight increase (Census, 1891, Part II, p. 376).

In the 1901 census the different Protestant denominations have been listed separately. In this table the column Protestant Christians includes Anglicans only, as the term "Anglican" may be seen as equivalent to "LMS Christian". About 5,000 people, belonging to minor denominations but possibly also connected with the LMS, have not been returned under this column.

APPENDIX III

Alphabetical List of LMS Missionaries in South Travancore 1806–1900[1] (giving, if known, date and place of birth and death, denomination, previous occupation, (missionary) education, date and place of service in Travancore and further remarks)

1. ABBS, John • 1810 Norwich—1888 Kirby Moorside, Yorkshire • assisted his father in boot and shoemaking • Cheshunt College • 1838–1859 Neyoor, Pareychaley.

2. ADDIS, William Bawn • 1800 Hambrook, near Bristol—1871 • shoemaker and leather business • Missionary College, Hoxton • 1827—1830 Nagercoil, Quilon • 1830–1861 for LMS in Coimbatore.

3. ALLAN, Alexander L. • 1854 Riccarton, Ayrshire—1928 Nagercoil • Evangelical Union College, Glasgow • 1884–1905 Nagercoil • married (1892) Annie L. Duthie, daughter of No. 11.

4. BACH, Thomas William • 1868 Worchester – ? • solicitor's clerk • New College, Hampstead • 1894–1899 Trivandrum • resigned on account of ill-health.

5. BAYLIS, Frederick • 1825 Rodborough, Gloucestershire—1877 Muttam • assistant to a chemist • Rotherham College • 1854–1877 Santhapuram, Neyoor • 1850–1853 for LMS in Madras, remarried (1865) Ann M. Cox, daughter of No. 6.

6. COX, John • 1811 Painswick, Gloucestershire—1895 Neyoor • Congregationalist • assisted his father in wool trade and business • Highbury College, London • 1838–1861 Trivandrum, Quilon • remarried (1861) Amy, female teacher Girls Boarding School.

7. CROW, William • 1797 Essex – ? • Congregationalist • apprentice to his stepfather, a butcher • Gosport Academy • 1823–1825 Quilon • returned on account of ill-health.

8. DENNIS, John Joll • 1830 Morrice Town, near Plymouth—1864 Nagercoil • Methodist • printer and foreman compositor in the Illustrated London News Office • Bedford College • 1856–1864 Nagercoil Printing Office.

9. DENNISON, James Everington • 1864 Bedford – ? • Congregationalist • schoolmaster • Teacher training course • 1892–1899 Nagercoil College • married (1898) Kate Derry, missionary in Nagercoil, No. 10.

10. DERRY, Kate • 1860 Launceston, Cornwall – ? • Congregationalist • teacher • Western College, Plymouth • 1892–1898 Nagercoil Zenana work • married (1898) J.E. Dennison, missionary in Nagercoil, No. 9.

11. DUTHIE, James D.D. • 1833 Stonehaven—1908 Bangalore • Presbyterian • clerk in an advocate's office • Bedford College • 1859–1908 Nagercoil Seminary, Nagercoil, Jamestown • 1856–1859 for LMS in Madras, married (1858) Sarah A. Lea, sister of W.K. Lea, missionary of Amoy.

[1] The data for this table have been derived from the LMS Archives, Candidates Papers 1796–1899, Boxes 1–18/mf. 150–651 and Sibree's Register of LMS Missionaries, LMS 1923; some additional information was received from Rev. J.T. Hardyman, archivist of the Council for World Mission, London, and from memorial stones placed in the walls of churches in Nagercoil and Neyoor.

12. EDMONDS, William John • 1868 Bletchingley in Surrey—1941 • stonemason • Hackney College London • 1898–1928 Quilon • 1892–1897 for LMS in Madagaskar.

13. EMLYN (JONES), James • 1838 Adpar, Cardiganshire—1917 Martandam • Western College and Highgate College • 1868–1890 Pareychaley.

14. FELLS, Arthur, MB CM • 1868 Ramsgate—1939 • Congregationalist • apprentice to a chemist and druggist • Edinburgh Medical Missionary Society, Edinburgh University • 1893–1905 Medical Mission Neyoor • friend of and influenced by No. 16.

15. FOSTER, Arthur Thomson • 1873 Bradford—1952 • Congregationalist • apprentice to a stuff merchant • Hackney College London • 1899–1932 Pareychaley.

16. FRY, Edwin Sargood, MB CM • 1858 Chelmsford—1929 • Congregationalist • apprentice, later assistant to a chemist • Edinburgh Medical Missionary Society • 1886–1892 Medical Mission Neyoor • married (1885) Anne C. Lowe, daughter of No. 28, in 1893 superintendent of the Edinburgh Medical Missionary Society.

17. GANNAWAY, James Frank • 1838 Wartlington – ? • Congregationalist • teacher running a private school • 1861–1864 Jamestown • returned on account of his wife's ill-health.

18. GILLIES, James Wardrop • 1862 Glasgow – ? • missionary in Ireland • Evangelical Union College, Glasgow, and St. Mungo's Medical College • 1892–1897 Quilon • married (1895) Margaret J. Maclean LMS missionary in Calcutta.

19. HACKER, Isaac Henry • 1848 Birmingham—1933 Kodaikanal • Spring Hill College, Mosely and Western College • 1878–1920 Neyoor, Trivandrum, Quilon • remarried (1887) Winifred D. Baylis, daughter of No. 5.

20. HARRIS, William M.A. • 1805 Glasgow—1833 Portsmouth • University of Glasgow • 1831–1832 Quilon • returned on account of ill-health.

21. HEWETT, Henry • 1864 Godstone in Surrey—1957 • gas and hot water fitter, whitesmith etc. • Hulme Cliff College, Derbyshire • 1893–1928 Vakkam, Attingal, Quilon, Nedungolam, Trivandrum.

22. JONES, Samuel • 1830 Warrington—1877 London • Rotherham College • 1870–1877 Nagercoil • 1859–1867 for LMS in Coimbatore, returned on sick certificate.

23. KNILL, Richard • 1787 Braunton, Devonshire—1857 • tailor • Gosport Academy • 1818–1819 Nagercoil • 1816–1818 for LMS in Madras, returned on account of the climate, became missionary in Russia.

24. KNOWLES, Joshua • 1850 Shuttleworth, Lancashire – ? • Methodist • employee in business • Lancashire College, Manchester • 1880–1898 Trivandrum, Quilon, Pareychaley.

25. LEE, William • 1841 Tiverton—1928 • employee in business • Bedford College and Highgate College • 1865–1884 Jamestown, Trivandrum, Nagercoil, Neyoor • returned on account of his wife's ill-health.

26. LEITCH, Charles Calder M.R.C.S.E. • 1822 Edinburgh—1854 Muttam • Presbyterian • clerk and accountant to a bank • United Presbyterian Theological Hall and Congregational Theological Academy in Glasgow and Royal Infirmary in Edinburgh • 1852–1854 Medical Mission Neyoor • sister and cousin working as missionaries in Madras.

27. LEWIS, Ebenezer • 1812 Aberystwyth—1873 • Congregationalist • Highbury College, London • 1846–1862 Santhapuram • 1840–1846 for LMS in Coimbatore

and Madras, returned on account of ill-health, in 1874 Mrs. Lewis was employed by LMS in Palamcottah.

28. LOWE, John L.R.C.S.E. • 1835 Aberdeenshire—1892 • Congregationalist • apprenticed as apothecary • Bedford College and Edinburgh Medical Missionary Society • 1861–1868 Medical Mission Neyoor • returned on account of his wife's ill-health, in 1871 superintendent of the Edinburgh Medical Missionary Society.

29. MABBS, Goodeve • 1835 London–1906 • Congregationalist • draughtsman and engraver on wood • Bedford College • 1865–1867 Nagercoil • 1862–1865 for LMS in Salem, retired on account of his wife's ill-health.

30. MACDONNELL, Margaret Eliza • 1861 Londonderry—1937 • Congregationalist • hospital nurse • training in Edinburgh Royal Infirmary • 1892–1903, 1907 – ? Medical Mission Neyoor.

31. MATEER, Samuel • 1835 Belfast—1893 Hastings • Presbyterian, later Methodist • bookkeeper at a linen and cotton manufacturing firm • Bedford College • 1859–1891 Pareychaley, Trivandrum, Quilon.

32. MAULT, Charles • 1791 Shropshire—1858 Stoke, near Coventry • Gosport Academy • 1819–1855 Nagercoil • married (1818) Martha Mead, sister of No. 33.

33. MEAD, Charles • 1792 Bristol—1873 Trivandrum • Methodist • trained as a printer • Gosport Academy • 1817–1851 Nagercoil, Neyoor • remarried (1819) Johanna C. Horst, daughter of a missionary in Tanjore, remarried again (1851) Lois Biddulph, daughter of an Indian catechist.

34. MILLER, Charles • 1805 Forfar—1841 Poonamallee, near Madras • Presbyterian • private teacher • Theological Seminary and University classes, Edinburgh • 1834–1841 Neyoor, Nagercoil Seminary.

35. MILLER, William • 1804 Thurso—1838 Nagercoil • Congregationalist • schoolmaster • Gosport Academy and Missionary College, Hoxton • 1827–1838 Quilon, Neyoor • married Mary Pitman, sister of LMS missionary in South Seas, remarried (1830) Sophia E. Horst, daughter of missionary in Tanjore, brother-in-law of No. 33.

36. NEWPORT, Georg Oliver • 1840 Henley-on-Thames—1894 Colombo • Cheshunt College • 1863–1877 Pareychaley, Nagercoil • remarried (1869) Rosa M. Lechler, daugher of LMS missionary in Salem, from 1877 for LMS in Salem.

37. OSBORNE, William Davey • 1860 St. Ives, Cornwall – ? • Congregationalist • pastor of Tutbury, Staffordshire • Nottingham Congregational Institute • 1893–1914 Vakkam, Attingal.

38. PARKER, Arthur • 1858 West Bromwich—1935 • Congregationalist • carpenter and blacksmith • Lancashire Independent College, Manchester • 1900–1926 Trivandrum • from 1888 for LMS in Benares.

39. PATTISON, James T. • 1811 London – ? • Highbury College, London • 1838–1844 Nagercoil Seminary, Quilon • recalled by LMS.

40. RAMSAY, Archibald, Dr. R.C.S.L. • 1806 London – ? • Congregationalist • hospital surgeon • 1838–1842 Medical Mission Neyoor, Nagercoil • entered Government service (1842) as court physician of the Travancore *Raja*.

41. RINGELTAUBE, Wilhelm Tobias • 1770 Scheidelwitz, Prussia-1816 at sea • Lutheran • Halle University • 1806–1816 Mayiladi, Palamcottah • in 1799 for SPCK in Calcutta, from 1804 for LMS in Tranquebar.

42. ROBERTS, J. • appointed by Travancore District Committee • died in Birmingham • former army schoolmaster and teacher for CMS in Kottayam •

1830–1834 Nagercoil Seminary • entered Government service (1834) as Director of the Government High School in Trivandrum, retired in 1855.

43. RUSSELL, James • 1806 Glasgow—1890 Aberystwyth • pastor of Rendall, Orkney Islands • Glasgow Theological Academy and classes at Glasgow University • 1838–1860 Nagercoil, Jamestown (formed by him).

44. SMITH, John • 1790 Coventry – ? • cabinet maker and carpenter • Gosport Academy • 1820–1824 Nagercoil, Quilon • returned on account of ill-health.

45. THOMPSON, Alfred • 1862 London – ? • Baptist • employee in the wholesale drapery and mantle trade • Regents Park College • 1888–1891 Quilon • returned on account of his wife's ill-health.

46. THOMPSON, James Charles • 1804 Tweedmarth, Durham—1850 Quilon • Presbyterian • apprentice to a printer • Gosport Academy and Missionary College, Hoxton • 1827–1850 Quilon.

47. THOMSON, Thomas Smith, L.R.C.P. & S.E. • 1843 Edinburgh-1884 Neyoor • Presbyterian • resident surgeon • Edinburgh University and Edinburgh Medical Mission Dispensary • 1893–1884 Medical Mission Neyoor • remarried (1878) Mrs. Cox-Baylis, see No. 5.

48. WHITEHOUSE, John Owen • 1815 Dorking, London—1907 • warehouse clerk • Cheshunt College • 1842–1857 Nagercoil Seminary, Nagercoil • married (1849) Sarah Mault, daughter of No. 32, after 1861 in LMS Foreign Secretariat, later LMS Director.

49. WILKINSON, J. Frederick • 1832 Trinidad—1918 Liverpool • Bedford College • 1860–1876 Neyoor, Santhapuram, Quilon, 1881–1883 Quilon, 1894–1896 honorary assistant to No. 11 in Nagercoil • 1876–1880 for LMS in Madras, married (1861) Mary E. Cox, daughter of No. 6.

50. WILLS, Harold Temple, M.A. B.Sc. • 1862 Bristol—1942 • Congregationalist • engaged in business with his father • Universities of Bristol, London and Cambridge • 1892–1915 Trivandrum • married (1896) Florence M. Duthie, daugher of No. 11, resigned on account of his wife's ill-health.

APPENDIX IV

LMS Annual Statistics for the Years 1858–1901[1]
showing the number of adhrents, increase or decrease, the number of Indian preachers, catechists etc., Indian schoolteachers male and female, schools, scholars and local contributions in Rs.

Year	Adherents	Increase/ Decrease	Preachers Catechists etc.	Teachers	Schools	Scholars Boys	Scholars Girls	Rs. Contributions
1858	16,939		404		185	6,570		
1859	18,493	+1,554	400		199	6,710		4,329
1860	18,624	+ 131	199	200	192	5,188	1,541	4,223
1861	22,688	+4,064	213	190	205	5,229	1,790	4,936
1862	23,828	+1,140	222	201	207	5,180	1,861	6,558
1863	24,142	+ 314	237	213	220	5,918	1,808	6,966
1864	25,788	+1,646	242	190	201	5,856	1,480	7,836
1865	26,736	+ 948	249	198	198	5,802	1,531	7,842
1866	28,440	+1,704	203		213	6,346	1,507	9,680
1867	32,362	+3,922	207		237	6,646	1,595	12,190
1868	33,729	+1,367	213		185	4,838	1,078	11,610
1869	32,746	− 983	214		194	4,781	970	12,050
1870	30,969	−1,777	221		161	4,168	883	9,050
1871	30,601	− 368	205		131	3,569	840	8,760
1872	30,094	− 507	188		124	3,297	750	8,591
1873	31,601	+1,507	191		133	3,774	911	9,380
1874	32,556	+ 955	190		138	4,089	915	10,440
1875	40,449	+7,893	193		146	5,722	1,397	11,850
1876	37.470	−2,979	188		169	6,086	2,954	11,910

1877	36,471	− 999	199		168	6,214	1,489	10,140
1878	38,120	+1,649	196		176	6,745	1,651	12,100
1879	37,841	− 279	188		178	7,420	1,860	6,260
1880	39,337	+1,496	179		179	7,716	1,851	13,100
1881	40,453	+1,116	177		198	8,193	2,188	11,680
1882	41,347	+ 894	175		206	8,321	2,375	10,590
1883	42,378	+1,031	175		216	8,632	2,644	11,102
1884	42,998	+ 620	182	317	230	8,779	2,729	11,450
1885	42,810	− 188	181		248	9,050	2,938	9,030
1886	44,053	+1,243	42		267	9,466	2,846	10,641
1887	45,176	+1,123	44		285	10,044	3,251	10,290
1888	44,633	− 543	44		295	9,832	3,397	10,490
1889	45,356	+ 723	185		311	10,560	3,504	15,800
1890	46,497	+1,141	259		321	10,869	3,779	15,440
1891	49,267	+2.770	282		330	10,971	3,795	18,081
1892	50,637	+1,370	290		363	12,209	4,184	18,970
1893	53,147	+2,510	306		412	13,000	4,552	19,421
1894	47,667	−5,480	273	556	411	13,544	4,323	20,651
1895	55,099	+7,432	320	558	372	11,928	4,742	19,761
1896	56,753	+1,654	334	531	388	12,441	4,833	23,060
1897	58,129	+1,376	351	504	351	11,766	4,423	30,060
1898	60,250	+2,121	359	508	339	11,492	5,007	22,390
1899	63,142	+2,892	359	506	341	11,352	4,206	23,631
1900	63,152	+ 10	371	511	358	10,585	4,705	23,291
1901	57,500	−5,652	383	513	281	11,707	4,834	17,322

[1] Source: *Annual Reports of the London Missionary Society* for the years mentioned. Statistics for the period before 1858 are confusing and defective, at one time omitting whole districts, at another time numbering only members in full communion.

APPENDIX V

Travancore Staie Income from Coffee 1852/53–1884/85[1]
(State Income from Land Sales, Land Revenue and Export of Coffee)

Year	*Land Sales Rs.*	*Land Revenue Rs.*	*Export Cwts.*[2]	*Export Duties Rs.*	*Value of Export Rs.*
1852/53			1.033		
1855/56			830		
1858/59			1,174		
1861/62			1,941		
1862/63			2,567		
1863/64			2,979		59,644
1864/65			3,965		80,221
1865/66			4,777		120,787
1866/67			9,655	10,577	211,542
1867/68			14,140	12,156	243,000
1868/69			12,865	12,567	251,300
1869/70		2,100	16,991	16,942	338,800
1870/71			27,095	27,242	544,800
1871/72	3,800		29,597	29,852	596,800
1872/73	5,444		41,636	41,963	839,000
1873/74	85,254		29,407	29,723	584,000
1874/75	214,761		26,031	26,224	524,000
1875/76			n.g.	abolished	786,696

1876/77		40	20	990,058
1877/78		39,737	20,092	803,700
1878/79	17,105	18,781	9,378	374,600
1879/80	18,773	45,700	22,084	883,100
1880/81	19,316	29,611	14,948	599,400
1881/82	25,630	40,484	20,877	835,200
1882/83	28,104	19,561	9,728	389,135
1883/84		13,708	13,565	225,704
1884/85		22,209	22,305	446,805

[1] Source: *Annual Reports on the Administration of Travancore* for the years mentioned.

[2] Cwts = 112 English Pounds, generally an abbreviation for hundredweight.

Glossary

anna	1/16 part of Rupee
a-varnas	untouchables, those not belonging to a *varna*
ayurvedic	belonging to the *Ayurveda*, a Indo-Aryan medical treatise
bazar	market
cadjan	dried leaf of the palmyra palm
Chera	name of large historical empire in south India
Cheramar/Cherumar	slightly deviant way of calling the ex-slaves
Chetti	merchant or trader
chuckram	tiny copper coin in Travancore 28 of which were equal to one rupee
chunam	lime
cottah	a measure of land (1,33 acre) as well as grain
cutcherry	a government office
division	largest administrative unit of Travancore 19th century
dewan	prime minister
dewan peishkar	government officer subordinate only to the *dewan* and in charge of a division
dharma	the social rules particular to each caste
Ezhava	caste of untouchable agriculturists and artisans, traditionally connected with the care of the palm trees
fanam	silver coin worth four *chuckrams*
harijan	lit. child of God, Gandhi's name for the untouchable
jati	birth or caste
Kaliyuga	fourth and present era of the world
kangany	labour recruiter and overseer
Kanikar	south Travancore hill tribe
karanavan	eldest male member and manager of a *taravad*
karma	the sum total of merits and demerits determining rebirth
Kshatriya	the warrior *varna*
kudumi	tuft of hair worn by Hindu men of certain castes
kuppayam	jacket with long sleeves worn by Syrian and Muslim women
Kuravar	untouchable caste said to originate from Tinnevelly
lakh	100,000
Mahabharata	classic Hindu *epos*
Mahar	Untouchable community in Maharashtra
maharaja	king
makkathayam	inheritance and descent through the male line
Malayalam	litt. hill country, language spoken in central and north Travancore
marumakkathayam	inheritance and descent through the female line
muditchi ravakkay	jacket with short sleeves made of fine cloth worn by Brahmin women

Mukkavar	fishing community on the coast
musnud	throne
Nadan	a prominent subsection of the *Shanar* caste
Nambudiri	caste of *Malayali* Brahmins
Nayar	matrilineal dominant caste in Travancore
pataneer	open vessel used for boiling the fresh toddy into palm sugar or jaggery
palanqin	covered litter for one person, carried usually by four or six men
pandal	provisional porch or booth used for meetings and festivities
Parasurama	mythological divine hero
Pariah	*Tamil*-speaking caste of (ex-)slaves
Pulaya	*Malayalam*-speaking caste of (ex-)slaves
puranas	Hindu classics
raja	prince
rani	princess
ravakkay	jacket devised for Christian women
Saivite	worshipper of the great Hindu god Shiva
Saliar	weavers caste
sambandham	marriage connection among matrilineal castes
samsara	the cycle of rebirth
sati	a woman's (self-)immolation on the funeral pile of her husband
Shanar	caste of untouchable palmyra palm tappers and land labourers, now called *Nadars*
shastra	Hindu law books
sirkar	government
star pagoda	gold coin worth 42 *fanams*
sudra	the lowest category of the *varna* system, in Travancore often synonymous with *Nayar*
tahsildar	government officer in charge of a *taluk*
tali	small gold or silver pendant tied round the neck of a girl on the occasion of a pre-puberty marriage
taluk	administrative unit beneath a division
taravad	joint-family and house of *Nayars*
uliyam	forced labour demanded by the state
uttupura	free boarding and lodging house for Brahmins
vakil	legal practitioner
varna	one of the four categories of the Hindu social hierarchy
zillah court	old name for district and sessions court

Bibliography

I. Missionary Sources

1. London Missionary Society

Since 1973 the LMS Archives, now incorporated in the Archives of the Council for World Mission, have been deposited in the Library of the *School of Oriental and African Studies* in London.

Most files are also available on microfiche in the library of the *Interuniversity Institute for Missiological and Ecumenical Research* in Leiden. Where the microfiche-edition has been consulted, in the notes a mf. number has been added to the original Box number.

Unpublished

Candidates Papers	: Boxes 1–18 (1796–1899, alphabetically)
India	: Outgoing Letters, Boxes 19, 21
	: Personal, Boxes 2, 3
	: Odds, Boxes 4–6, 15–18 (Travancore : Reports, Letters, Papers)
Travancore	: Incoming Letters, Boxes 1–19 (1817/99)
	: Reports, Boxes 1–7 (1866/1902).

Missionary Portraits and Pictures India (mainly photographs).

The *Ecclesiastical Archives at the United Theological College in Bangalore* contain several files and papers in relation to the LMS mission in Travancore:

LMS 62–66: Travancore District Committee Correspondence (1828–1903).

LMS 79–81: Travancore District Committee Minute Books (1875–1909).

LMS 101: Photos, 1 album.

Manuscripts

Abbs, John, 1861. "Travancore, Manuscript History", in LMS Archives, Odds, Box 5.

Duthie. James, no date. "Travancore Mission 1805–73", manuscript given by the author to Rev. George Parker, who handed it to the librarian of the LMS 1953, in LMS Archives, Odds, Box 17.

The *Ecclesiastical Archives* (Bangalore) contain the following manuscripts:

LMS 95: "Histories" of LMS work in south Travancore, containing: □ Manuscript history of Nagercoil Seminary, not signed, about 1905. □ Parker, Mrs. B. "Nagercoil Lace Industry", about 1919. □ Official address by Matthias, former student of Nagercoil Seminary, held at Centenary Meeting, 1906.

LMS 96: Copies of the Official Papers ... (see under II.3).

LMS 97: Jacob, J.A. no date. "History of the LMS in Travancore", typescript (pp. 1–48 and 231–334 are missing).

LMS 98: Parker, G. no date. "History of Mission Fields", typescript, (also in LMS Archives, Odds, Box 17).

Published

Annual Report of the London Missionary Society (or: Report of the Directors to the Missionary Society), 1800–1900, London.

Annual Report of the Travancore District Committee, in connection with the London Missionary Society for the year ... Nagercoil: LMS Press. The issues of 1858–1872, 1879–1881 and 1883 can be found in the Bangalore *Ecclesiastical Archives* (a complete run from 1858–1900 has been preserved in the library of *Scott Christian College*, Nagercoil).

Brief Statement of the Gross Outrages recently committed in Travancore by the heathen natives on their Christian countrymen, London: London Missionary Society 1859.

Sibree, James, 1923. *A Register of Missionaries, Deputations, etc. from 1796 to 1923*. London: London Missionary Society.

The Missionary Magazine and Chronicle, from 1867 continued as *The Chronicle of the London Missionary Society*.

2. CHURCH MISSIONARY SOCIETY

Letters, Journals etc. from Rev. Septimus Hobbs, Missionary Tamil Cooly Mission 1856–1862, File C Ce/O 70.

Travancore + Cochin Papers 1880–1882, File G2 I 5/O.

Annual Report of the Church Missionary Society (or: Proceedings of the Church Missionary Society for Africa and the East), London.

3. INTERNATIONAL MISSIONARY COUNCIL AND CONFERENCE OF BRITISH MISSIONARY SOCIETIES (IMC/CBMS) – JOINT ARCHIVES AFRICA & INDIA 1910–1945

South India: Report of the Mass Movement Commission, Mysore 1919, Box 411.

Travancore: The Travancore Ezhava Situation, Confidential Report by Bishop of Dornakal, 1936, Box 406.

4. GENERAL

The Indian Evangelical Review: a quarterly journal of missionary thought and effort, Bombay, Vol. I, 1874 ff.

Mededeelingen vanwege het Nederlandsche Zendelinggenootschap, Vol. XXIX 1885–Vol. XXXII 1888.

II. Government Sources

1. TRAVANCORE GOVERNMENT

Census of Travancore 1875, 1891, 1901 and 1931 (the 1881 census was not sent to England, neither has it appeared in print).

Annual Report on the Administration of Travancore, from the year M.E. 1041 (A.D. 1865–66) to M.E. 1076 (A.D. 1900–1901), Trivandrum.

2. MADRAS GOVERNMENT

Crown Representative's Records: Madras States Agency (Confidential Reports, Disposals etc., on Travancore and Cochin by the British Resident).

3. BRITISH GOVERNMENT

"Copies of the Official Papers sent from India touching the recent disturbances in Travancore", India Office, August 5, 1859, in *Parliamentary Papers* 1859, Session II, XXV, No. 158, 353.

III. OTHER SOURCES

Regional Records Survey Committee, 1970/1972. *The History of the Freedom Movement in Kerala*, 2 Vols. Trivandrum: Government Press.

The Travancore Memorials and Counter Memorials, reprinted from the Madras Times, July 1891.

IV. LITERATURE

Abbs, John 1870. *Twenty-two Years' Missionary Experience in Travancore*, London: John Snow & Co.

Agur, C.M. 1903. *Church History of Travancore*, Madras: SPS Press.

Alexander, K.C. 1972. "The Neo-Christians of Kerala", in Mahar, J. Michael (Ed.), *The Untouchables in Contemporary India*, Tucson: The University of Arizona Press.

——— 1977. "The Problem of Caste in the Christian Churches of Kerala", in Singh, Harjinder (Ed.), *Caste among Non-Hindus in India*, New Delhi: National Publishing House.

Allen, Charles. 1979[2]. *Raj: a scrapbook of British India 1877–1947 Harmondsworth: Penguin Books.*

Alter, James P. 1974. "Liberty, Equality, Fraternity: themes in the Anglo-Saxon Protestant missions and the church in north India 1800–1914", in *Indian Church History Review*, VIII: 1, pp. 14–40.

Ayrookuzhiel, A.M. Abraham. 1983. "The Religious Resources of the Dalits in the Context of their Struggle (an overview of the Kerala scene)", in Chatterji, Saral K. (Ed.), *Essays in Celebration of the CISRS Silver Jubilee*, Madras.

Bandarage, Asoka. 1983. *Colonialism in Sri Lanka: the political economy of the Kandyan Highlands 1833–1886*, Berlin etc.: Mouton.

Becker, C. 1980. *History of the Catholic Missions in North-East India (1890–1915)*, (translated from German original, published in 1923) Calcutta: KLM.

Béteille, André. 1972. "Pollution and Poverty", in Michael Mahar, J. (Ed.), *The Untouchables in Contemporary India*, Tucson: the University of Arizona Press, pp. 411–21.

Birrell, Charles M. 1860. *The Life of the Rev. Richard Knill of St. Petersburgh etc.*, London: Nisbet & Co.

Boel, J. 1975. *Christian Mission in India: a sociological analysis*, Amsterdam: Graduate Press.

Bucher, Hubert. 1980. *Spirits and Power: an analysis of Shona cosmology*, Oxford: Oxford University Press.

Caldwell, R. 1982 (reprint of 1881). *A History of Tinnevelly*, New Delhi: Asian Educational Services.

Chandramohan, P. 1987. "Popular Culture and Socio-Religious Reform: Narayana Guru and the Ezhavas of Travancore", in *Studies in History*, New Series, III: 1, pp. 57–75.

Cox, John. 1857. *Travancore: Its Present Ruin Shown and the Remedy Sought, in a correspondence with the Government of Madras in the years 1855–1857*, Nagercoil: LMS Press.

David, S. Immanuel. 1986. "History of Christianity in India: changing perspectives", in *Indian Church History Review*, XX: 1, pp. 5–13.

Duff, Alexander. 1839. *India and India Mission: including sketches of the gigantic system of hinduism*, Edinburgh: Johnstone.

Dumont, Louis. 1970. *Homo Hierarchicus: the caste system and its implications*, London: Paladin.

Duthie, J. 1906. *Reminiscences,* Madras.

Embree, A.T. 1962. *Charles Grant and British Rule in India*, New York: Columbia University Press.

End, T. van den 1983. "Dutch Protestant Mission Activity: a survey", in *Itinerario* VII: 1, pp. 86–108.

Etherington, Norman. 1983. "Missionaries and the Intellectual History of Africa: a historical survey", in *Itinerario* VII: 2, pp. 116–144.

Ferguson, A.M. (compiled by). 1868. *The Ceylon Directory Calendar and Compendium of Useful Information for 1866–68*, Colombo.

Ferguson, A.M. & J. (compiled by). 1878. *The Planting Directory for India and Ceylon*, with a list of coffee, tea, cinchona and other plantations in India and Ceylon etc., Colombo.

Forrester, Duncan B. 1977. "The Depressed Classes and Conversion to Christianity, 1860–1960", in Oddie, G.A. (Ed.), *Religion in South Asia: religious conversion and revival movements in South Asia in medieval and modern times*, New Delhi: Manohar.

——— 1980. *Caste and Christianity: attitudes and policies on caste of Anglo-Saxon Protestant missions in India*, London: Curzon Press.

Frykenberg, R.E. 1978. "Conversion and Crises of Conscience under Company Raj in South India", paper submitted to VIth European Conference on Modern South Asian Studies, Paris.

——— 1980. "On the Study of Conversion Movements: a review article and a theoretical note", in *The Indian Economic and Social History Review*, XVII: 1, pp. 121–39.

——— 1985. "Caste, Morality, and Western Religion under the Raj", in *Modern Asian Studies*, XIX: 2, pp. 321–43.

Fuller, C.J. 1976[a]. *The Nayars Today*, Cambridge: Cambridge University Press.

——— 1976[b]. "Kerala Christians and the Caste System", in *Man*, XI, pp. 53–70.

Gladstone, J.W. 1976. "19th Century Mass Movement in South Travancore: a result of social liberation", in *Indian Church History Review*, X: 1, pp. 53–66.

——— 1984. *Protestant Christianity and People's Movements in Kerala: a study of Christian mass movements in relation to neo-Hindu socio-religious movements in Kerala, 1850–1936*, Trivandrum: The Seminary Publications.

——— 1986. "Christian Missionary Work and Socio-Religious Movements in Kerala, 1850–1910", in *Indian Church History Review*, XX: 1, pp. 30–43.

Goodall, Norman. 1954. *A History of the London Missionary Society 1895–1945*, London: Oxford University Press.

Hacker, I.H. 1887. *Memoirs of Thomas Smith Thomson, LRCP, LRCS, Medical Missionary at Neyoor, Travancore, South India*, London: Religious Tract Society.

——— 1908. *A Hundred Years in Travancore 1806–1906: a history and description of the work done by the LMS in Travancore, South India*, London: H.R. Allenson.

Hardgrave, Robert L. Jr. 1969. *The Nadars of Tamilnad: the political culture of a community in change*, Berkeley: University of California Press.

Heimsath, Charles H. 1978. "The Functions of Hindu Social Reformers: with special reference to Kerala", in *The Indian Economic and Social History Review*, XV: 1, pp. 21–39.

Hjelje, Benedicte. 1967. "Slavery and Agricultural Bondage in south India in the Nineteenth Century", in *The Scandinavian Economic History Review*, XV: 1, 2, pp. 71–126.

Horne, C. Silvester 1895. *The Story of the LMS 1795–1895*, London: John Snow & Co.

Horsley, W.H. 1839. *Memoir of Travancore: historical and statistical, compiled from various authentic records and personal observation*, Trevandrum: Sirkar Press.

Horton, Robin. 1971. "African Conversion", in *Africa*, Vol. XLI, pp. 85–108.

Hospital, Clifford G. 1979. "Clothes and Caste in Nineteenth Century Kerala", in *Indian Church History Review*, XIII: 2, pp. 146–157.

Ingham, Kenneth. 1956. *Reformers in India: an account of the work of Christian missionaries on behalf of social reform*, Cambridge.

Isaac, T.M. Thomas & Tharakan, P.K. Michael. 1986. *An Enquiry into the Historical Roots of Industrial Backwardness of Kerala: a study of Travancore Region*, Working Paper No. 215, Trivandrum: Centre for Development Studies.

Jeffrey, Robin. 1974. "The Social Origins of a Caste Association 1875–1905: the founding of the SNDP-Yogam", in *South Asia*, IV, pp. 39–60.

——— 1976. *The Decline of Nayar Dominance: society and politics in Travancore, 1847–1908*, New Delhi [etc.]: Vikas.

Kooiman, Dick. 1982. "Poverty and Untouchability in Kerala: a historical study based on missionary sources", in *Indian Church History Review*, XVI: 1, pp. 10–36.

——— 1983. "Untouchablility in India through the Missionary's Eye", in *Itinerario* VII: 1, pp. 115–25.

——— van den Muyzenberg, Otto and van der Veer, Peter (Eds.) 1984a. *Conversion, Competition and Conflict: essays on the role of religion in Asia*, Anthropological Studies Nr. 6, Amsterdam: Free University Press.

——— 1984b. "The Gospel of Coffee: mission, education and employment in 19th century Travancore", in *Economic and Political Weekly*, XIX: 35, pp. 1535–44.

——— 1984c. "Conversion and Socio-Cultural Change: a case study of south Travancore", in *Journal of Kerala Studies*, XI: 1–4, pp. 1–23.

——— 1985. "Social and Economic Backgrounds of Nineteenth Century London Missionaries in Southern Travancore", in *Indian Church History Review*, XIX: 2, pp. 99–127.

——— 1988. "Change of Religion as a Way to Survival", in Quarles van Ufford, Ph. and Schoffeleers, M. (Eds.). *Religion and Development: Towards an integrated approach*, Amsterdam: Free University Press, pp. 167–185.

Krishna Iyer, L.A. 1937–41. *The Travancore Tribes and Castes*, 3 Vols. Trivandrum: Government Press.

Kumar, Dharma. 1965. *Land and Caste in South India: agricultural labour in the Madras Presidency during the nineteenth century*, Cambridge: Cambridge University Press.

Kuper, Adam. 1979. "The Magician and the Missionary", in van den Berghe, P.L. (Ed.), *The Liberal Dilemma in South Africa*, London: Tavistock, pp. 77–96.

Kurup, K.B. 1980. *Toddy Tappers: a study*, Amsterdam: Indo-Dutch Kerala Research Project, Interim Report No. 8.

Kurup, K.K.N. 1984. "The Colonial Investment and the Abolition of Slavery", in *Journal of Kerala Studies*, XI: 1–4, pp. 187–99.

Kusuman, K.K. 1973. *Slavery in Travancore*, Trivandrum: Kerala Historical Society.

Laird, Michael A. 1972. *Missionaries and Education in Bengal 1793–1837*, Oxford: Clarendon Press.

Lewis, Frederick. 1926. *Sixty-four Years in Ceylon: reminiscences of life and adventure*, Colombo.

Logan, William. 1951 (1887). *Malabar*, Madras, 2 Vols.

Lowe, John. 1886. *Medical Missions: their place and power*, London

Luke, P.Y. and Carman, J.B. 1968. *Village Christians and Hindu Culture*, London: Lutterworth Press.

Maltby, F.N. 1861. "Public Works in Travancore", in *Madras Journal of Literature and Science*, VI New Series, pp. 127–38.

Manickam, S. 1977. *The Social Setting of Christian Conversion in South India: the impact of the Wesleyan Methodist missionaries on the Trichy Tanjore diocese with special reference to the Harijan communities of the mass movement area 1820–1947*, Wiesbaden: Steiner.

——— 1979. "Grants-in-Aid and Christian Missions in the Madras Presidency 1854–1947", in *Indian Church History Review*, XIII: 2, pp. 123–146.

Markham, Clements R. 1866. *Report on the Coffee-planting district of Wynaad*, no place.

Mateer, Samuel, 1871. *The Land of Charity: a descriptive account of Travancore and its people*, London: John Snow & Co.

——— 1883[a]. *Native Life in Travancore*, London: W.H. Allen & Co.

——— 1883[b]. "Nepotism in Travancore", in *Journal of the Anthropological Institute* XII, pp. 288–306.

——— (1886). *The Gospel in South India, or the religious life, experience and character of the Hindu Christians*, London: Religious Tract Society.

——— no date. "The Pariah Caste in Travancore", in LMS Archives, Odds, Box 15/mf. 1099–1100 (also in *Journal of the Royal Asiatic Society*, XVI New Series 1884, pp. 180–95).

Mathew, George, 1982. "Politicisation of Religion: conversions to Islam in Tamil Nadu", in *Economic and Political Weekly*, XVII: 25, pp. 1027, ff. and XVII: 26, pp. 1068 ff.

Mayhew, Arthur. 1929. *Christianity and the Government of India: an examination of the Christian forces at work in the administration of India and of the mutual relations of the British government and Christian missions 1600–1920*, London: Faber & Gwyer.

Mencher, Joan P. 1966[a]. "Kerala and Madras: a comparative study of ecology and social structure", in *Ethnology* V: 2, pp. 135–71.

——— 1966[b]. "Namboodiri Brahmins: an analysis of a traditional elite in Kerala", in *Journal of Asian and African Studies* I, pp. 183–96.

Miller, Eric J. 1954. "Caste and Territory in Malabar", in *American Anthropologist* LVI, pp. 410–20.

Millie, P.D., 1878. *Thirty Years Ago or Reminiscences of the Early Days of Coffee Planting in Ceylon*, Colombo.

Muller, J. 1913. "Industrial Missionary Work in India: the Basel industrial missions", in *International Review of Missions*, January.

Murdoch, John. (compiled by) 1870[2]. *Indian Missionary Manual-hints to young missionaries in India, with lists of books*, London.

Nagam Aiya, V. 1906. *The Travancore State Manual*, 3 Vols. Trivandrum: Government Press.

Namboodiripad, E.M.S. 1967. *Kerala: Yesterday, Today and Tomorrow* Calcutta: National Book Agency.

Nehru, Jawaharlal 1949. *The Unity of India*, New York.

Oddie, G.A. 1979. *Social Protest in India: British Protestant Missionaries and Social Reforms 1850–1900*, New Delhi: Manohar.

Pandit, Nalini, 1979. "Caste and Class in Maharashtra", in *Economic and Political Weekly*, XIV: 7, pp. 429 ff.

Panikkar, A.K. 1969. "The Travancore Rebellion, 1809", in *Journal of Indian History* XLVII: 1, pp. 159–72.

Panikkar, K.M. 1967[7] (1953). *Asia and Western Dominance: a survey of the Vasco Da Gama epoch of Asian history 1498–1945*, London: Allen & Unwin.

The Planting Directory of South India. 1896, Madras.

Pullapilly, Cyriac K. 1976. "The Izhavas of Kerala and their Historic Struggle for Acceptance in the Hindu Society", in *Journal of Asian and African Studies* XI: 1–2, pp. 24–46.

Rajaratnam, S. 1961. "The Growth of Plantation Agriculture in Ceylon 1886–1931", in *The Ceylon Journal of Historical and Social Studies*, IV: 1, pp. 2, ff.

Rajendran, G. 1974. *The Ezhava Community and Kerala Politics*, Trivandrum: The Kerala Academy of Political Science.

Richter, Julius. 1908. *A History of Missions in India*, Edinburgh etc.: Oliphant Anderson & Ferrier (transl. from German edition of 1906).

Roberts, M.W. 1966. "Indian Estate Labour in Ceylon during the Coffee Period (1830–1880)", in *The Indian Economic and Social History Review*, III: 1, pp. 1–34, III: 2, pp. 101–26.

Robinson, William 1902. *Ringeltaube, the Rishi: the pioneer missionary of the London Missionary Society in Travancore*, Sheffield.

Samaraweera, Vijaya. 1981. "Masters and Servants in Sri Lankan Plantations: labour laws and labour control in an emergent export economy", in *The Indian Economic and Social History Review*, XVIII: 2, pp. 123–58.

Saradamoni, K. 1980. *Emergence of a Slave Caste: Pulayas of Kerala* New Delhi: People's Publishing House.

Schenk, Hans. 1986. *Views on Alleppey: socio-historical and socio-spatial perspectives on an industrial port town in Kerala, South India*, Ph.D. Thesis University of Amsterdam.

Sen Gupta, Kanti Prasanna. 1971. *The Christian Missionaries in Bengal 1793–1833*, Calcutta: Mukhopadyay.

Sherring, M.A. 1884. *The History of Protestant Missions in India, from their Commencement in 1706 to 1881*, London: The Religious Tract Society.

Shetty, V.T. Rajshekar. 1978. *Dalit Movement in Karnataka*, Madras: The Christian Literature Society.

Silva, K.M. de. 1961. "Indian Immigration to Ceylon: the first phase, *c.* 1840–1855", in *Ceylon Journal of Historical and Social Studies* IV: 1, pp. 106–37.

——— 1965. *Social Policy and Missionary Organizations in Ceylon 1840–1855*, London: Longmans.

Smith, David. 1856. *Memoir and Remains of the Late Rev. Charles C. Leitch, Missionary at Neyoor*, Edinburgh & London.

Srinivas, M.N. 1965 (1952). *Religion and Society among the Coorgs of South India*, London: Asia Publishing House.

——— 1962. *Caste in Modern India and other Essays*, London: Asia Publishing House.

——— 1969 (1966). *Social Change in Modern India*, Berkeley: University of California Press.

Stein, Burton. 1985. "State Formation and Economy Reconsidered", in *Modern Asian Studies* XIX: 3, pp. 387–413.

Tharakan, P.K. Michael. 1984. *Socio-Economic Factors in Educational Development: the case of nineteenth century Travancore*, Working Paper No. 190, Trivandrum: Centre for Development Studies.

Thurston, Edgar. 1909. *Castes and Tribes of Southern India*, 7 Vols. Madras: Government Press.

Tinker, H. 1974. *A New System of Slavery: the export of Indian labour overseas, 1830–1920*, London: Oxford University Press.

Varghese, T.C. 1970. *Agrarian Change and Economic Consequences: land tenures in Kerala 1850–1960*, Bombay & Madras: Allied Publishers.

Warren, Max. 1967. *Social History and Christian Mission*, London: SCM Press Ltd.

Wesumperuma, D. 1978. "Unindentured Indian Labour Overseas: plantation labour in British Ceylon", paper submitted to VIth European Conference on Modern South Asian Studies, Paris.

Wilson, K. 1982. *The Twice Alienated: Culture of Dalit Christians*, Hyderabad: Booklinks Corp.

Witz, Cornelia. 1985. *Religionspolitik in Britisch-Indien 1793–1813: Christliches sendungsbewusstsein und achtung Hinduistischer tradition im widerstreit*, Wiesbaden: Steiner.

Wolf, Eric R. 1982. *Europe and the People without History*, Berkeley etc.: University of California Press.

Yesudas, R.N. 1975. *A People's Revolt in Travancore: a backward class movement for social freedom*, Trivandrum: Kerala Historical Society.

——— 1977. *Colonel John Munro in Travancore*, Trivandrum: Kerala Historical Society.

——— 1980. *The History of the London Missionary Society in Travancore 1806–1908*, Trivandrum: Kerala Historical Society.

V. Unpublished Theses

Gladstone, J.W. 1975. "The Social Impact of the Protestant Missionary Work in South Travancore in the 19th Century", Master Thesis United Theological College, Bangalore.

Hector, S.S. 1979. "History of the Protestant Mission in the Kanyakumari District 1806–1947", Ph.D. Thesis Madurai Kamaraj University.

Paulose, E.M. 1980. "The Protestant Missionaries and Social Reforms in Travancore 1806–1865", dissertation submitted as a partial fulfilment for the degree of Master of Philosophy of the University of Calicut, Department of History.

Index